WHAT IS OPEN?

Accelerating Answers for Football's Most Important Game Planning & Play Calling Question

Dub Maddox

FIRST EDITION

ISBN: 978-1-946466-67-9

Library of Congress Control Number: 2019937691

Designed by Wendy Trubia

Published by

3741 Linden Ave. SE, Grand Rapids, MI 49548

Printed in the United States of America

To the relationships that made this book possible...

To my Lord and Savior Jesus Christ, I hope the readers see your creative fingerprints in this book.

To my beautiful wife Tanya Maddox, God answers prayer, you are everything I wanted and more.

To my newborn son, you gave me the strength to keep pushing forward. I cannot wait to be your dad.

To my parents, your encouragement made me believe that I could do anything. Thank you for loving me.

To Darin Slack, a phone call and a plane ticket changed my life. Thank you for showing me the way.

To Rick Jones, you taught me how to coach and that "little things" matter. Thank you for hiring me.

To Trandy Birch, you protected me and believed in me. Thank you for being the big brother I never had.

To Allan Trimble, your empathy and empowerment made R4 possible.You define "servant leader."

To JC Boice, your friendship and partnership made a way when there seemed no way. You are a warrior.

To Will Hewlett, your drive to always get better inspires me. You are the best QB coach I know.

To Rod Robison, you were there from the start. You're the best man a brother could have.

To Reid Roe, you planted the vision for R4. Your passion carried me when I needed it the most.

To Jonny Ulibarri, your insight and support continue to move R4 forward. Thankful to fight with you.

To Doug Greenwood, your step of faith took R4 to another level. I will never forget our time together.

To the quarterbacks I have coached, Mark Ginther, Sawyer Kollmorgen, Hunter Collins, Kyle Alexander, Steven Litwiller, Cooper Nunnley, Ian Corwin and Garrett Williams. Thank you for letting me coach you. The bond of being in battle together can never be broken. I am a better coach because of you.

To all the coaches who I have worked with and against. This book doesn't happen without you.

Thank you.

As Iron sharpens Iron, so one person sharpens another. Proverbs 27:17

TABLE OF CONTENTS

What is Open?

INTRODUCTION

Lost in Space and Time

INTRODUCTION

Lost in Space and Time

I will never forget the feeling of walking out of the coaches meeting room. I was sick to my stomach. We just finished our first Sunday afternoon game-plan meeting. I was a 23-year-old rookie coach at the largest high school in Oklahoma (Broken Arrow HS). My job was to coach the slot backs and wide receivers in a flex bone offense. We just spent four hours in a staff meeting and it might as well have been in Chinese.

The goal of the game-planning meeting was to determine "What is open?" Coaches were communicating their opinions and strategies in terms I had never heard before. "Shade, 5, 9" "Double Eagle" "Spoke Safety" "Pirate" "Cross Pop" "Corner Hammer" were just a few of the terms being thrown around the room. This was before Google, mind you, so you couldn't just pick up a smartphone and Google or YouTube the answers.

I was lost. I simply couldn't process and communicate with the other coaches in the room. The offensive goal was to create and attack "open" space against the defense. My problem (and yours)? The process to define "What is open" was specific to the select few who understood the secret language. They were on the inside and I wanted into the club. I needed a cipher to break the secret code, but it didn't exist. I needed a new set of eyes that could see the space that the coaches were referring to on the whiteboard and game film, but I didn't have them. I needed a mental model that revealed their thought processes behind the decision-making to what plays would best attack an opponent... but none was given.

I was almost fired after that first year of coaching. Our head coach had evaluation meetings at the end of the season and my review didn't go well. In the meeting, my boss gave me some advice that I will never forget. "If you want to excel as a coach in this game, 'knowledge' is your greatest weapon. You must never stop learning."

Thankfully, I was given a chance in the offseason to earn the head coach's trust back, but the clock was ticking. I had a short amount of time to prove myself. My quest to learn how to better understand the game of football quickly began. I needed to find out how to determine "What is open."

THE EXPLICIT APPROACH

My search began in the digital age of the early 2000s. This period saw an explosion of available football knowledge that was once reserved for the elite inner circles of the professional coaching communities. The rise of the Internet allowed the novice coach to peek behind the curtain and gain access to information that was once off limits. The access to this hallowed football data surged again with the development of smartphones and social media. The ability to gain access to large databases of football knowledge opened the door to more explicit learning.

Explicit Learning (thinking) is a verbal conscious acquisition of data, rules, and strategy through memorization. "Knowing WHAT to do."

Explicit learning is conscious classroom book-learning. We learn explicitly as a child by memorizing the rules of multiplication tables, spelling words, or speaking a foreign language. Explicit learning is rule-based knowledge that can be coded with language in the form of words and numbers. It is often organized in a stimulus-response IF/THEN format. Explicit learning in the human brain requires a high bandwidth of space storage in the brain and time to memorize and store it for long term memory. This limits the speed at which the knowledge can be learned and recalled.

The benefit of explicit learning is that it can give you a seat at the table with the experts, but it doesn't mean you will be allowed to stay there. In learning a foreign language, memorization of linguistic structures, rules, and exceptions can allow you to "know WHAT to do" in sentence structure, but it doesn't give you the ability to "know HOW to do" it quickly and blend it within a native environment.

Similarly, just memorizing the base data of football doesn't equate to mastery in coaching football. For example, I learned explicitly from playbooks that a Curl-Flat concept is designed to place a Flat defender in conflict. I use this data to formulate an IF/THEN coaching cue for my quarterback to read the Flat defender.

IF the flat defender covers the Flat route, THEN throw the Curl route.

IF the flat defender covers the Curl route, THEN throw the Flat route.

What I quickly discovered was that if the defender moved directly to the Flat route or the Curl route, we had good success with the concept. However, our execution of the Curl-Flat concept diminished when a new variable was introduced. In one game the Flat defender didn't cover the Flat route or the Curl route.

He just stood there.

My quarterback had not been taught or ever experienced what to do in this situation. He locked up and threw an interception for a touchdown in a playoff game.

This forced me to add another rule to the explicit knowledge database for the Curl-Flat concept.

IF the flat defender doesn't move, THEN reset to the backside concept.

The rules didn't stop there. Every time there was failure in execution, a new IF/THEN rule was created to address the issue. Before the year was finished we had **more than 20 IF/THEN rules** that the quarterback had to process on just one play. While the addition of IF/THEN rules provided the solutions for a myriad of situations, they quickly overloaded my quarterback with information that his brain couldn't quickly process under pressure. I was creating a quarterback that was good at verbalizing what to do in the film room but couldn't translate it to execution on the field. Simply put, knowledge space and time was the limiting factor to the explicit approach. There wasn't enough time to learn and process all the IF/THEN information and apply them in a real-world environment under pressure.

The roadblock of space and time forced me to try another method of learning.

THE IMPLICIT APPROACH

To speed up the learning curve in football, I put down the playbooks and attended numerous coaching clinics and visited different universities to immerse myself under experts in the football world. If I could learn the patterns and principals that experts had developed through experience I could shortcut the vast knowledge memorization time that it takes to learn explicitly. Learning their methods could give me context to quickly connect the football dots of discernment. Access to experts opened a door to implicit learning.

Implicit Learning (without thinking) is a non-verbal unconscious acquisition of knowledge, perspectives, and beliefs through experience. "Knowing HOW to do."

Implicit learning is unconscious shared learning. An example of implicit learning would be in how we learned to speak our native language or riding a bicycle as a child. We were not taught the grammatical rules of language or the physics of motion to learn these techniques. We simply were immersed with others who were proficient in a skill and learned through mimicking and sweeping statements. Trial and error provided feedback that promoted learning by guided self-discovery.

Implicit learning from an expert who knows how to do a task is highly personal and hard to articulate in words. An expert has years of experience to develop expertise but is often unable to describe the technical principals behind what he knows. Therefore, it is difficult to communicate. For example, I learned this common coaching cue from passing game expert coaches. **Throw to grass...**

This sweeping statement was a visual conceptual cue that provided a mental model for the quarterback to predict the best open route. This implicit approach eliminated the myriad, explicit IF/THEN rules that overloaded my quarterback in games. It allowed the quarterback to self-discover through trial and error what open looked like. This is the benefit of implicit learning. It provides the learner with a subconscious accelerated "knowing HOW to do" a skill in real-time.

Implicit learning might seem like the most effective method of learning. However, it lacks rules, definitive language and a process that prevent the instructional content to be easily understood, taught and transferred to others. In the absence of explicit context, we are left to draw on our own conclusions of how we perceive the world in a specialized domain. This can lead to misinterpretations and high-risk, bias-based decision errors in given situations.

Unfortunately, this low bandwidth of language leaves the learning space empty. This, in turn, forces a requirement of time through trial and error repetitions to learn implicitly. In a competitive environment like football, there is not a lot of time given to experience learning through failure. Repetitive failures can result in the loss of starting positions, games, and careers.

Once again, space and time was an enemy and forced me to try another method of learning.

A SPECIALIZED SYSTEMS BASED APPROACH

I quickly discovered that the boundaries of space (bandwidth) and time created a learning gap that prevents the functioning and flow of explicit and implicit learning in a real-world environment. The average coaching career in football is 30 years. The average playing career is 6 years. How do you get 30 years of knowledge to crossover into a player in 6 years? Moreover, how do you do it with a rookie coach on your staff? Is it possible to download 30+ years of explicit and implicit knowledge into a person in a short amount of time in which they can process and execute it in the real-world while under pressure?

Time is the most precious resource we have as humans. Without a bridge to connect the two learning approaches, many coaches use systems to fill the time gap. It doesn't matter if you are coaching offense, defense or just a position, every coach runs a system. Specialized systems are a subsystem of a domain that reduces the bandwidth of explicit knowledge needed to achieve a goal. Like a piece of a pie, they operate using relevant data, with unique concepts and philosophies that function within the rules of the whole domain.

Due to the pressures and limits of time in the football domain, many coaches focus on learning the game through a specialized subsystem. This is done by immersing oneself under an expert mentor. The challenge is that specialized system expert knowledge is specific to an offensive or defensive system. Some examples of specialized offensive systems in football would be the West Coast, Air-Raid, Flex-Bone, or Wing-T offenses.

These subsystems reduce the time burden to know all the explicit data of the game and focus on only information pertinent to the system. These specialized subsystems are influenced by the overall football coaching tree from which the coaching expert learned the game. The problem with specialized football systems is that they are culturally specific to an inner circle of experts within the group and rely heavily on the expert's implicit knowledge that was learned through years of experience. While this method allows a coach to become an expert in a distinct system, it limits his ability to adapt across different philosophies, talent levels, and unexpected situations that occur within the evolving environment of the game.

This is the issue that was addressed in the book Adapt or Die. The football domain is like a living organism. It evolves and grows every year. As a result, coaches who learn through a specialized system lack the tools necessary to quickly adapt to the changes of personnel and strategies that occur in the game over time. Specialized system coaches see the game through the eyes and methods of their mentors instead of perceiving the reality of the game as it is occurring in real-time. There are many examples of this every year in football. Offensive and Defensive systems that once dominated become stagnant because the rules of the subsystem are not fluid to handle the explicit and implicit information necessary to change.

ARE YOU WILLING TO DIE ON THIS HILL?

I experienced this first hand early in my coaching career. In my second year as a coach, we changed from a Flex Bone offensive system to a No-Huddle Spread system. The No-Huddle Spread offense was a specialized system that was quickly becoming popular in the 21st century. We learned the system under Randy Walker, the Head Coach at Northwestern. This subsystem was designed to reduce the amount of explicit information required to process in the game. Spreading out the defense to run the football made it easier to process box numbers and increased spatial awareness of where to attack the defense. The no-huddle tempo forced the defense into static looks that made the implicit decision-making process much smoother.

This system quickly produced offensive records and in the second year took us to the first state-final appearance in school history. This system greatly benefitted a young coach by reducing the explicit knowledge burden to know everything about the game. I quickly became biased that the No-Huddle Spread offensive system was the best system in football and the only one worth running. My perception of reality was heavily influenced by the mentors I was coaching under and the success we were experiencing.

Two years later I took a job at Palmetto Ridge High School in Naples, Florida. It was a brand-new high school playing a varsity schedule with mostly sophomores. The head coach was an expert in the Single Wing offensive system. The offensive coordinator was an expert in a hybrid unbalanced Spread Single Wing system. I was a young "know it all" coach that though he was an expert in the Spread No-Huddle system. Every coach in the room was a self-imposed expert in a specialized system that operated within the domain of football. The problem was that each system had its own explicit and implicit approaches that functioned within a culturally specific language, rules, and decision-making procedures.

Every staff meeting was a battle of ego that might as well have been in English, Chinese, and French. Each coach was willing to die on a hill for what they believed was the best system to teach the game of football. The burden of proof wasn't in the process explaining the "why" but it was in the prizes that they had won doing it the way that they had learned. Coaches weren't willing to invest the time necessary to learn an entirely new way of doing things. Space and time again was the enemy. I witnessed in those meetings how the ideology of specialized systems fragment staffs all over the country.

To no avail, we submitted to the Head Coach and ran the Single Wing offense. We went 5-5 that year, which was a great season for a young inexperienced team. The biggest lesson I learned was that my preconceived bias in the No-Huddle Spread offensive system being the best was shattered. However, bigger questions burned in my heart after that season.

> Is there a way to bridge the explicit and implicit knowledge gap of space and time it takes to become an expert?
>
> Is there a way to network the best practices in every specialized system in the football domain into one holistic system?
>
> Is there a way to accelerate decision-making under pressure at an expert level in the football domain?
>
> Is there a way to justify the "why" behind decision-making within football systems with scientific and mathematical proof?
>
> Is there a way to easily transfer expert football knowledge to grow a novice into an expert?
>
> Is there a way to quickly know "What is Open..."

ARTIFICIAL INTELLIGENCE AND THE R4 EXPERT SYSTEM

I've heard it said that when you hit a creative roadblock, it's best to look outside your domain to find a solution. As a biology major in college, I thrived on finding the simple connections of science that allow the complex to come to life. The life source-code of a DNA strand is made of 4 simple nitrogenous bases. These bases of Adenine, Cytosine, Thymine, and Guanine can only pair specifically with one another. Adenine can only bond with Thymine and Cytosine can only bond with Guanine. These simple non-negotiable rules provide the building blocks to fathom the foundation of the complex world of biology. I desperately needed to find these types of foot-holds for football.

In the search for a scientific solution, we investigated a new technology that was beginning to emerge. It was artificial intelligence. Artificial intelligence (AI) is an area of computer science the creates machines that think, reason, and react like humans. The creation of artificial intelligence requires scientists to reverse engineer the human brain. The branch of AI that was developed to understand human learning and thinking is called Expert systems. Expert systems are computer applications that accelerate and solve complex decision-making problems at the level of extraordinary human expertise.

The expert system was the answer that I had been looking for but didn't know even existed.

Deconstructing the expert system model produced the road map to developing a holistic solution that was missing for football. However, creating a machine that could inform the coach or player what to do wasn't the goal. If we could learn through AI how an expert brain thinks and operates, we could engineer better learning methods and strategies to accelerate our brain's functioning within a football domain. AI is built to possess the elite capabilities of human intelligence. This requires elite visual, verbal, and cognitive skills. If we know how to create those capabilities through machine learning, then we can apply that process to produce and enhance those qualities in our own lives.

Expert systems are made of 3 core components. They are the Knowledge Base, Interface, and Inference Engine. (Fig. 0-1)

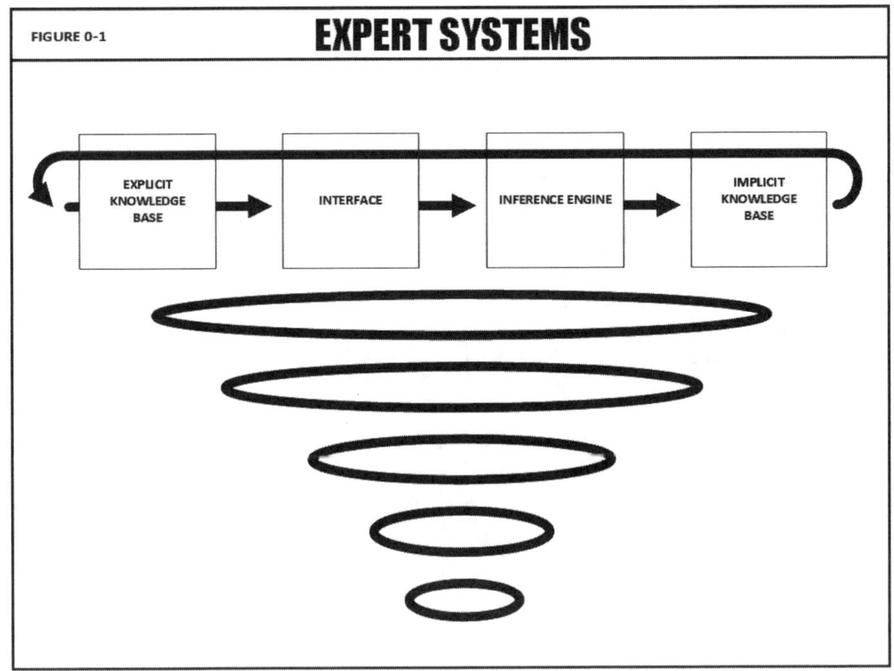

These components code data in a domain and create a mechanism that allows information learning to be accelerated and understood like a human expert.

Knowledge Base – A store of factual knowledge that is specific to a domain (football).

There are 2 categories that make up the knowledge base. They are factual knowledge (Explicit) and heuristic knowledge (Implicit). Explicit knowledge is all the coded rules and strategy that occurs within the game of football. Heuristic (Implicit) knowledge is all the uncoded mental models of information that a coach gains through experience. These are the two areas under which most coaches attempt to learn the game. The problem is space (bandwidth) and time limitations inhibit accelerated processing of information.

Interface – A common language that provides frame-of-reference tools that accelerate the distillation of data into information that can be easily understood and communicated.

The interface is a mechanism of tools that organize and code the data within the factual (Explicit) knowledge. This mechanism provides verbal and visual frames of reference to distill the vast amount of information within a domain. This allows information to be easily understood by the user. The interface is a bridge that crosses the learning gap and connects the factual (Explicit) expert knowledge to the heuristic (Implicit) expert knowledge.

Inference Engine – A process of IF/THEN rules applied to the knowledge base to explain how the expert system arrived at the solution and can deduce the "why" behind the solution.

The inference engine is the mechanism that accelerates decision-making. It is a process that identifies a pattern of non-negotiables in a given situation to inform the user of the best decision to make based on probabilities of factual (Explicit) knowledge and heuristic (Implicit) knowledge. The inference engine provides probability decision-making platforms that are connected by IF/THEN/ELSE statements. This allows a football user to understand and tell the story behind the best decision to make. The probability platforms were named Rhythm-Read-Rush-Release. This was the origin of the R4 expert system.

These 3 core components provided the building blocks to develop an expert system specific to the domain of football. This was a daunting task but worth the risk.

This book is broken down into four parts.

Part I - We cover the two major components that create the R4 interface. This will help the player understand how to create mental models that accelerate decision-making under pressure.

Part II - We will discover the relationships of personnel, formations, and scheme. Then we will show how the R4 inference engine accelerates the ability to understand the best personnel, formations, and scheme to use for any given situation.

Part III - We will lay out how the R4 interface and inference engine work together to develop the R4 grid. Then we will show how the grids work together to make a play-call sheet that accelerates play-call decision-making and practice scripts against an opponent.

Part IV - We will identify common behaviors that breakdown staff culture and show how the R4 system can bring a staff together and change the game.

Let's begin.

CHAPTER 1

WHAT IS OPEN?

H.A.L.O. Effect

WHAT IS OPEN?

H.A.L.O. Effect

In 2012 I was invited to a private coaching clinic at the University of Auburn. It was a collaborative clinic for a select group of high school and small college coaches from the southeast. The afternoon session was devoted to game-planning and play-calling. Coach Gus Malzahn's lead offensive analyst covered the Auburn offensive system. The coach took us through their game-planning process, play-call sheet and how they conducted play-calls during the game.

One of his in-game duties was drawing every defensive look they were getting to their formations during the game. He was then in charge of transposing the looks on a whiteboard in the locker room at half time. He talked about the genius of Coach Malzahn and how quickly he could look at a diagram under pressure and immediately know where to attack and what adjustment to make. "He just knew what is open."

Intrigued by this comment I raised my hand and asked, "Does Coach Malzahn have a way to teach you how he determines what is open?"

He paused for a few seconds to contemplate the question. It was as if he never even thought about the possibility of possessing this strength. He then responded with a smile, "No, but if he did, that would be awesome!"

I was excited by this answer because I knew that the R4 expert system could make this a reality for coaches, players, and even fans.

A key takeaway from this clinic was how the language and decision-making processes that operate football systems is heavily dependent on the head coach's or coordinator's expertise. This is the bottleneck that occurs in subsystems all over the country. Without an interface and inference engine to connect the explicit to the implicit expert knowledge, perceptions of space and time between players and assistants are scattered.

> *We do not perceive the world we see, we see the world we know how to perceive.*
>
> -Humberto Maturana

This quote is a summary of the Santiago Theory of Cognition. Humans, unlike machines, are living systems. They do not record reality like a video camera. Humans react with reality to produce perceptional awareness. The issue is that human perceptions are based on what they individually know and what experiences they have had. This is where the disconnect of cognition occurs. In football, what a coach may think is the best offense to run, or play-call to make, is based on his view of reality. When one human tells another human what is real, they are making a demand for obedience. This submission inhibits innovation and acceleration of knowledge transfer.

If we have different views on reality, which we probably do because of the experiences we've had and what we know, then there is going to be friction and a limit to how fast and far we can go together as a team. However, if it is possible to view reality from the same lens, we could accelerate the flow of information and knowledge and create a collective intelligence to produce the best decisions within a given domain.

The interface and inference engine of an expert system makes this possible. These mechanisms provide the mental tools, language and process to produce mental models that communicate verbally and visually what is occurring in the reality of the domain environment.

We will start with the interface.

The interface provides a pattern recognition process that bridges the gap of explicit expert knowledge and implicit expert experience. This is the missing link in the game-planning and play-calling process of football systems. The highest need for coaches and players is to perceive, process, and communicate space and time at an expert level of speed. This begins by identifying the goals within a domain.

The goal in the football domain is to own space.

The goal of the defense is to cover space – or in R4 terms CAP space.

The goal of the offense is to create space – or in R4 terms UNCAP space.

The interface extracts non-negotiables from base knowledge that is relevant to achieving the goal. Non-negotiables are the information that is most important in a situation. The tools that distill this information are called frames of reference. A frame of reference is a stable regularity in an environment that allows measurement and judgments to be made.

DICTATING SPACE – FORMATIONS

Offensive formations are a frame of reference that dictates the intent of owning space. In the football domain, space is expressed as run or route space. Run-space is formed in gaps. Gaps between 2 linemen create space. Gaps are labeled with letters starting with an A between the center and guard and work out to B, C, D, and E from there. Bringing a player within 2 yds of a down lineman creates an additional gap. Formations will present anywhere from 6-10 gaps of space.

Route-space is formed in tubes. There are 5 vertical tubes in football. There are 5 tubes because that is the maximum number of vertical threats that can be released downfield on a given pass play used to attack vertical space. Formations dictate the number of tubes that can be immediately attacked. (FIG. 1-1)

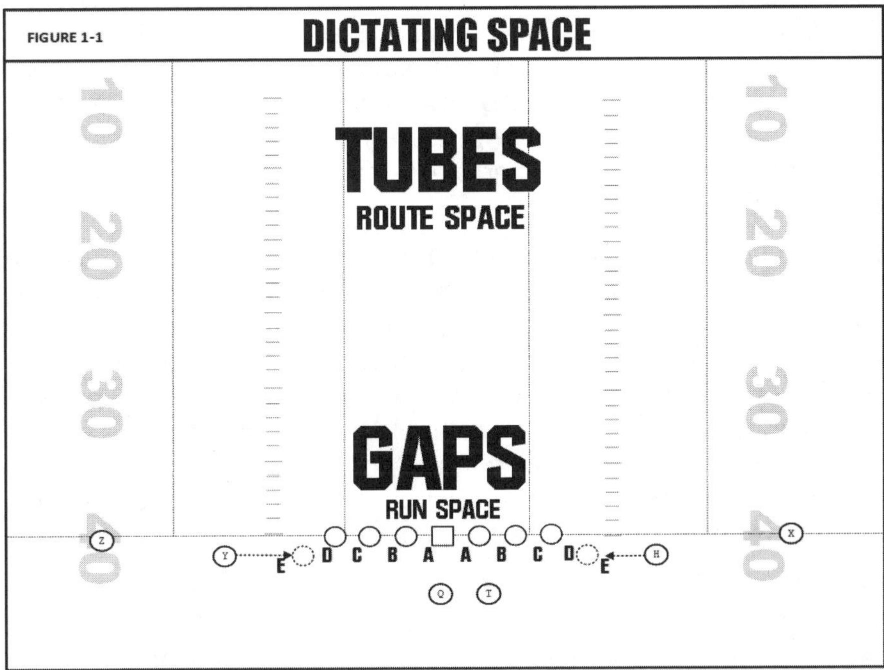

Offensive formations dictate the run and route space that must be defended. Traditional football teaching loosely defines space, but without clear frames of reference, one coach's definition of space may differ from another. In the absence of a clear definition of who is right... how can we know where run space ends and route space begins? How can we clearly communicate positions of defenders and the space they intend to cover without clear boundaries?

DEFINING SPACE – H.A.L.O.

The inability of determining positions in space presents the highest obstacle to overcome for many occupations. In the aviation field, the term is called spatial disorientation. Spatial disorientation is the inability to determine a person's position, location and motion relative to their environment. This condition results in almost half of flight accidents for fighter pilots in high-performance aircraft. Most result in a fatality. Furthermore, these accidents occurred in optimal flight conditions during the day with high visibility.

The alarming fact of these fatal crashes is that they occurred with pilots who averaged 30 years old, with 10 years of cockpit experience. They also had obtained 1,500 hours of instructor time and in the previous 3 months had flown an average of 25 times. The takeaway is that no amount of expertise, training, or experience negates issues with spatial disorientation.

The military has invested millions of dollars to develop technology to help overcome spatial disorientation. The modern fighter pilot has auto-correct features, helmet visor displays, and 3D visual guides. These advancements provide new safeguards and project a massive amount of flight information. However, these advancements present their own set of problems. The technology narrows the pilot's field of view, the visuals use symbols that are not universal, and the displays are not intuitive. The result is an overload of information that prevents the pilot from accelerating decision-making.

Similarly, coaches and players will also struggle with spatial disorientation throughout their careers. As the aerospace industry discovered, more information is not always better. Many coaches and players overload themselves with information only to spiral out of control when the conditions of the environment change. The ability to anticipate these changes requires tools that can orient the user to the reality of the environment.

The R4 interface is the football mechanism that provides stable regularities in the environment to counter spatial disorientation. The first interface tool is called the HALO. The H.A.L.O. is a verbal acronym that provides consistent visual frames of reference for any formation. The HALO boundaries clearly define the run and route space for any formation. It also allows coaches and players to recalibrate and read the reality of "what is open" in real-time. (FIG. 1-2)

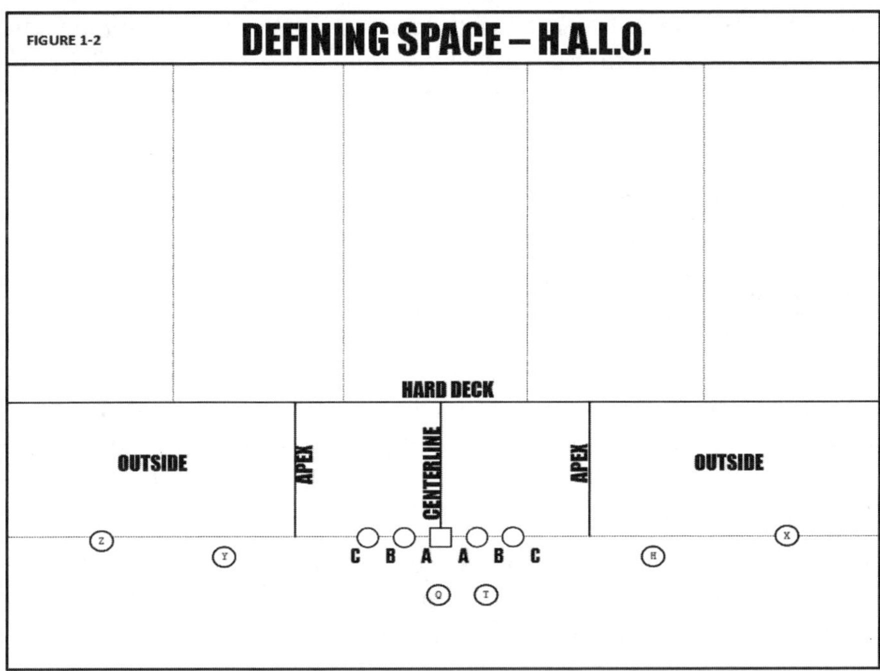

The H in HALO stands for **Hard Deck.** The Hard Deck reveals vertical-route space. The Hard Deck is a transition line into vertical space. The Hard Deck is a horizontal line that originates 7-yds from the line of scrimmage. This is the minimum distance in which a receiver can threaten a defender on rhythm-throws in 1.8 seconds (last step of QB drop). The Hard Deck line is fluid and can move up to 10 yards at the coach's discretion if the receivers can gain a higher range of yards on rhythm.

The A in HALO stands for the **Apex.** The Apex is the boundary line separating run space from flat tube-space. The Apex line is the midpoint between the end man on the line of scrimmage and the 1st eligible wide receiver. The Apex line is 2 yds outside the end man on the line of scrimmage if no wide receiver is outside of him. The Apex line is therefore fluid and will move based on the formation and the splits of the receivers.

The L in HALO stands for the **Line of Center.** The Line of Center is critical because it defines the number of defenders to a side of a formation. This is used when scheming concepts to attack defensive man-advantage to a side of space. This line runs through the center.

The O in HALO stands for **Outside space.** The Outside space defines horizontal tube space. The outside space is very important to highlight because it is space that contains a mixture of run and route space properties. For example, receivers who are located outside the Apex line create an immediate space threat for the defense to defend. If the Outside space is void of a defender for each receiver, then the offense can immediately attack the space with quick-pass screens or outside-run sweep concepts.

Overlaying the HALO interface tool on a formation clears the blurred lines of space that must be defended. (FIG. 1-3)

The HALO reveals that there are 15 total spaces that a defense must defend. 5 Vertical tubes + 4 immediate outside threats + 6 run gaps of run space = 15 spaces. The defense only has 11 players to defend these 15 spaces. This math reveals that there are 4 areas space advantage for the offense to immediately attack.

These spaces are called **Bubbles.** Bubbles are areas of space in the HALO that are void of a defender. Bubbles represent the highest priority of space to be attacked by the offense.

In (Fig. 1-4), the defense has 11 defenders to CAP 15 spaces. The HALO reveals the 4 Bubbles.

Next let's look at a 3 x 1 formation to see if the bubbles of space have changed. (Fig. 1-5)

The Hard Deck reveals that there are still 5 Vertical tubes of route space available. The Apex and Centerline reveals that there are 6 gaps of run space (3 on each side). The Outside space shows 1 immediate threat to the left of the formation and 3 immediate threats to the right of the

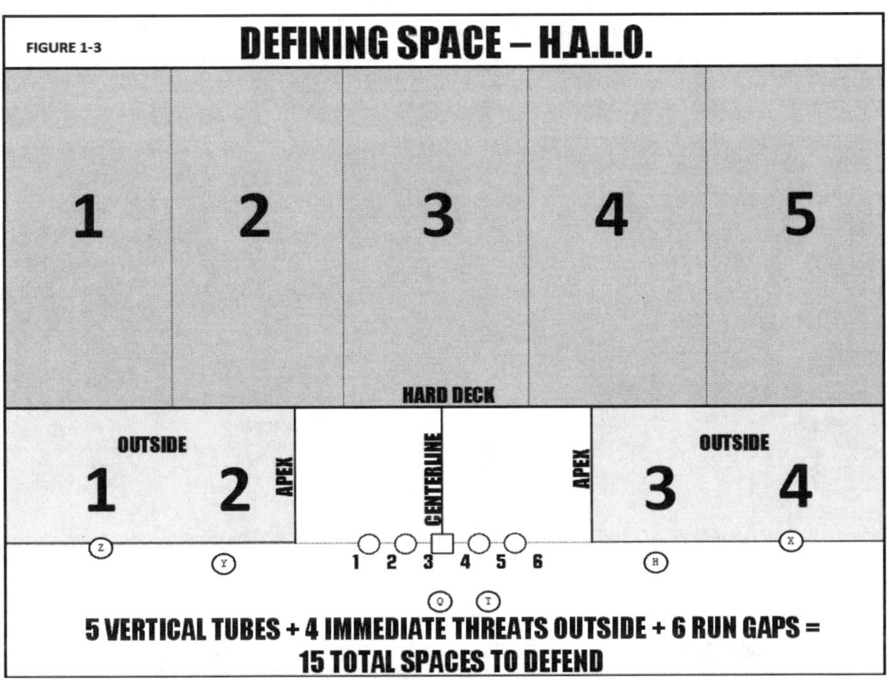
FIGURE 1-3
DEFINING SPACE – H.A.L.O.
1
2
3
4
5
HARD DECK
OUTSIDE
1
2
APEX
CENTERLINE
APEX
OUTSIDE
3
4
Z
Y
1 2 3 4 5 6
H
X
Q
T
5 VERTICAL TUBES + 4 IMMEDIATE THREATS OUTSIDE + 6 RUN GAPS =
15 TOTAL SPACES TO DEFEND

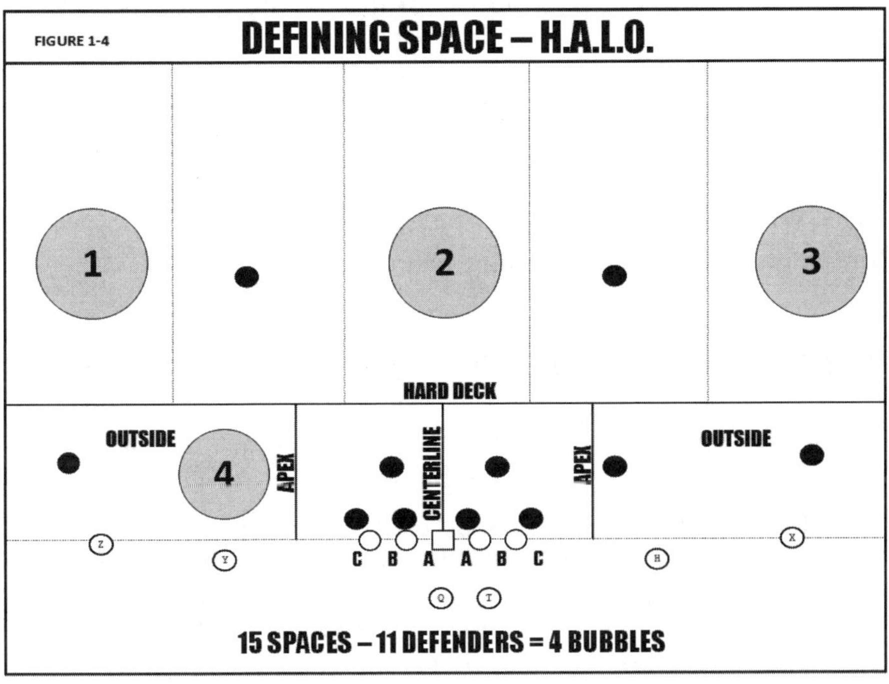
FIGURE 1-4
DEFINING SPACE – H.A.L.O.
1
2
3
HARD DECK
OUTSIDE
4
APEX
CENTERLINE
APEX
OUTSIDE
Z
Y
C B A A B C
H
X
Q
T
15 SPACES – 11 DEFENDERS = 4 BUBBLES

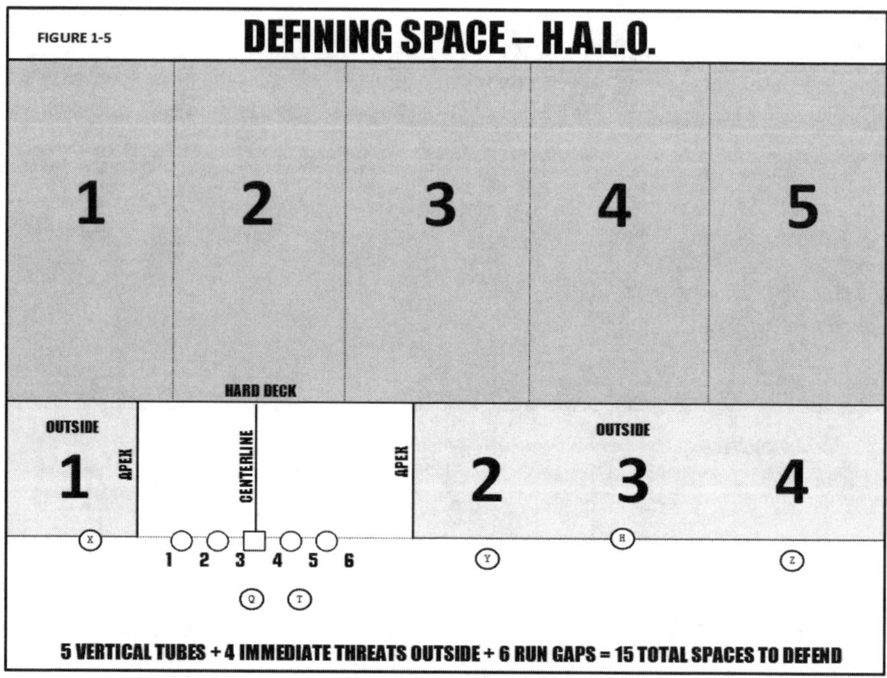

formation. While the distribution of immediate route threats has changed, the total Outside space threat still totals 4 spaces. The HALO again shows that there are 15 total spaces that a defense must defend. 5 Vertical tubes + 4 immediate outside threats + 6 run gaps of run space = 15 spaces.

In (Fig. 1-6), the defense has 11 defenders to CAP 15 spaces.
The HALO reveals the 4 Bubbles of space are still present even if the formation or location on the field changes.

DISCOVERING SPACE RELATIONSHIPS – BOX AND BUBBLES

The relationship between the movement of defenders is directly correlated to the movement of the 4 Bubbles of space.

The intent of defender placement is relative to the priority threats that a formation presents. The highest priority threat to the defense is run space within a formation. The HALO increases the spatial awareness of run space with clear boundaries that form the run BOX. The BOX is the heart of the formation and represents the easiest way for the of-

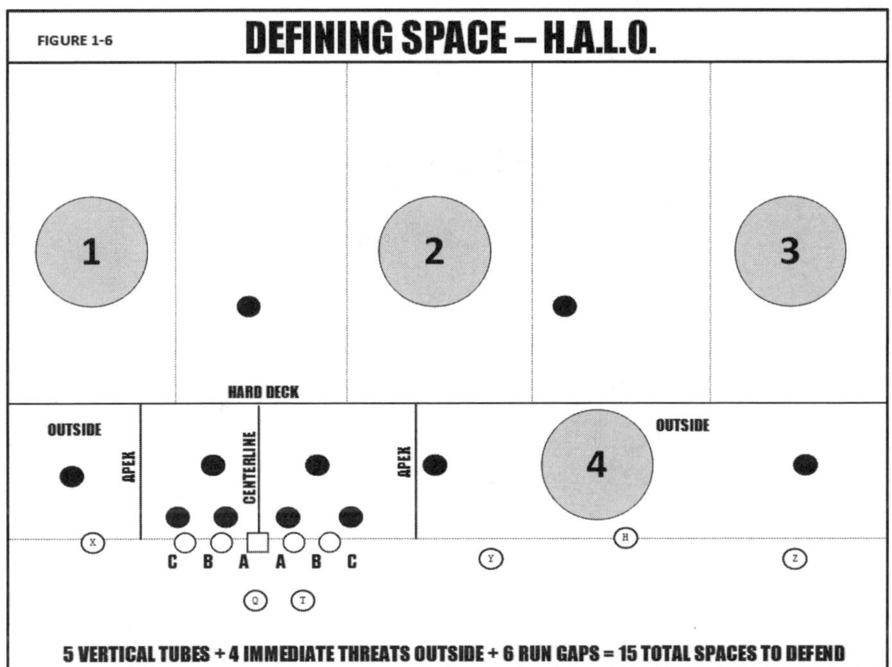

fense to advance the ball. Therefore, the defense must maintain a count of defenders who equals the number of run gaps in the BOX. (Fig. 1-7)

The BOX count of defenders initiates the game-planning process. This is how the shell game of football begins. If there is no BUBBLE in the BOX, then the offensive priority would be to attack an UNCAPPED BUBBLE of route space in the tubes.

For example, if we look at the original 2 x 2 Formation the HALO reveals that there are no Bubbles of space in the BOX.

If the offense attacks the fourth Bubble over the Y receiver, the defense may next move a defender out of the BOX to CAP this Bubble. (Fig. 1-8)

The relationship of these movements shows that if the defender moves out of the run BOX to CAP a tube that he also UNCAPS a run Gap. Capping Tubes, Uncaps Gaps. If a defender leaves a tube to CAP a run gap, then he UNCAPS that route tube. Capping Gaps, Uncaps Tubes. (FIG. 1-9)

At a minimum, there are always 4 Bubbles of space advantage given to the offense. However, there can be additional Bubbles present if the

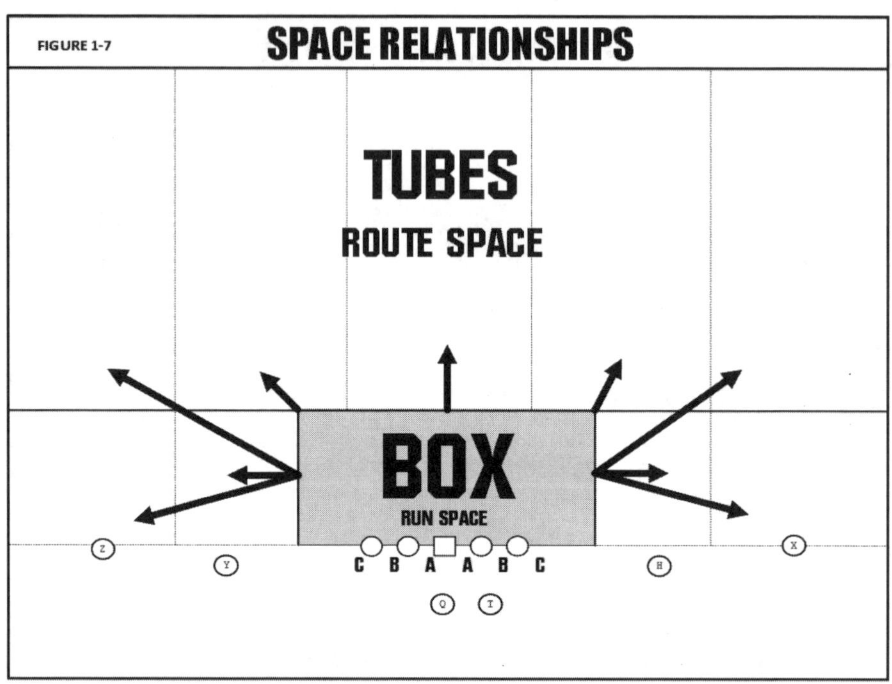
FIGURE 1-7
SPACE RELATIONSHIPS
TUBES
ROUTE SPACE
BOX
RUN SPACE
Z
Y
C B A A B C
Q T
H
X

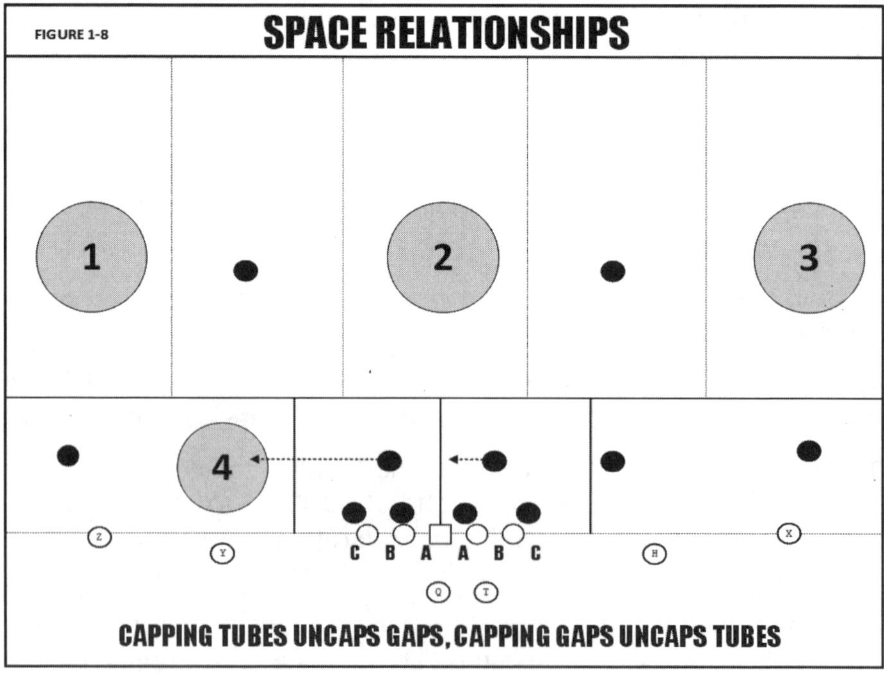
FIGURE 1-8
SPACE RELATIONSHIPS
1
2
3
4
Z
Y
C B A A B C
Q T
H
X
CAPPING TUBES UNCAPS GAPS, CAPPING GAPS UNCAPS TUBES

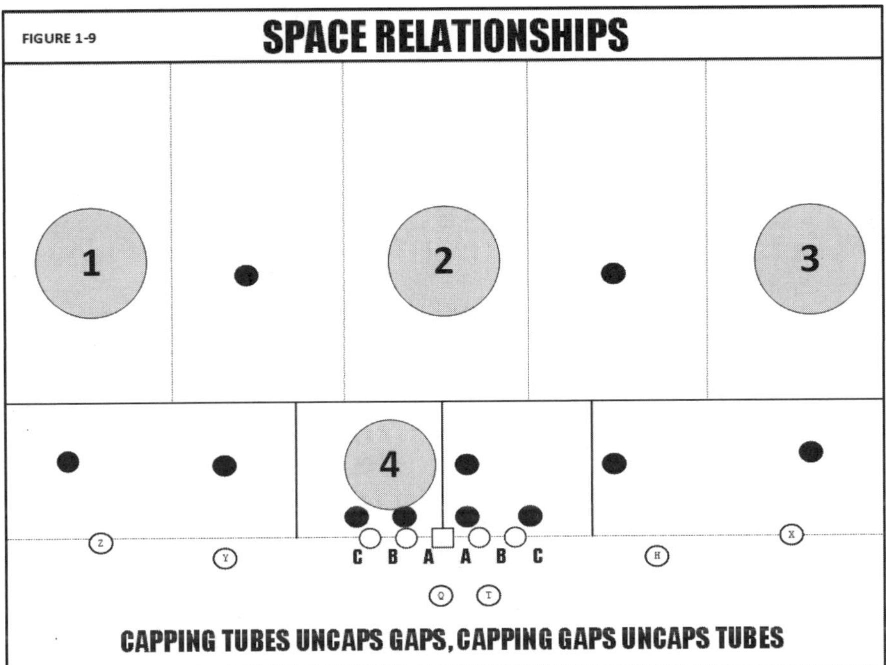

defense is misaligned or attempts to overload an area of run or route space due to an offensive mismatch. For example, if the offense has a superior run game and the defense is outmatched or anticipates a run play, they may decide to add an additional defender to the run BOX. (FIG. 1-10)

THE PERSONNEL EFFECT ON SPACE

We have just discovered the Bubbles of space opportunity that are available for the offense. However, the next concern is determining if changing personnel or personnel alignment affect the Bubbles of space. We previously looked at a 2 x 2 and 3 x 1 formation out of 10 Personnel.

11 PERSONNEL

Now let's look at 11 Personnel grouping and different formations we can get in with it. The first formation we will use is a 3 x 1 formation. (Fig. 1-11)

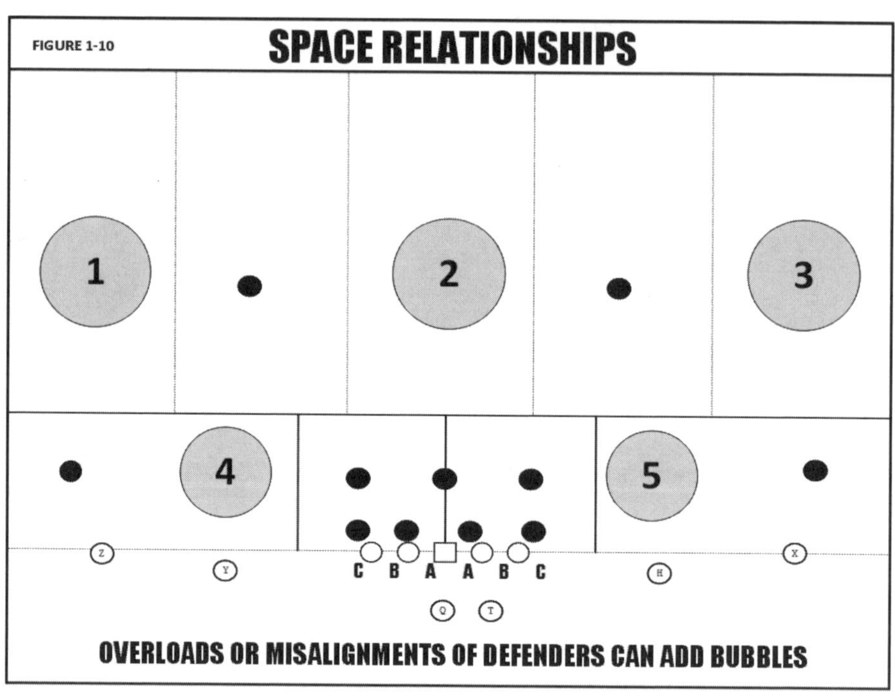
FIGURE 1-10
SPACE RELATIONSHIPS
1
2
3
4
5
Z
Y
C B A A B C
H
X
Q T
OVERLOADS OR MISALIGNMENTS OF DEFENDERS CAN ADD BUBBLES

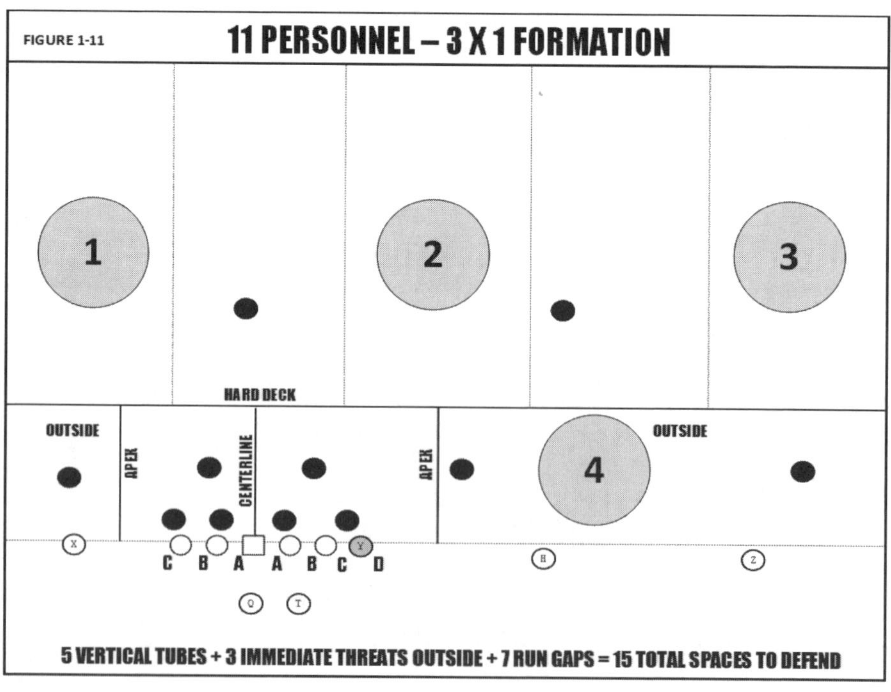
FIGURE 1-11
11 PERSONNEL – 3 X 1 FORMATION
1
2
3
HARD DECK
OUTSIDE
APEX
CENTERLINE
APEX
4
OUTSIDE
X
Y
C B A A B C D
H
Z
Q T
5 VERTICAL TUBES + 3 IMMEDIATE THREATS OUTSIDE + 7 RUN GAPS = 15 TOTAL SPACES TO DEFEND

When we add a tight end, we add a run gap inside the BOX. This extra run gap can still release and attack a vertical tube, so the 5 vertical tube threats still remain. The extra Gap now presents 7 total gaps to defend. We have 1 receiver in the outside tube to the left and 2 receivers in the outside tube to the right. This presents a total of 3 immediate threats in the outside tube. 5 tubes + 7 gaps + 3 in the outside tubes = 15 spaces to defend. With only 11 players to defend 15 spaces the offense still has 4 bubbles of space opportunity.

If we move the TE over to a create a 2 x 2 Formation, we still have 5 vertical tube threats and 7 run gaps in the BOX. (FIG. 1-12)

There is 1 receiver in the outside tube to the left and 2 receivers to the outside tube to the right. This still presents 3 immediate threats in the outside tube. 5 tubes + 7 gaps + 3 in outside tubes = 15 spaces to defend. 15 spaces – 11 defenders = 4 bubbles.

If we move the boundary WR over and look at a 3 x 1 nub tight end formation we still have 5 vertical tube threats, + 7 run gaps. (FIG. 1-13) There is no immediate route space threat to defend in the outside tube to the left because pre-snap no receiver is in that tube. The tight end

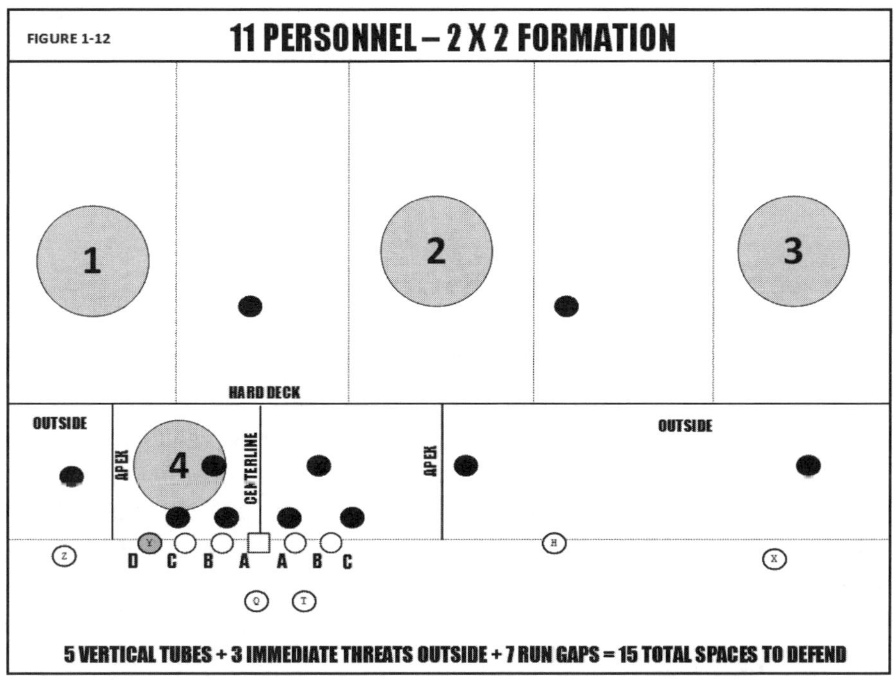

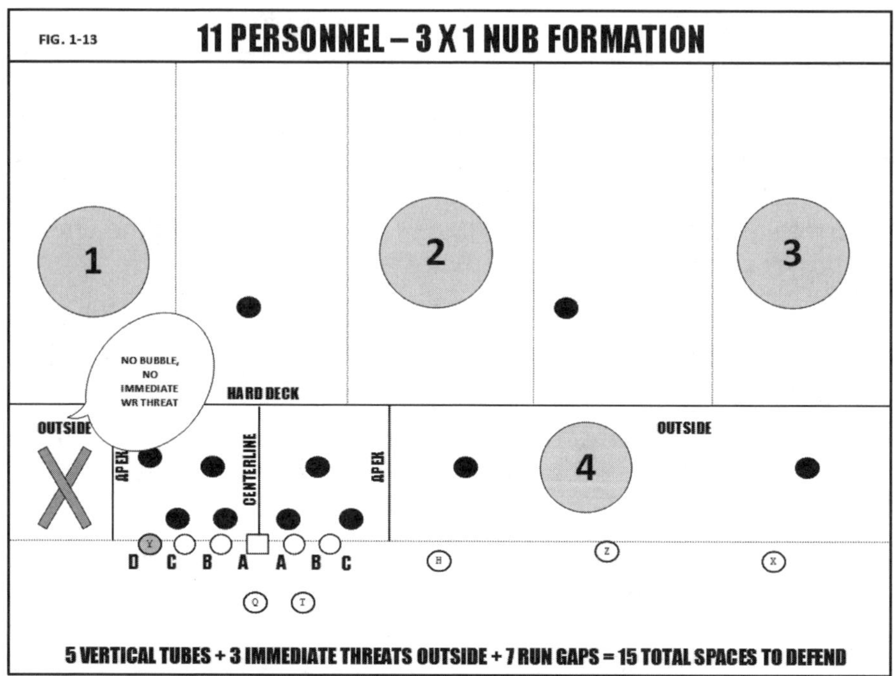

is not an immediate outside tube threat because he is capped by a D gap defender. The offense would have to scheme to get the tight end or receiver threat into this space post-snap. We will discuss scheme strategies to accomplish this later. 5 tubes + 7 gaps + 3 in outside tubes = 15 spaces to defend. 15 spaces – 11 defenders = 4 bubbles.

12 PERSONNEL

If we use 12 Personnel and look at a 2 x 2 Formation we still have 5 vertical tube threats. (FIG. 1-14)

By adding an additional tight end, we create 8 run gaps. We have 1 receiver threat in the outside tube to the left and 1 receiver in the outside tube to the right. This is a total of 2 receiver threats in the outside tubes. 5 tubes + 8 gaps + 2 in outside tubes = 15 spaces to defend. 15 spaces – 11 defenders = 4 bubbles.

If we move the receiver over to a 3 x 1 tight end nub formation, we still have 5 vertical tube threats and 8 run gaps. (FIG. 1-15)

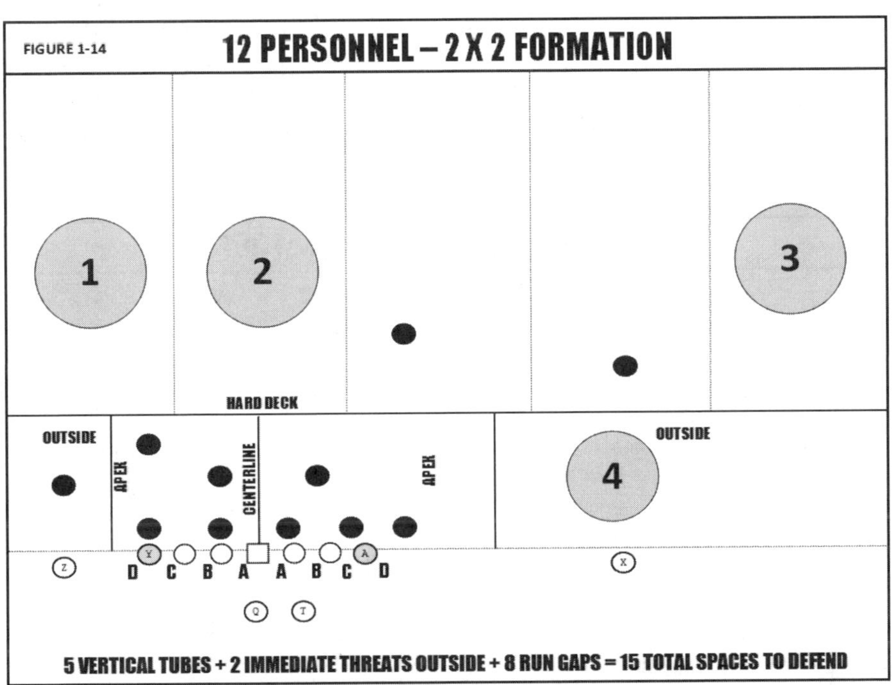
FIGURE 1-14
12 PERSONNEL – 2 X 2 FORMATION
1
2
3
HARD DECK
OUTSIDE
APEX
CENTERLINE
APEX
OUTSIDE
4
Y
A
D C B A A B C D
Z
X
Q
T
5 VERTICAL TUBES + 2 IMMEDIATE THREATS OUTSIDE + 8 RUN GAPS = 15 TOTAL SPACES TO DEFEND

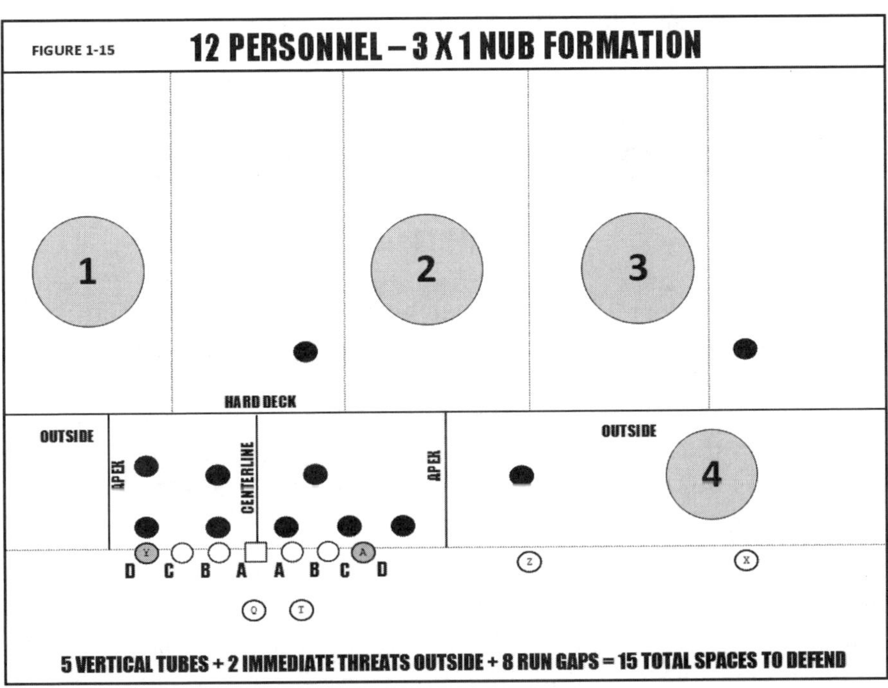
FIGURE 1-15
12 PERSONNEL – 3 X 1 NUB FORMATION
1
2
3
HARD DECK
OUTSIDE
APEX
CENTERLINE
APEX
OUTSIDE
4
Y
A
D C B A A B C D
Z
X
Q
T
5 VERTICAL TUBES + 2 IMMEDIATE THREATS OUTSIDE + 8 RUN GAPS = 15 TOTAL SPACES TO DEFEND

There is no immediate receiver threat to the outside tube to the left. Again, this is not an immediate space to be defended. There are 2 immediate threats to the outside tube to the right. 5 tubes + 8 gaps + 2 in outside tubes = 15 spaces to defend. 15 spaces – 11 defenders = 4 bubbles.

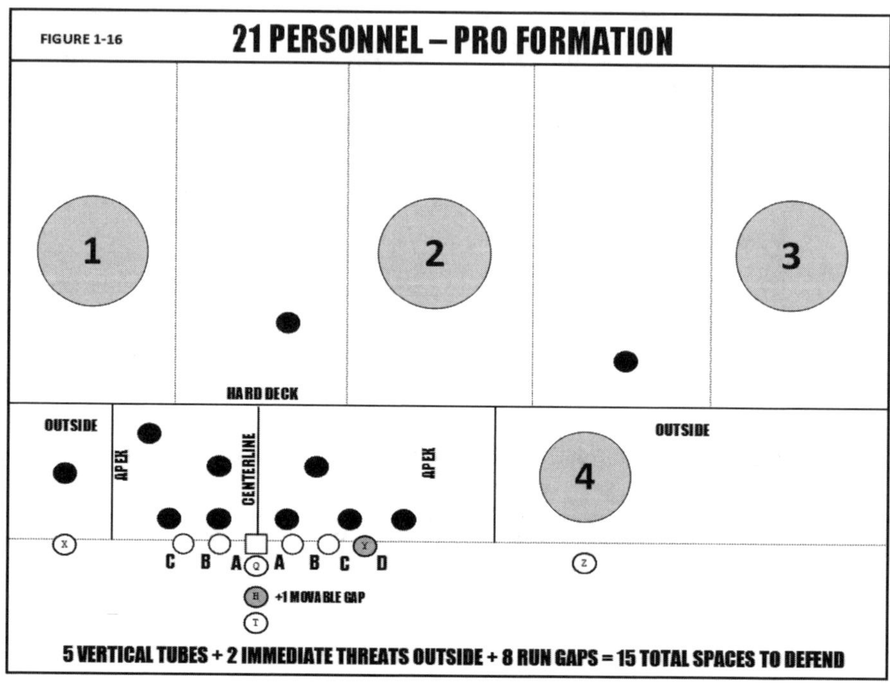

21 PERSONNEL

Next, we will look at 21 Personnel in a Pro formation. (FIG. 1-16) We can still release 5 players into each of the 5 vertical tubes. The tight end and fullback give us 8 run gaps that the defense must defend. We have 1 receiver in the outside tube to the left and 1 receiver in the outside tube to the right for a total of 2 in the outside tubes. 5 vertical tube threats + 8 run gaps + 2 in the outside tube = 15 spaces. 15 spaces – 11 players = 4 bubbles.

If we move the receiver over to a Slot Formation we still have 5 vertical tube threats + 8 run gaps + 2 receivers in the outside tube. (FIG. 1-17) Once again, the outside space to the left is not an immediate space to be defended because no pre-snap receiver threat is lined up in that

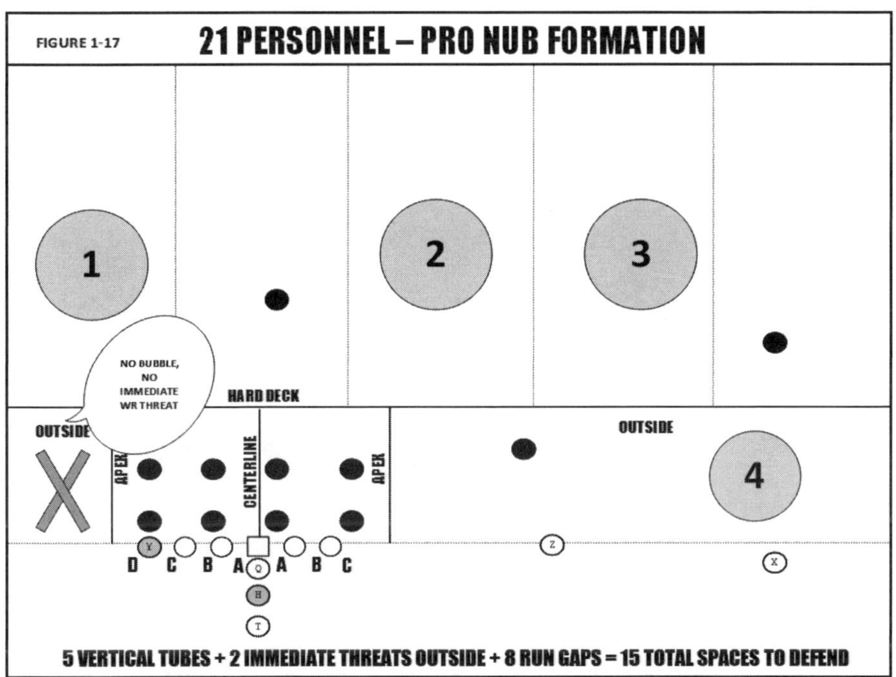

space. 5 tubes + 8 gaps + 2 in the outside tubes = 15 spaces. 15 spaces – 11 players = 4 bubbles.

22 PERSONNEL

Next, we will look at 22 Personnel in a double tight end and full back formation. (FIG. 1-18)

We still have 5 vertical tube threats. The 2 tight ends along with a full back provide 9 run gaps for the defense to defend. There is no receiver in the outside tube to the left. There is only 1 receiver in the outside tube to the right. 5 tubes + 9 gaps + 1 in outside tubes = 15 spaces. 15 spaces – 11 players = 4 bubbles.

32 PERSONNEL

Finally, we will look at a 32 Personnel double-wing formation. (FIG. 1-19)

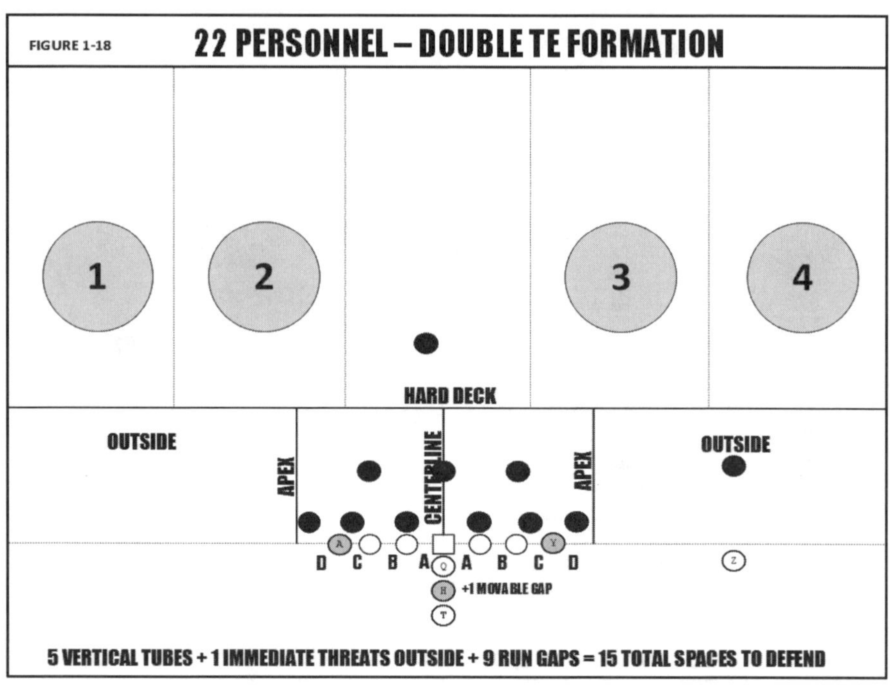
FIGURE 1-18
22 PERSONNEL – DOUBLE TE FORMATION
1
2
3
4
HARD DECK
OUTSIDE
APEX
CENTERLINE
APEX
OUTSIDE
D C B A A B C D
+1 MOVABLE GAP
5 VERTICAL TUBES + 1 IMMEDIATE THREATS OUTSIDE + 9 RUN GAPS = 15 TOTAL SPACES TO DEFEND

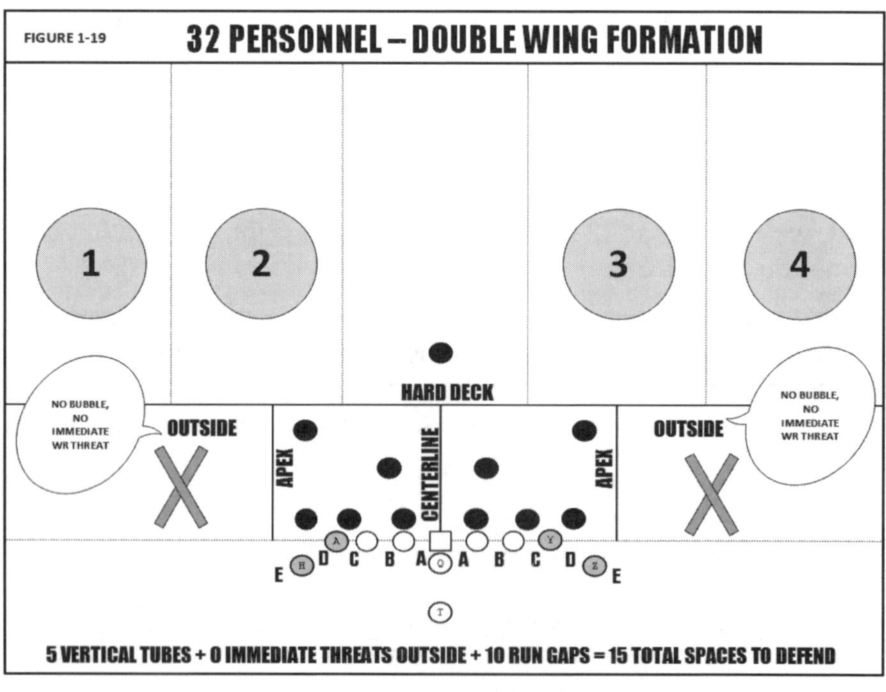
FIGURE 1-19
32 PERSONNEL – DOUBLE WING FORMATION
1
2
3
4
HARD DECK
NO BUBBLE, NO IMMEDIATE WR THREAT
OUTSIDE
APEX
CENTERLINE
APEX
OUTSIDE
NO BUBBLE, NO IMMEDIATE WR THREAT
E D C B A A B C D E
5 VERTICAL TUBES + 0 IMMEDIATE THREATS OUTSIDE + 10 RUN GAPS = 15 TOTAL SPACES TO DEFEND

We still have 5 vertical tube threats. The 2 tight ends and 2 full backs provide 10 run gaps to be defended. There are no receivers in the outside tubes to the left or the right. 5 vertical tubes + 10 run gaps + 0 Outside Tubes = 15 spaces. 15 spaces - 11 players = 4 bubbles.

What we have learned so far is that changing personnel will shift immediate space threats within the HALO, but it does not change the number of spaces on the field to be defended. There are always 15 spaces that the defense must defend no matter what the personnel or formation. With only 11 players to defend those 15 spaces, there is a minimum of 4 bubbles of UNCAPPED space advantage for the offense.

FINDING OPEN

Here are some critical space relationships that the HALO interface tool reveals to better define "What is Open?"

- A defense cannot simultaneously defend all run and route space. There is always opportunity for the offense.
- A bubble is formed in the absence of a defender in that space. In other words, a Bubble is a space that is void of a defender.
- Bubbles are immediate space that is available to the offense.
- With only 11 players to cover 15 spaces a formation presents, there is always a minimum of 4 bubbles for the offense.
- Additional bubbles of space can form by an overload of defenders in a space or by defensive misalignment.
- Personnel can immediately shift space threats, but it doesn't change the number of spaces that a defense must defend.

CHAPTER 2

MENTAL MODELS
Negative Space Advantage

MENTAL MODELS

Negative Space Advantage

An increase of visual information does not provide a standalone revelation to what is open. It's how you process the information that defines what is open. Mental models are visual pictures that accelerate cognition of what is open in real-time. They are the foundation that experts use to gain mastery within a domain. The interface tool of the HALO allows novice users to access these frames of reference to achieve an expert ability of mental model constructs. Mental models allow the user to accelerate decision-making through pattern recognition. Once the HALO is overlaid on to the formation, a mental model of run space in the Box and route space in the tubes can be clearly defined for the offense. A clear definition informs and communicates an understanding of "what is open." This is the beginning of receiving the gift of pattern recognition. The ability to see what others don't.

"OPEN" SPACE IS NEGATIVE SPACE

An example of the benefit in mental models can be seen in the FedEx logo. (FIG. 2-1)

When Lindon Leader created the logo, he used the E and X as a frame of reference to reveal a pattern of open space in the shape of an arrow. The hidden arrow was a symbol for speed and precision. In the art world, open space between images is called negative space. Artists may use open space between images to form hidden pictures. When you know the picture to look for and the frames of reference that creates it, the picture is no longer hidden. Your eyes are drawn to the open space without thinking. The result is intuition.

Intuition is nothing more than pattern recognition. In the absence of

FIGURE 2-1 **NEGATIVE SPACE ADVANTAGE**

stable regularities in the environment, intuition cannot be communicated or accelerated. The HALO provides the first step in building the bridge to making this possible. Football is played in a three-dimensional domain but building the intuition bridge begins on a two-dimensional platform.

The platform for information transfer between coaches and players is usually a whiteboard or video screen. Such platforms lack the stable regularities that the HALO provides to see space from the same perspective. The HALO provides a medium to see space advantage quickly from the same perspective. This provides the non-negotiables to determine what matters most in decision-making on play design and execution. The result is building better mental models to process spatial awareness in a whole new way.

Building mental models requires practice. The starting point is drawing a diagram of the field or printing out sheets of paper with the field on it. There is an area on FIG. 2-2 to practice drawing if you would like. (Fig. 2-2)

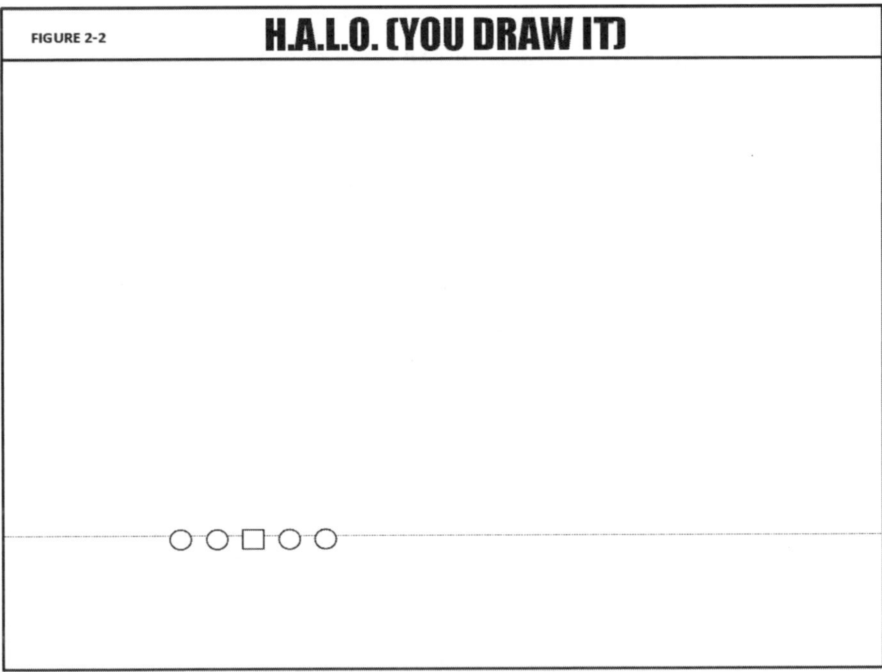

Next, draw a formation on the field. When drawing the HALO, draw the:

1. Horizontal HARD DECK line. The baseline for the HARD DECK is at 7 yds.

2. The APEX line. The APEX line to the left is the mid-point from the end man on the line of scrimmage to the 1st eligible receiver.

3. The LINE of center. The centerline runs through the center to the HARD DECK line and splits the formation in half. The OUTSIDE space is the flat tube area outside each APEX line.

The final frames of reference to be drawn are the 5 vertical tubes. Draw the:

1. The Crossover Tube. The crossover tube is vertical and originates out of the offensive tackles in the formation. Draw a vertical line upwards that is just outside the hip of each offensive tackle on the line of scrimmage. The field is 53.3 yds wide divided by 5 tubes, making each tube around 10 ½ yds in width.

2. If your formation is on a hash, then there will be 3 vertical tubes to the field and 1 tube to the boundary between the crossover tube.

3. If you are in the middle of the field there will be 2 tubes to the left and 2 tubes to the right of the crossover tube.

The next step to practice is drawing in a defense of defenders against the formation. You can fill in whatever defense you choose. After the defense is filled-in, you can begin the practice of training your eyes to search for the Bubbles of space advantage.

LEARN FROM EXPERT SCAN STRATEGIES

The scan path of the eyes should be in a specific pattern. This has been proven through research between expert and intermediate chess players. Experts make fewer eye fixations by focusing on relevant pieces in relation to frames of reference. This produces a pattern of selective saccadic scans that informs the best move. The result is accelerated decision making by matching patterns of preexisting mental models. In other words, expert chess players have a consistent scan strategy when it comes to identifying space opportunity.

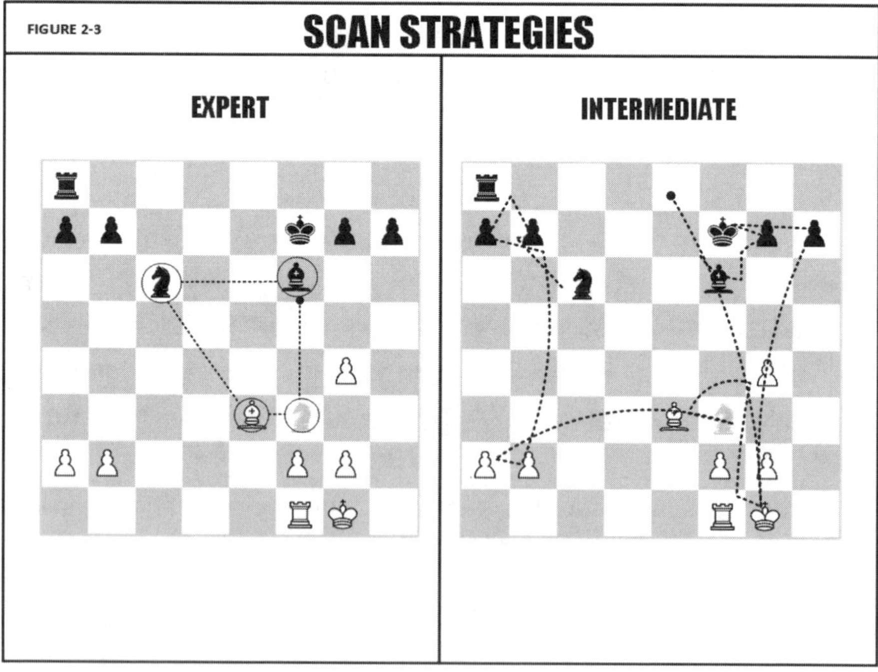

(FIG. 2-3) shows the difference between expert and intermediate chess players. Intermediate players tend to fixate on every piece on the board, moving visually from piece to piece at a time. The scan path is muddled and in no order. Expert chess players fixate with a greater focus on relevant pieces rather than intermediates. The relevant pieces contain critical relationships that reveal patterns of intent. This allows the expert to access and update the correct mental model to increase his spatial awareness of what is occurring on the chess board. By knowing what the key pieces are and the patterns of relationships that they reveal, a user can develop a prioritized scan path that accelerates decision-making.

It is important that coaches and players emulate this advantage in football. The most relevant defenders in football are the ones that frequently adjust to change the space advantage on the field. These defenders are the safeties and outside linebackers. (FIG. 2-4)

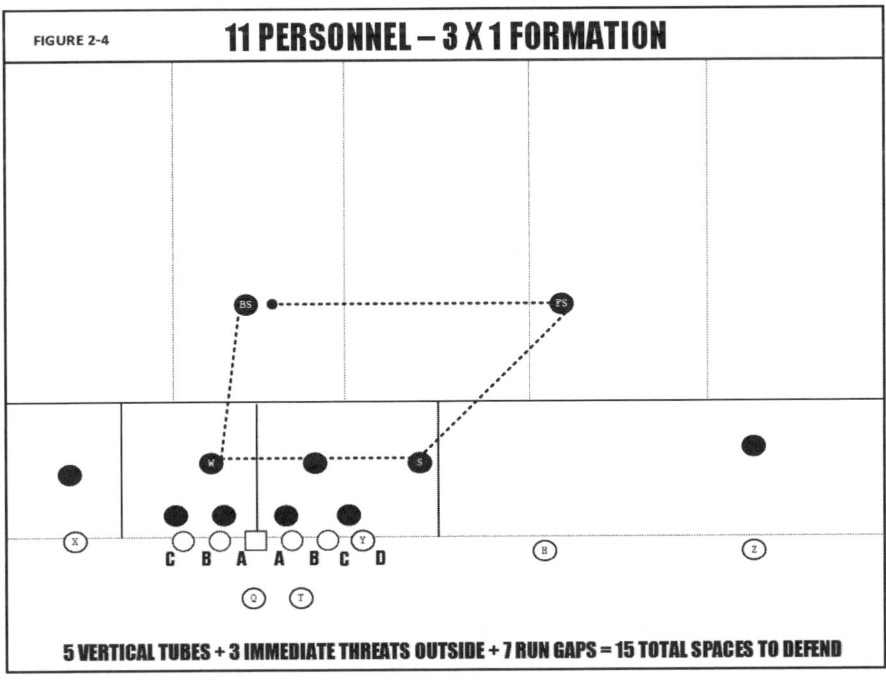

These four key defenders are referred to as dual-read defenders. This means that they can have both run box and route tube responsibilities. This relationship binds these four players together as they are the primary adjusters within a defensive structure. A movement of one of these defenders across a HALO boundary elicits a move with the rest of these key defenders in the group. (FIG. 2-5)

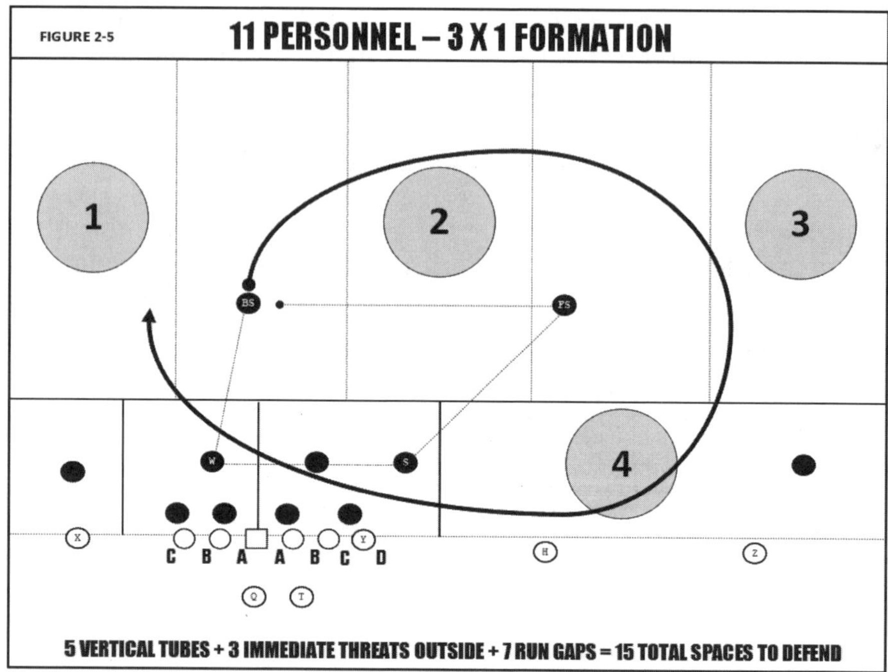

This allows users to develop an expert scan path strategy that mimics expert chess players. The first fixation begins with the boundary or weakside safety. The position of this defender determines the location and movements of the remaining defenders in the group. From this point, the saccadic movement of the eyes will move in a rotation around the HALO frames of reference. As the eyes make this scan, fixations will move from the boundary safety to the field safety to the field-side outside linebacker to the weakside outside linebacker.

The football domain contains pieces that are active, unlike static pieces on a chess board. This requires a scan path that must be smoother to process movements as the positions of space are calculated. To account for this movement, a circular scan path is used when processing spatial awareness while watching film or a play on the field. As this circular scan path occurs, the eyes and brain should identify the Bubbles of space advantage that are void of a defender.

When training scan paths, it is best to first remain in the shallow end of the pool of processing. After practicing the process of identifying static bubbles on a piece of paper, take this practice to video of a game on film. Stop the film when watching a game and use drawing tools on your computer to overlay the HALO onto the screen. Practice the circular search strategy using the key fixation points of defenders. This practice will enhance the mental model snapshots stored in the memory of the mind.

The exercise of creating two-dimensional, pre-snap mental models creates a baseline of spatial awareness, but they are not the end-all. Football is not played on a whiteboard, piece of paper or video screen. It's a three-dimensional world full of chaotic movement under a fixed amount of time. These snapshots of critical observed information against frames of reference must determine current and future meaning for the user.

The purpose of creating pre-snap mental models is to increase intuition of post-snap defender movements. Decision-making is simplified if the post-snap movements match up with the pre-snap mental models. The challenge in football occurs when the movement of defenders is different or the information that was anticipated is missing. For example, what is happening in your brain when you look at this? (FIG. 2-6)

FIGURE 2-6 **NEGATIVE SPACE ADVANTAGE**

Is the open space of the arrow still there? Right now, your mind is crossing over from the unconscious implicit "without thinking" to activating the conscious "thinking" part of your brain. Your slower conscious mind is comparing the missing X frame of reference with the mental model frames of reference of the original FedEx logo. It's through this connection of comparison that you will start to see that the arrow of open space reappears. You have just created a new mental model that reveals an open arrow of space. (FIG. 2-7)

FIGURE 2-7 **NEGATIVE SPACE ADVANTAGE**

This cognitive action is what takes place in the mind when watching or playing the game of football. In absence of the R4 frames of reference, the mind struggles with making sense of the reality of space availability in real-time. This requires 10,000 hours of reps to gain an implicit understanding of what is occurring in front of our eyes. The HALO interface tools short-cut this time constraint.

The practice of using the HALO within the two-dimensional models informs the feel of the three-dimensional environment. The physical reps of writing and drawing the frames of reference engraves them in the mental models of the mind and allows this process to be overlaid in real-time when viewing the game on the field.

This takes us to the next level of practice within the domain. The acceleration of intuition carryover occurs by watching football plays live on video. Watch a live game without using the HALO tool. Try to quickly use the circular search strategy and see if you can identify the 4 Bubbles of space implicitly before the play begins. Let the play develop in real-time and then rewind the film and pause it to see if you were correct. Pausing the video may require you to overlay the HALO to explicitly determine the bubbles. This is the process that builds the bridge of accelerated learning and soon you will no longer need to slow down the film.

The final level of practice is to use this circular scan strategy on the field. It doesn't matter if you are in the coach's box, in the stands, on the sideline or as a player on the field. After each play, use your mind to quickly identify the Bubbles on the field. If you struggle with a play, go back practicing with film and slow it down so the mind can inform the space. Interject the HALO if needed. Over time you will accelerate your ability to intuitively know the Bubbles that are open.

CHAPTER 3

GAME PLANNING THE CAP

Coverage, Alignment, Personnel

GAME PLANNING THE CAP

Coverage, Alignment, Personnel

Diagnosing the Bubbles of negative-space advantage is not a stand-alone marker for mastery in football. It is the front door into the game-planning and play-calling process that the R4 expert system provides. It doesn't take an expert to identify Bubbles and draw a play that can exploit it. Any novice can achieve that. Game-planning and play-calling at an expert level requires a user to understand how to develop deeper mental models that tell the story of post-snap pattern movements and what those relationships mean.

This dilemma requires an offensive coach with another intuitive tool that the R4 interface provides. It is called the CAP. The goal of the defense is to CAP space. The CAP is an acronym action word that describes the strategic intent of how this goal is achieved. The 3 core strategies are COVERAGE, ALIGNMENT, and PERSONNEL. The CAP interface tool provides a process to predict the highest probability of space advantage for the offense. If we know the defensive weapons of intent to CAP space, then the offense can flip the script. This allows us to use those weapons against them to create and UNCAP space.

The primary concern of defense is to **eliminate explosive plays.** Mike Eayrs, former Head of Research & Development for the Green Bay Packers, shares some of the following research about the NFL. An explosive yardage gain is considered a 16-yard pass or a 12-yard run. The explosive yardage gain distance is mathematically considered to be a minimum number of yards needed to statistically raise the scoring probability on a drive.

Teams executing an average NFL drive (NFL avg. drive is 6-6.5 plays) without a single explosive yardage gain play on that drive scored a touchdown 0% of the time, and a field goal 9% of the time. Zero Explosive plays = 9% scoring probability (Score 1 out of 10 drives).

Teams executing an average drive (NFL avg. drive 6-6.5 plays) with a **single** explosive yardage gain play during that drive scored a touchdown 29% of the time, and a field goal 20% of the time. 1 explosive play = 49% scoring probability (Score 1 out of 2 drives).

Teams executing an average drive (NFL avg. drive 6-6.5 plays) with **2** explosive yardage gain plays during that drive scored a touchdown 52% of the time, and a field goal 25% of the time. 2 Explosive plays = 77% scoring probability (3 out of 4 drives). While turnover ratio is number one, the positive explosive yardage gain play ratio has never been lower than 4th as a correlate of winning games in each of the past 30+ years of statistical analysis in the NFL.

Going a step further, the NFL team that secures both a positive turnover ratio and a positive explosive yardage gain play ratio in a game wins 91% of the time.

Therefore, these stats show that the highest priority of defense. The core strategy is to CAP all available run gaps to eliminate explosive runs, as well as all immediate vertical threats, to eliminate explosive passes.

COVERAGE

The CAP interface guides the user through a step-by-step offensive game-planning process. It begins by processing COVERAGE. *Coverage* is the vertical leverage position of defenders above and below the Hard Deck to cap run and route space. The defense can only defend 11 of the 15 spaces on the field. Therefore, it must place a priority on the spaces that will hurt them the most. The coverage the defense chooses to play initiates the strategy in which the defenders intend to prevent explosive runs and passes.

Let's look at this diagram to illustrate how coverage reveals the space that the defense intends to CAP. (FIG. 3-1)

In this 2 x 2 Formation, the BOX reveals 6 gaps of immediate run space that the defense must defend and 4 vertical tubes of immediate route space to defend. These immediate threats determine what coverage the defense will call. The COVERAGE determines the number of defenders available above the Hard Deck to CAP immediate vertical threats in TUBES.

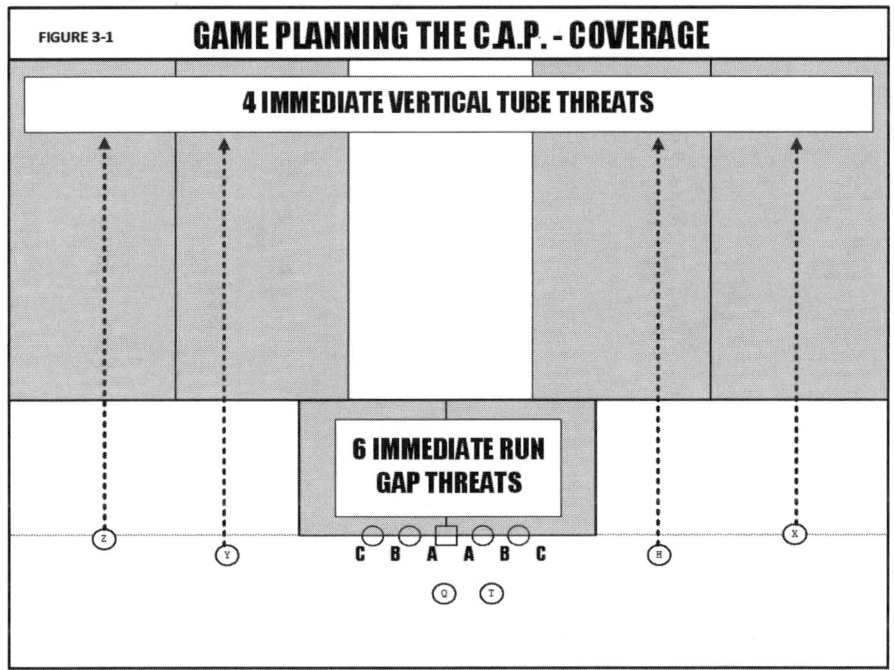

The COVERAGE also determines the number of defenders available below the HARD DECK to assist the front in capping OUTSIDE tube-space or run gaps in the BOX SPACE. Let's say the defense has called a coverage that places 5 defenders above the HARD DECK capping each of the 5 vertical tubes. While it is highly unlikely we would ever see this coverage, this picture provides a starting point in our understanding of what space should be prioritized to defend. (Fig. 3-2)

As we look at the HALO, we see 4 bubbles of space available to attack.

There are 2 bubbles in the run box and 2 in the outside flat tubes. The highest priority of the defense is to CAP immediate run space. As a result, the defense must call a coverage that places defenders in the BOX to cap this space. We previously discussed space relationships and revealed how CAPPING gaps UNCAPS tubes. (FIG. 3-3)

Notice that the bubbles of space have moved because of adjusting the COVERAGE. This defensive look is more consistent with what we see in football. By bringing 2 more defenders into the RUN BOX, the defense has CAPPED all 6 immediate run gaps. They have also maintained their priority of CAPPING immediate vertical route space in the process.

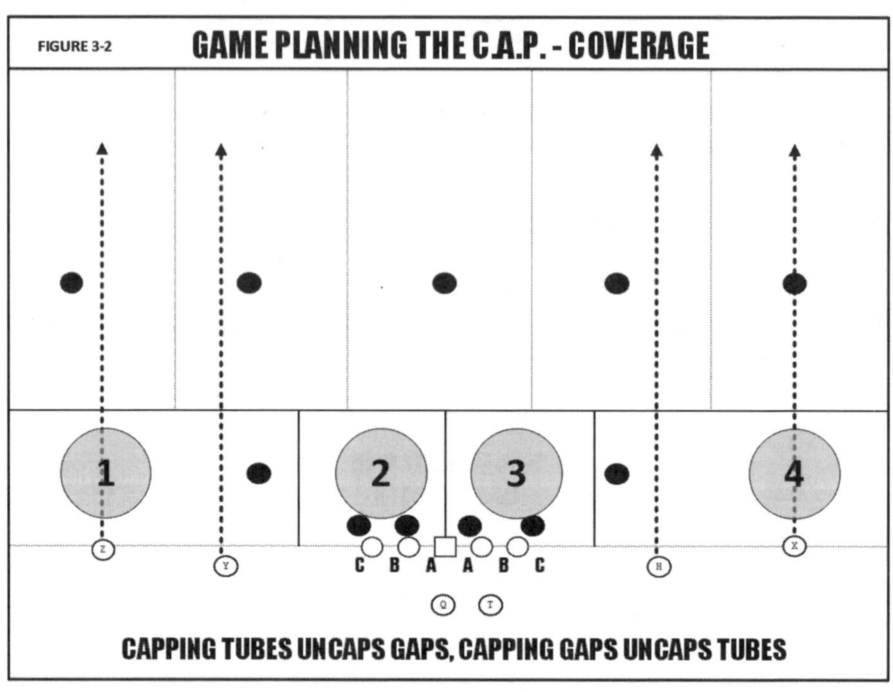
FIGURE 3-2
GAME PLANNING THE C.A.P. - COVERAGE
1
2
3
4
Z
Y
C B A A B C
H
X
Q T
CAPPING TUBES UNCAPS GAPS, CAPPING GAPS UNCAPS TUBES

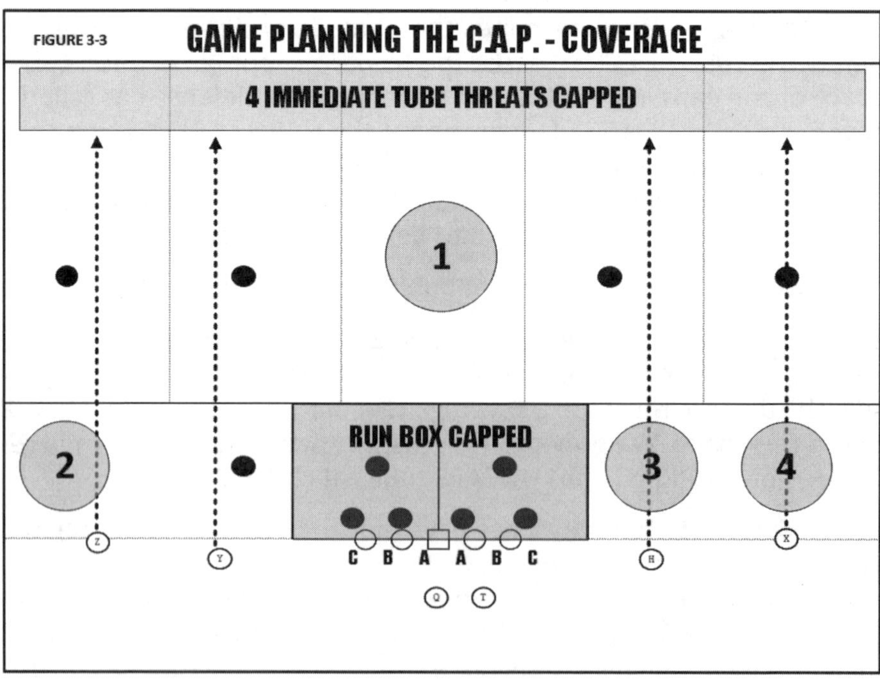
FIGURE 3-3
GAME PLANNING THE C.A.P. - COVERAGE
4 IMMEDIATE TUBE THREATS CAPPED
1
RUN BOX CAPPED
2
3
4
Z
Y
C B A A B C
H
X
Q T

As you look above the Hard Deck, you will notice that there are 4 defenders in each tube over the immediate vertical threats at receiver.

This is where the game-planning process begins. Coverage dictates the bubbles-of-space advantage to the offense. Therefore, the game-planning process for the offense should always begin with play design that attacks the Bubbles. In this diagram, the best advantage would be attacking the Bubbles to the outside flat tube to the right. (FIG. 3-4)

Let's say we decide to throw a quick game Fade-Out route combination to attack the uncapped space. This would be a sound concept to attack the Bubbles.

The defense is not going to continue to let the offense have free access to this space, so it will adjust their coverage accordingly to CAP it. (FIG. 3-5)

And this is where the shell game is played. The COVERAGE that the defense employs determines where they are. The offense must stay one step ahead of the defense in determining their intent to CAP space with COVERAGE adjustments. It is easier for the offensive coach to get in the mind of a defensive coach using the HALO to reveal Bubbles.

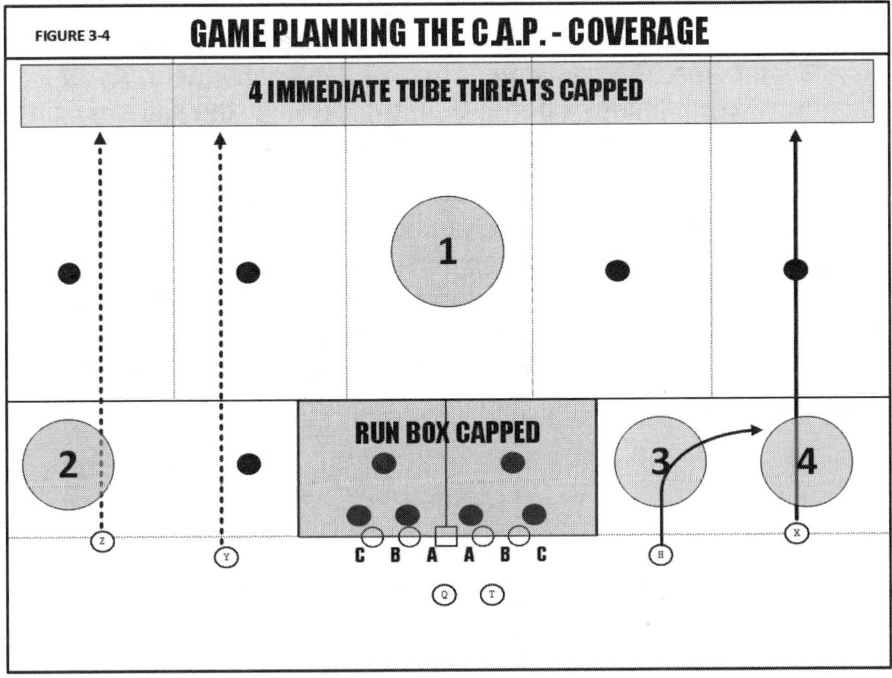

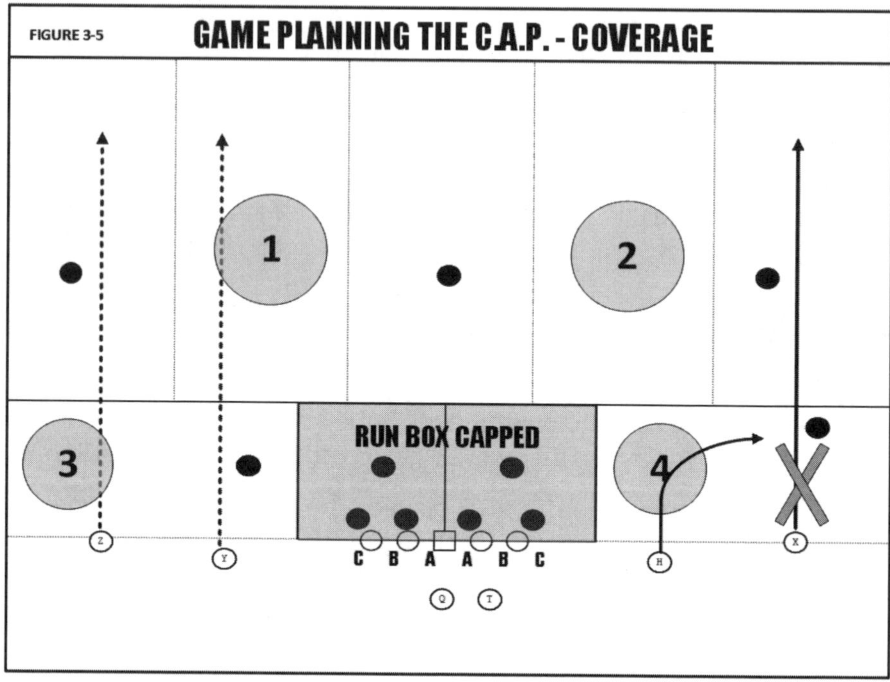

Being able to determine what COVERAGE adjustment the defense will have to make to CAP Bubbles allows the offense to have the next-best play-called *before the adjustment to take it away happens.* As long as the offensive personnel is better than the defense, the ball can be advanced into these Bubbles to generate explosive plays.

The first step in game-planning is creating plays that attack Bubbles. However, the process cannot stop there. Good defensive coaches will know their BUBBLE weaknesses better than you. They will position their defenders to create Bubbles in areas or around offensive players that lack the skill-sets to attack them. When this occurs, an offensive coach must scheme to create space. This requires examining the next layer of the CAP process.

ALIGNMENT

One of the biggest examples of the need for scheming space is shown when the offense attempts to run the football. Running the football is the easiest way to advance the ball and generate an explosive play. The highest priority of the defense is to eliminate explosive runs. Therefore, there are rarely any Bubbles of free run space given to an offense. This is because the 2nd core strategy of defense is to maintain a +1 man-advantage in areas of the offensive strength, or attack intent. Man-advantage CAPs Bubbles of space and allows the defense to move post-snap to CAP preexisting Bubbles of space faster. The defense gains a man-advantage by using Alignments to position a defender in these areas. *Alignment* is what the A in the CAP acronym stands for.

Alignment is the horizontal leverage position of defenders to a side to CAP run and route space. The defense achieves a man-advantage when it gains 1 more defender than the offense has to a side of space. The offense neutralizes man-advantage when it has the same number of players as the defense has to a side. Man-advantage reveals space that must be schemed to be neutralized and gained back by the offense.

The key frame of reference in determining man-advantage is the LINE OF CENTER in the HALO. The line of center (a.k.a. centerline) divides the formation into 2 sides of run and route space. This presents 4 total areas of space that a defense must defend. (FIG. 3-6)

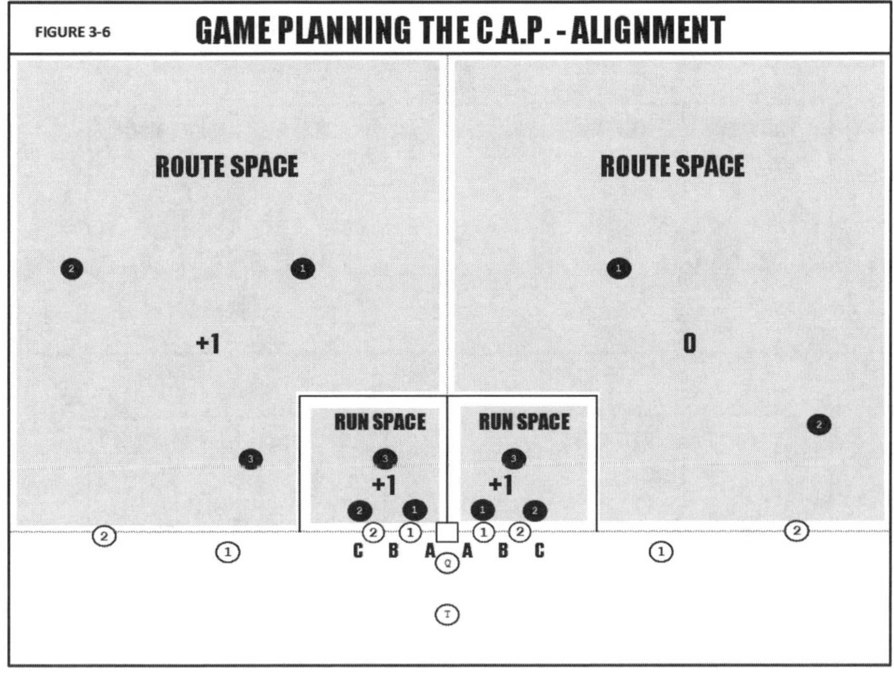

In the run space to the left, there is a 2-man offensive line surface that presents 3 gaps of run space. The defense has 3 defenders over the 2-man offensive line surface. This gives the defense a +1 man-advantage that CAPS all the gaps to the left side of run space.

In the run space to the right, there is a 2-man offensive line surface that also presents 3 gaps of run space. The defense has 3 defenders over the 2-man offensive line surface. This gives the defense a +1 man-advantage that CAPs all the gaps to the right side of run space.

In the route space to the left, there are 2 receivers that present 2 immediate threats to the route space. The defense has 3 defenders over the 2 immediate receiver threats. This gives the defense a +1 man-advantage that increases their ability to CAP the available route space to the left.

In the route space to the right, there are 2 receivers that present 2 immediate threats to the route space. The defense has 2 defenders over the 2 immediate receiver threats. This presents a neutral man-advantage to the route space to the right side. A neutral count can place the man-advantage into the offense's favor.

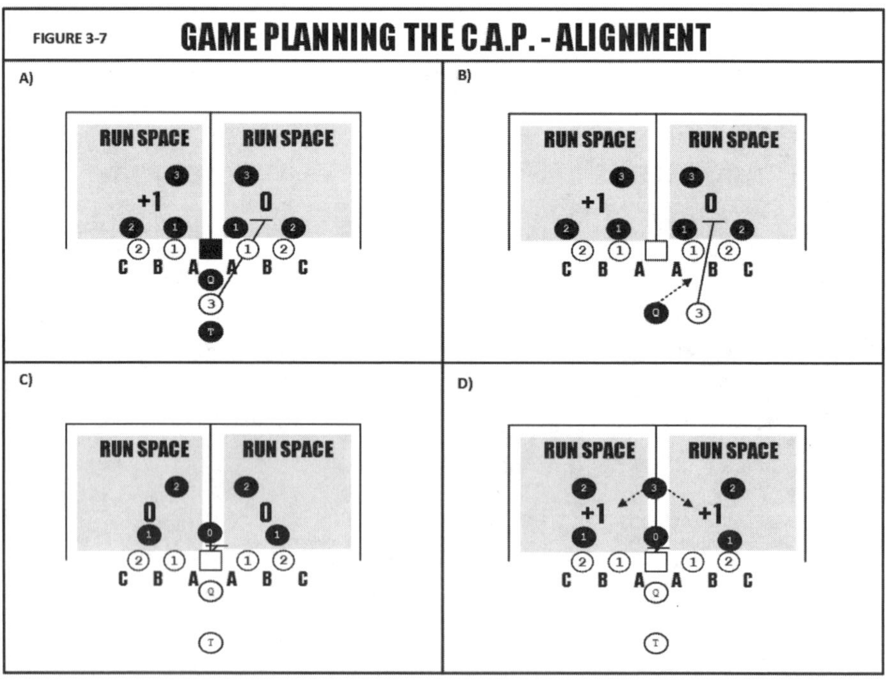

Because there are 11 defenders vs. 11 offensive players, the defense cannot maintain a +1 man-advantage on all 4 sides of run and route space. This makes it critical for the offense to find where the man-advantage is neutral and should be considered a high-priority space to attack in the game-plan.

CALCULATING MAN-ADVANTAGE USING THE RULES OF THE CENTERLINE

Calculating man-advantage starts with how players are positioned on the centerline. The CENTERLINE is a key frame of reference that reveals the crossover capabilities of players to occupy another side of space. Players who are positioned on the CENTERLINE can move post-snap in either direction to change the man-advantage count. Therefore, it is critical to understand how these actions can change the numbers. The first man-advantage rule to remember is: (FIG. 3-7)

A. Offensive players on the CENTERLINE (other than lead blockers) are non-advantage players. They will not be included in the pre-snap advantage count. In (DIAGRAM A) the full back is included in the man-advantage count to the side of space he inserts into. This is because he is a lead blocker in the Run scheme that is being used. The quarterback and running back are non-advantage players because they are not being used as lead blockers on the play.

B. An offset RB is a non-advantage player (unless he is being used on a play as a lead blocker) In (DIAGRAM B) the running back is included in the man-advantage count to the side of space he inserts into. This is because he is a lead blocker in the run scheme being used. The quarterback is a non-advantage player because he is not being used as a lead blocker on the play.

C. A single run box defender on the centerline who can be neutralized by the center is a non-advantage player. In (DIAGRAM C) the nose guard over the center is not considered in the man-advantage count if he can be blocked by the center. However, if the nose tackle was a dominant defender and could not be single blocked by the center, then offense should consider the nose tackle a man-advantage player to both sides of run space.

D. Run box defenders on the centerline who cannot be blocked by the center are man-advantage players to both sides of run space. Man-advantage for unblocked defenders aligned on the centerline must be determined post-snap to the side they will be included. In (DIAGRAM D) the middle linebacker is on the centerline and cannot be blocked by the offensive center. This allows him to be included as a man-advantage player to each side of run space.

The positioning of defenders on the Hard Deck, apex or centerline must also be considered when calculating man-advantage to a side of space. (FIG. 3-8)

For example, a safety who is on the HARD DECK line pre-snap can move post-snap in the run box or drop into route space to the right. He must be considered as a man-advantage player to both spaces on the right.

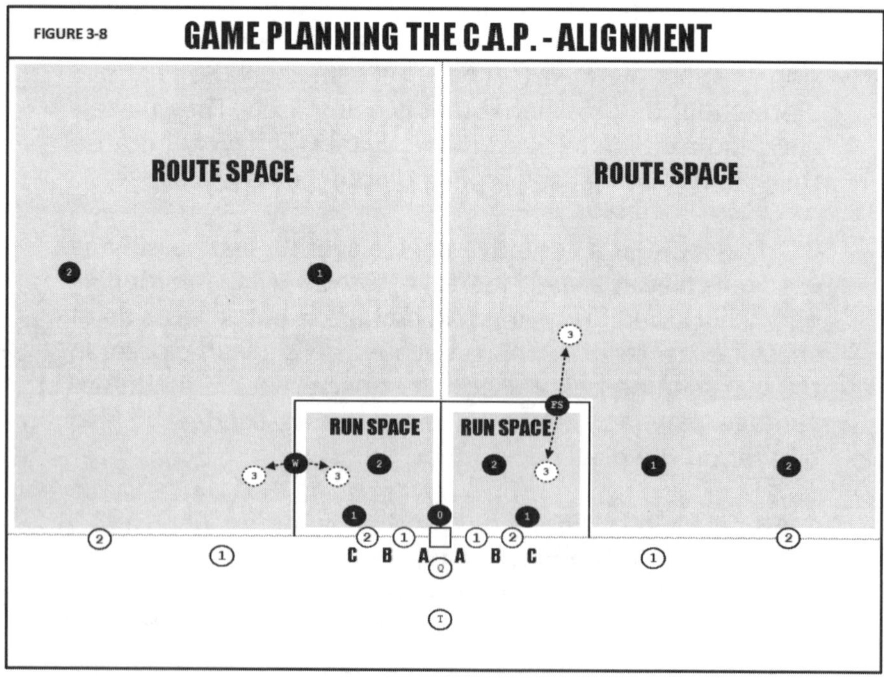

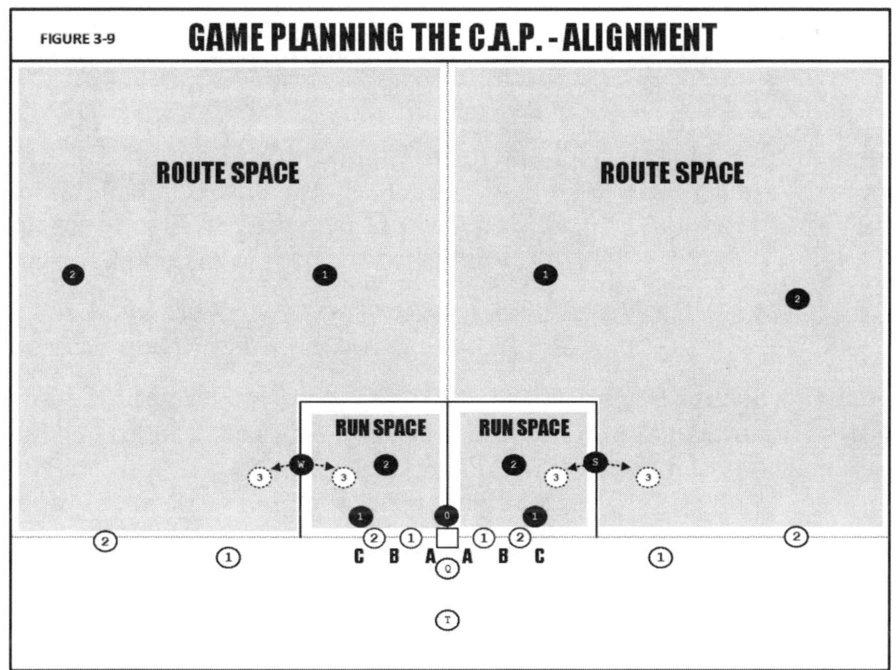

Another example shows that a defender who is on the APEX line can move post-snap in the run box or as well as into OUTSIDE space. Therefore, he must be considered as a man-advantage player to each side of space. (FIG. 3-9)

The final example is a safety who is on the centerline pre-snap can move post-snap to either side of route space. This movement changes the man-advantage count to favor the route space that a defender moves into. (FIG. 3-10)

Understanding and applying these rules are critical in the game-planning process. Defenders who are on the Hard Deck, apex or centerline must be schemed by a play to dictate the man-advantage movement to a side of space. These alignments require an offensive coach to understand how play schemes can dictate the movement of defenders who are positioned on a HALO frame of reference. In the next chapters, we will cover 3 schemes strategies that accelerate a user's ability to accomplish this task at an expert level.

Scheming concepts that attack Bubbles of space and neutralize man-advantage are considered by many to be one of the fun parts of coach-

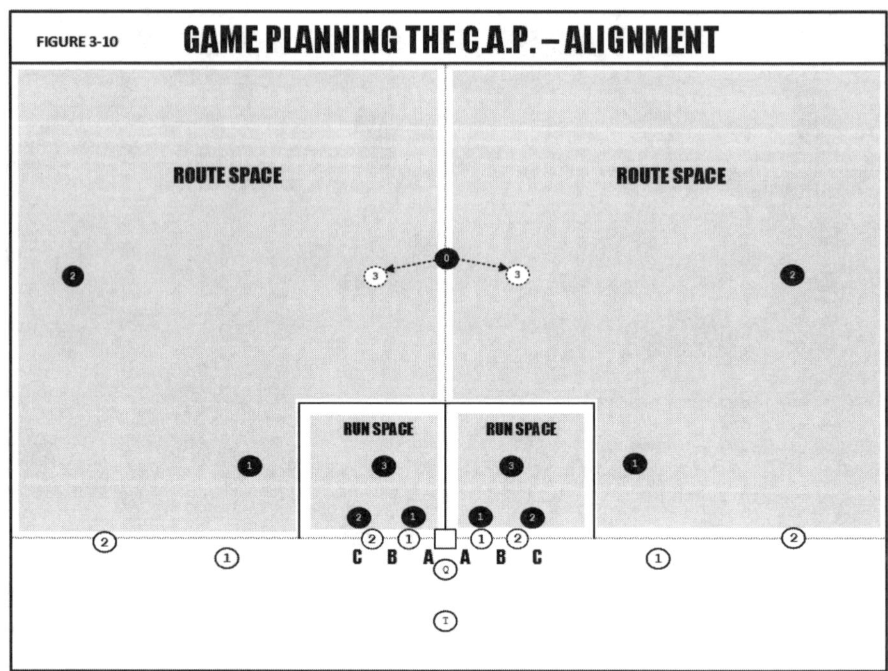

ing. However, drawing up effective concepts on a whiteboard does not guarantee success. The most overlooked part of coaching is not taking into consideration the players who execute the plays along with the players the plays are attacking. Therefore, a coach must focus more on the last layer of the CAP process more than the others.

PERSONNEL

Personnel is the most important phase of game-planning. It is the one variable that will change every week. A coach can draw a perfect play that attacks a coverage BUBBLE or neutralizes the MAN-ADVANTAGE in the alignment of a front. However, there is no guarantee of success if the offensive and opposing personnel is not taken into consideration within a play design.

There are three key issues that hinder a coach's ability to properly evaluate opposing personnel.

1. Coaches are not sure what specific traits to evaluate. There are many characteristics that can be evaluated when game-planning. The problem is that there is only so much

time to execute a grade for each ability. Therefore, a coach must know the non-negotiable traits to grade when grading the personnel ability of an opponent.

2. Coaches do not have a consistent grading process that can be duplicated by others. Many coaches may have enough experience to watch film and know the strengths and weaknesses of an opponent. However, they do not have a process and language that can be used to teach others how to execute this ability. Furthermore, while they may be able to break down a position group effectively, they do not have a process that can break down an entire defense adequately.

3. Coaches do not have the countermeasures needed to attack opponent strengths and weaknesses. Many coaches may have a few strategic ideas on how to attack the personnel ability of an opponent. However, a master coach must have a library of countermoves stored in memory that can be recalled to determine the BEST scheme to employ against personnel strengths and weaknesses. The central theme to mastery in scheme is through an understanding of the relationships between countermeasures that are employed against personnel strengths and weaknesses.

Let's look at a couple of examples to show why properly grading personnel is critical in scheming. Let's say we are running a 3 x 1 formation out of 11 Personnel. (FIG. 3-11)

The defense has shown on film the tendency to play Cover 1 with an Under Front. We decide to scheme our four-man Snag concept against it. The corner-route in the Snag concept should easily be able to attack the Bubbles of space to the field. Nonetheless, if we stop at this point, we are missing critical intel that could confirm if this concept has a probability of success.

ACCELERATORS

We refer to the ability or talent of personnel as ACCELERATORS. We call them accelerators because an athlete is not going to change who he is in a short amount of time. Therefore, the evaluation of an athlete's

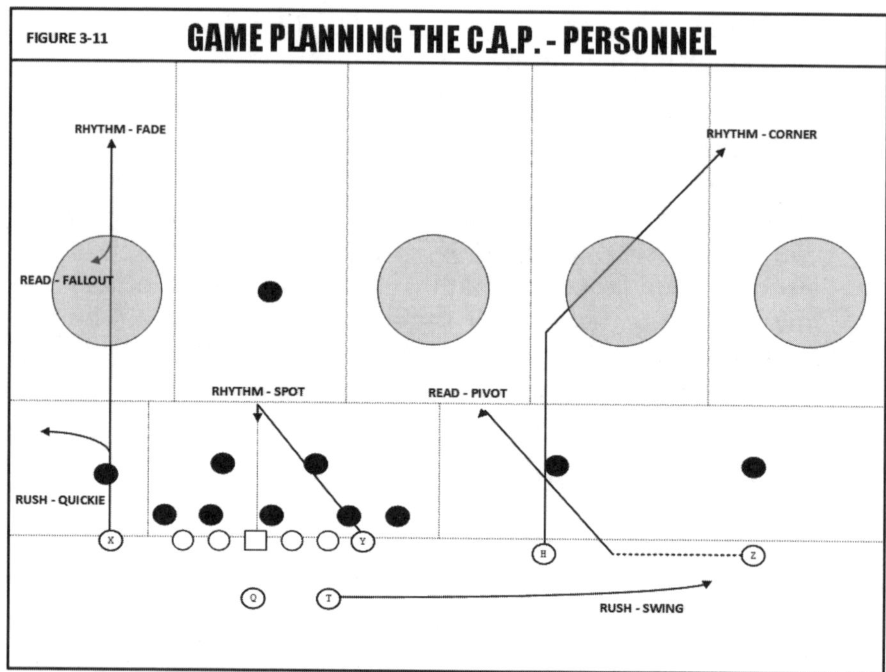

ability to defend space makes up who he is. If we grade this ability properly then we can use this information as a mental decision-making accelerator in determining how to best attack his abilities or lack thereof.

Grading accelerators is like extracting evidence from a crime scene. Some crime scenes will have a lot of evidence to sort through and therefore the detective can walk away with confidence on how the crime was committed. However, some crime scenes have minimal evidence and therefore can make it difficult to determine how the crime occurred. It is important to remember when grading accelerators to not get bogged down. Extract the information that you can from the film you have and move on. For some games, you may have no film to grade. Other games may consist of offensive schemes that you do not run. Everything is information if you know what to look for.

PASS ACCELERATORS

There are two categories of personnel accelerator grading that are required when breaking down a defense. They are pass accelerators and run accelerators.

The primary pass accelerator grades are CUSHION, COLLISION, and CLOSURE.

CUSHION - The defender's ability to maintain a minimum of 4-yards of vertical space over a receiver.

COLLISION - The defender's delay or disruption of the stem or release of a route.

CLOSURE - The defender's ability to break on a route and make a play on the ball.

A defender is either a Cushion or Collision player. Film breakdown within existing coverages will inform the coach on which type of pass accelerator a specific defender is playing with. Grading a defender's ability to maintain Cushion or execute Collision is vital.

CUSHION

Cushion can be graded by watching film. It begins by collecting clips of receivers who are running vertical routes against specific defenders. The clips should be organized by type of coverage. If you are not sure what coverage is being played, then sort clips by man and zone technique. A coach will select like clips and play each until the quarterback hits the last step of his drop. This is a critical point in the timeline in which cushion is measured. (FIG. 3-12)

If the defensive back has more than 4 yards of cushion at the last step of the quarterback drop, then we give him a positive cushion grade. If the defensive back is even at 4 yards, we give him a neutral cushion grade. If the defensive back is less than 4 yards, we give him a negative cushion grade.

Cushion grades help inform the coach which type of routes should be used to attack a defensive back. Positive cushion grades report that quick-game and intermediate routes may be more effective. Neutral cushion grades can go either way and require the coach to look closely at the closure ability of a defensive back. Negative cushion grades communicate that vertical and double move routes are optimal.

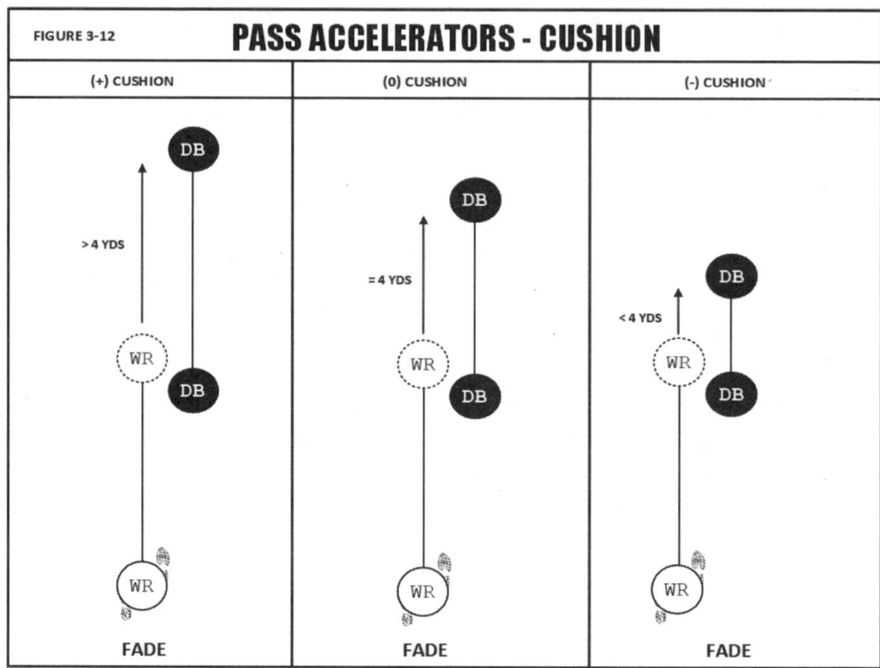

COLLISION

Collision is graded on the same timeline as Cushion. Collision is measured between a defender and receiver on or before the last step of the quarterback's drop. (FIG. 3-13)

If a receiver is delayed or disrupted off his initial route stem, then a positive collision grade is given. If a defensive back attempts to collision a receiver but the receiver can defeat it with a proper release, then a neutral grade is given. If a defensive back does not attempt to collision a receiver, then a negative collision grade is given.

Collision grades help inform the coach which type of scheme strategies or route adjustments should be used to counter a specific grade. Positive collision grades may require a coach to use motions or stack splits to help a receiver delete a defender's collision ability. Neutral collision grades can inform a coach to incorporate release strategies that are effective to defeat the collision action. Negative collision grades can guide the coach to the optimal defender to attack within a play.

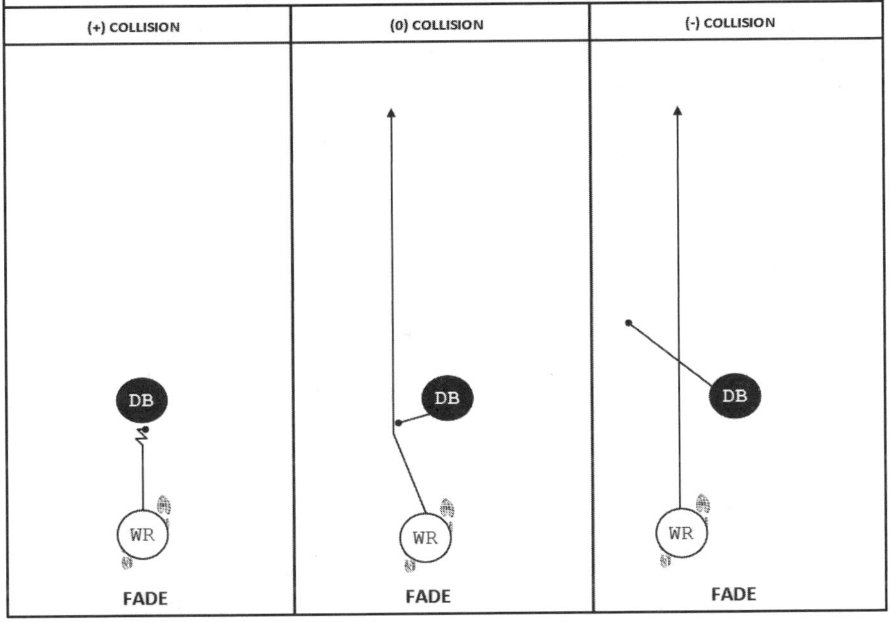

FIGURE 3-13 **PASS ACCELERATORS - COLLISION**

(+) COLLISION	(0) COLLISION	(-) COLLISION
DB WR FADE	DB WR FADE	DB WR FADE

CLOSURE

Closure is one of the most important grades to account for when game-planning. Grading closure begins at the break of the route. If the route is a vertical fade or seam route, then the grading begins when the throwing motion of the quarterback begins. (FIG. 3-14)

If a defensive back closes space and can make a play on the ball or is immediately able to make a tackle on the reception, then he receives a positive closure grade. If no space is gained out of the break or the same amount of space remains after the ball is thrown, then the defensive back receives a neutral grade. If a receiver creates space out of the break or after the ball is thrown, then the defensive back earns a negative closure grade.

Closure grades reveal a defensive back's talent level of recovery to gain a dominant position to defend the route and the ball. A defensive back with a consistent positive closure grade is a player who must be attacked with caution. These players are aggressive and usually susceptible to

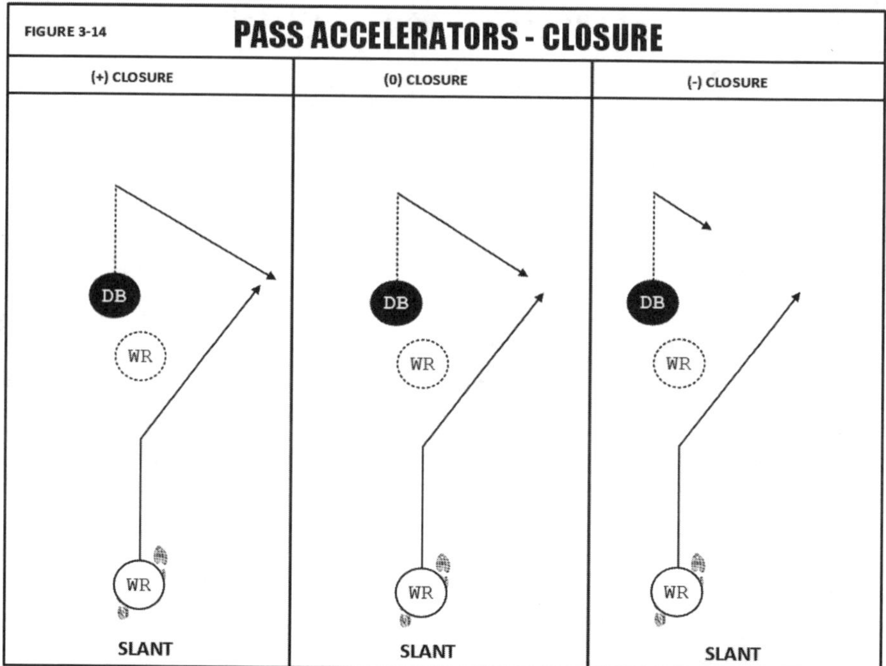

double moves. A coach may want to use routes to clear out these defenders, so they can create space to attack areas they have been removed from. Defenders with neutral or negative closure grades represent defenders that game-plans should be centered around.

GAME-PLANNING PASS ACCELERATORS

Let's go back to the original play that we had game-planned against Cover 1 with an Under Front. We were running a four-man Snag Concept out of a 3 x 1 formation. The highest priority route being used to attack the Bubbles of space within the coverage was the rhythm-corner route. The accelerator grades for the defender who was manned up over the corner route showed he had a consistent positive collision grade. (FIG. 3-15)

This positive grade should alert the coach that he must use a technique or scheme strategy to overcome this accelerator weapon. A lack of adjustment will increase the probability that the route will incur collision and destroy the space creation of the concept. One technique that can help neutralize a positive collision grade is by using a different release off the line of scrimmage. A slide release is effective here. The slide release can help the receiver avoid collision and allow the defender to win route-side space of the corner at the top of the route.

It is important to note that adding a slide release will prevent the corner route from being thrown on rhythm. This release changes the route to a read route. Therefore, the coach must inform the quarterback that when using this release adjustment to counter collision, his progression timing must change. The quarterback will Rhythm the Spot route, Read the Corner route, and Rush the Swing route by the running back.

This is just one example of how grading accelerators provide a checks-and-balances system to the game-planning process. In the absence of grading accelerators, there is no frame of reference to determine if a scheme will withstand the personnel it is designed to attack. The accelerators provide context in determining if a play will work or what adjustments need to be added to increase the probability of success.

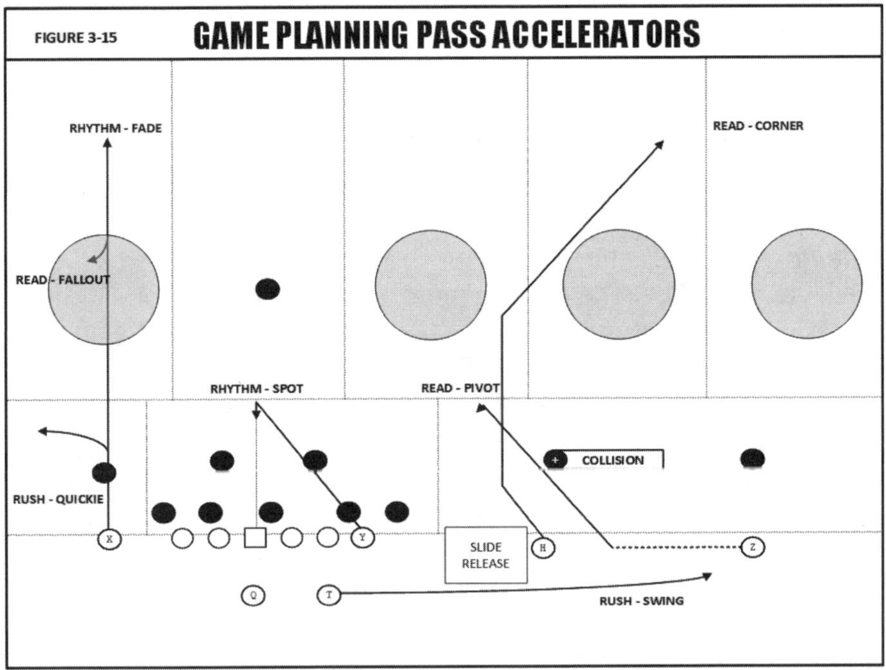

RUN ACCELERATORS

The next family of accelerators to grade are the run accelerators. There are four types of run accelerators. They are **PENETRATE, PIN, PLUG, and PURSUIT.**

The Penetration Accelerators – CAP vertical run space behind the line of scrimmage.

The Plug Accelerators – CAP vertical run space under the Hard Deck to the play side of the centerline.

The Pin Accelerators – CAP horizontal run space inside the apex line.

The Pursuit Accelerators – CAP horizontal run space across the centerline. (FIG. 3-16)

These accelerators are measured as follows:

PENETRATE – The post-snap position of a 1st level defender in relation to the line of scrimmage.

PLUG – The post-snap position of a play side 2nd level defender in relation to the line of scrimmage.

PIN – The post-snap position of any defender in relation to the end man on the line of scrimmage.

PURSUIT – The post-snap position of a play side 2nd level defender in relation to the centerline.

A defense must excel in these four run accelerator phases to CAP all available run space. The offense must neutralize at least one or more of these run accelerator weapons to achieve positive yards gained on a given run play. Proper grading of these run accelerators helps to inform a coach on the best scheme strategies for attacking run accelerator weaknesses and counter run accelerator strengths.

Grading run accelerators must be broken into two categories: Vertical runs and Horizontal runs. Vertical runs are any run that is designed to attack between the tackles. Examples would be Inside Zone, Wide Zone, Power, Counter, and Iso schemes. Horizontal runs are designed to attack the outside space only. Examples would be Outside Zone, Toss Sweep, Jet Sweep, etc.

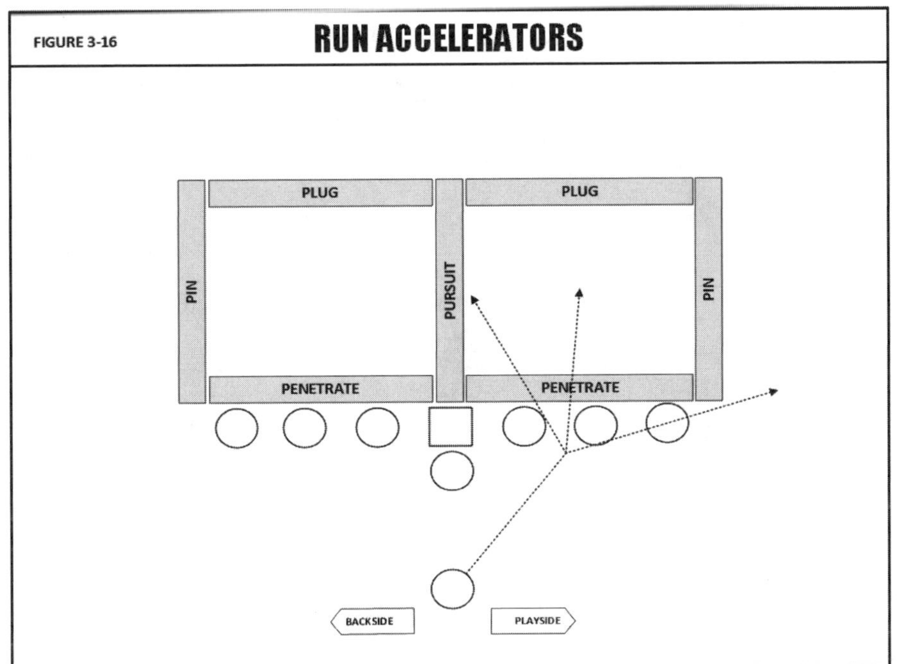

PENETRATION

Penetration is the first line of defense and starting point in the grading process of run accelerators. If an offense cannot neutralize penetration, then it will be very difficult to run the ball. A defender is classified as a penetrator if he is on the line of scrimmage with his head up to inside alignment between the E.M.O.L.S. The measurement of penetration begins on the snap and stops when the ball-carrier is at the line of scrimmage. (Fig. 3-17)

A positive penetration grade is given to a defender who penetrates at or beyond the line of scrimmage and redirects or tackles the ball-carrier. A neutral penetration grade is given to a defender who penetrates at the line of scrimmage and gets blocked or misses a tackle. A negative penetration grade is given to a defender who gets blocked beyond the line of scrimmage.

It is important to make note of the type of block that a defender is attacking when grading penetration. A consistent negative penetration grade on base blocks can free up other blockers to be used on double-

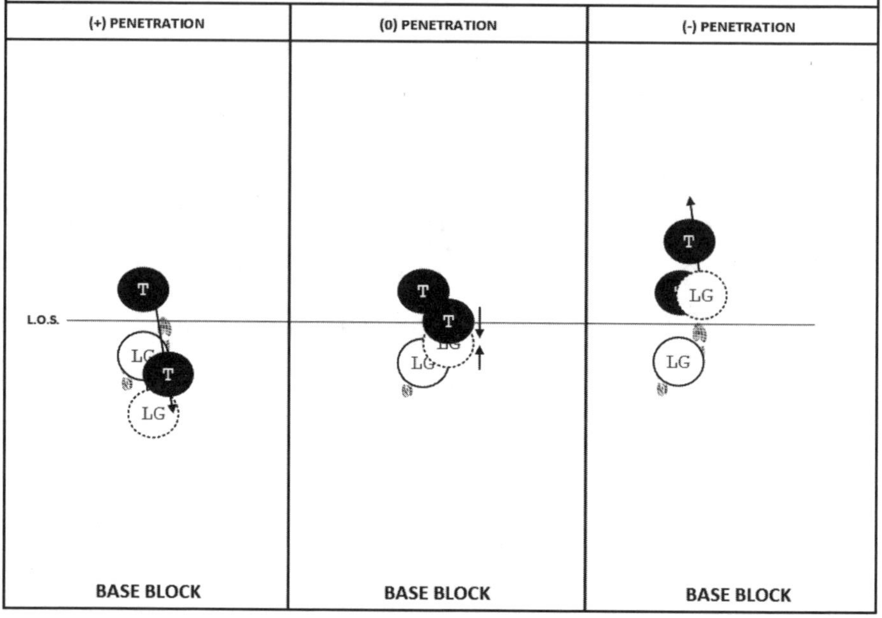

FIGURE 3-17 **RUN ACCELERATORS - PENETRATE**

(+) PENETRATION	(0) PENETRATION	(-) PENETRATION
BASE BLOCK	BASE BLOCK	BASE BLOCK

teams. It can also inform the coach to use more man or gap schemes. Conversely, if a defender has a consistent positive penetration grade against a base block it can spotlight a need for a double-team.

PLUG

Plug is the second line of defense to eliminate play-side vertical run space. Plug players are primarily play-side inside linebackers. Plug players must read offensive run keys and properly fit to CAP the correct run gap. The grading of the Plug accelerator begins when the running back is at the line of scrimmage. A coach will stop the film at this point, then determine the location and execution of the plug-player based on the following rules. (FIG. 3-18)

Defenders who plug their gap at the line of scrimmage and redirect or tackle the ball carrier are given a positive Plug grade. Defenders who plug their gap but get blocked or miss a tackle receive a neutral Plug grade. Defenders who plug the run gap or hesitate and get blocked earn a negative Plug grade.

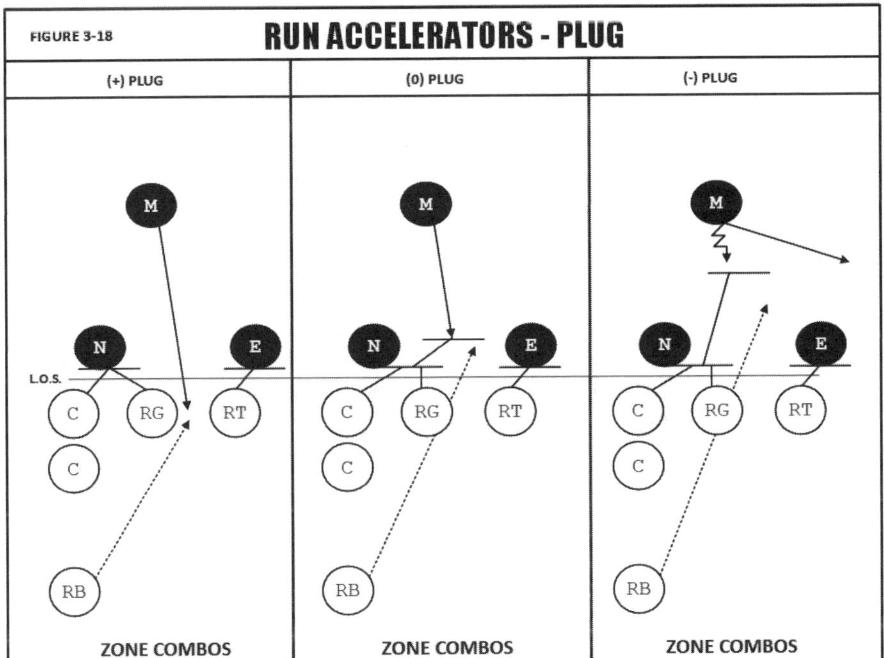

Inside linebacker accelerator roles change based on their alignment with the play. If they are lined up to the play-side of the run, they are graded as Plug players. If they are lined up away from the run, then they are Pursuit players. Therefore, inside linebackers will have both Plug and Pursuit grades when game-planning an opponent.

PIN

Pin is the first line of defense to eliminate horizontal run space. Force and Contain are other terms that are used in football to describe the Pin accelerator. A Pin player is the first defender who is lined up outside the end man on the line of scrimmage. The Pin accelerator is graded when the running back is at the line of scrimmage. (FIG. 3-19)

A defender who pins the gap outside the EMOL and redirects or tackles the ball carrier at or behind the line of scrimmage receives a positive Pin accelerator grade. A defender who pins the gap outside the EMOL but gets blocked or misses a tackle receives a neutral Pin accelerator grade. A defender who is attempting to pin the gap outside the EMOL

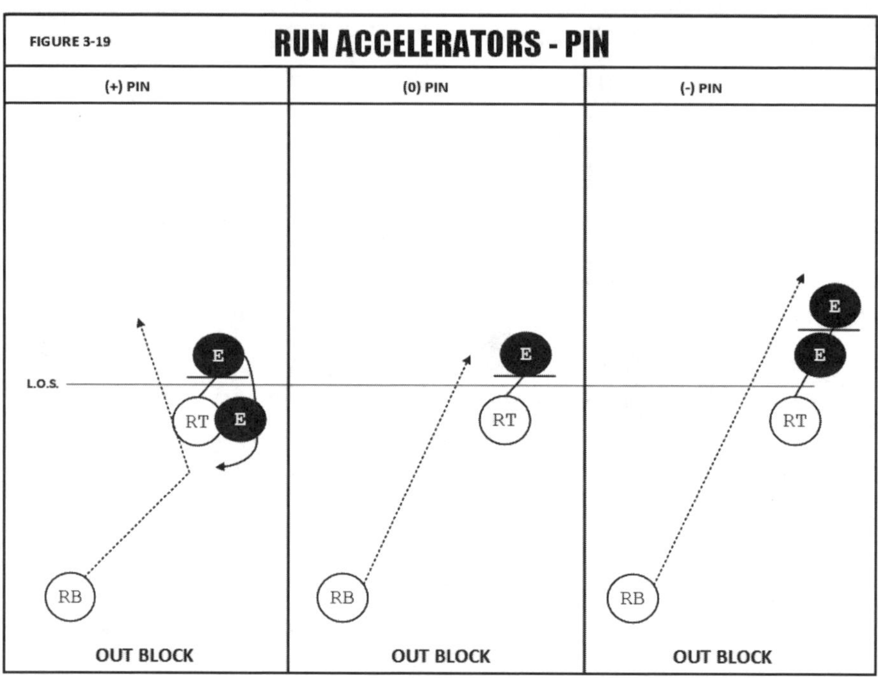
FIGURE 3-19
RUN ACCELERATORS - PIN
(+) PIN
(0) PIN
(-) PIN
L.O.S.
E
E
RT
RB
OUT BLOCK
E
RT
RB
OUT BLOCK
E
E
RT
RB
OUT BLOCK

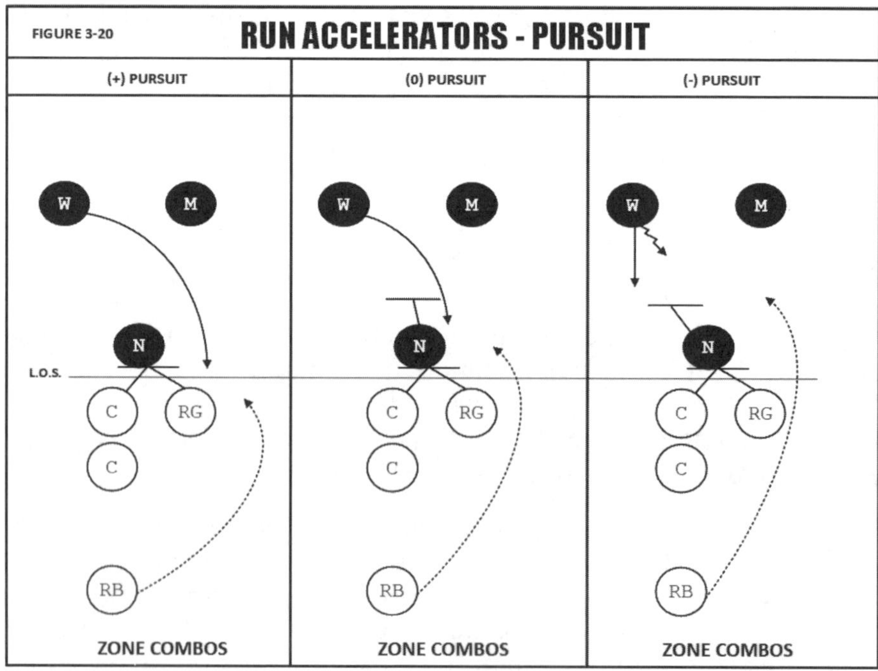
FIGURE 3-20
RUN ACCELERATORS - PURSUIT
(+) PURSUIT
(0) PURSUIT
(-) PURSUIT
W
M
N
L.O.S.
C
RG
C
RB
ZONE COMBOS
W
M
N
C
RG
C
RB
ZONE COMBOS
W
M
N
C
RG
C
RB
ZONE COMBOS

but gets blocked beyond the line of scrimmage earns a negative Pin accelerator grade.

PURSUIT

Pursuit is the backside second-level defender who is responsible for CAPPING horizontal cutback space at the centerline. The backside inside linebacker is the primary Pursuit player on defense. The Pursuit accelerator is graded when the running back reaches the line of scrimmage. Pursuit accelerators become man-advantage players when they cross the centerline. Therefore, grading and cueing their post-snap actions can reveal big play opportunities. (Fig. 3-20)

A defender who pursues with a proper angle that results in a redirection or tackle of the ball carrier is given a positive Pursuit accelerator grade. A defender who pursues with a proper angle but gets blocked or misses a tackle is given a neutral Pursuit accelerator grade. A defender who pursues with an improper angle and UNCAPS run space is given a negative Pursuit accelerator grade.

GAME-PLANNING RUN ACCELERATORS

Game-planning runs concepts to attack defensive alignments usually begins with determining which side of run space contain the man-advantage. A defense will typically maintain a +1 man-advantage to each side of run space. However, there are times when the coverage attached with the front alignment won't allow for an immediate man-advantage count in the box. (FIG. 3-21)

For example, in (DIAGRAM A), it shows that the man-advantage to the right side of run space is neutral. The defense is playing an Odd Front. Game-planning begins by attacking where the man-advantage is neutral. We decide to run a 1 back power concept to attack this side of run space. The final step in the run game-planning process is to confirm that the run accelerators will hold up against this 1 back power scheme.

When you look at the run accelerator grades (Fig. 3-21 B) you will notice that the play-side defender who is playing in a 4 technique is a positive penetrator. This could make the base block by the right tackle very

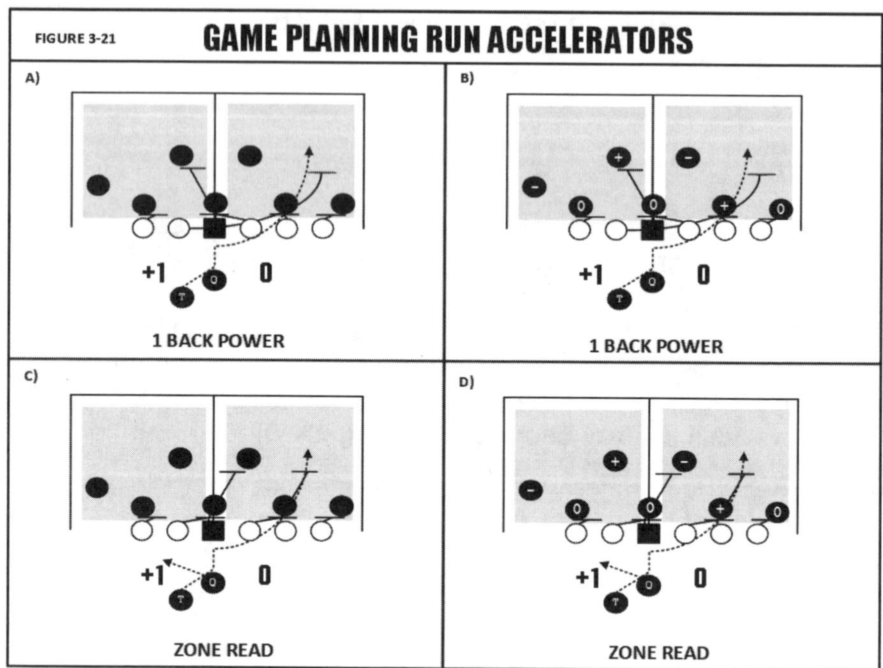

difficult to execute. Another grade that stands out is the backside pursuit player. He has a positive pursuit accelerator grade. This shows that the defender may be exceptional at working over the centerline and defeating the double-team between the right guard and center.

Analyzing these grades closely can increase a coach's intuitive ability to see problems that occur before they happen in real-time. This sets the stage to look at a run concept that better neutralizes the positive run accelerator grades. For example, (Fig. 3-21 C) a frontside inside zone double-team can provide help to the right tackle on the positive penetrating 4 technique. The plug player has a negative plug grade, which can allow the double-team to stay on longer. The backside double-teams between the left guard and center has an angle that is more favorable to cut off the positive pursuit player.

(Fig. 3.21 D) The inside zone read concept contains blocking schemes and angles that better neutralize the positive penetration and pursuit grades of the opponent. A coach can have a sound concept drawn up to beat a defensive front alignment. However, in the absence of personnel accelerator grades to confirm if the play is executable, a coach will have to wait until the game to determine if the play will be successful. Waiting until game-time makes it difficult to make the necessary adjustments to overcome the personnel accelerator strengths. Therefore, proper grading is the most important phase of the game-planning process.

CHAPTER 4

SCHEME STRATEGIES

Fake, Flow and Flood

SCHEME STRATEGIES

Fake, Flow, and Flood

The next step in the game-planning process requires crossing over into the R4 inference engine. The inference engine is an IF/THEN decision-making process that informs the user of the best decision to make based on probabilities within the mental model knowledge base that was created by the interface. The goal in game-planning is to decide which is the best play to attack and own space. To decide what the "best" play is, we need a non-negotiable understanding of the qualities that make up good plays.

The qualities that make up the "best" plays are ones that:

1. Attacks or creates Bubbles of space
2. Neutralizes or gains a +1 MAN-ADVANTAGE to a side of space
3. Attacks PERSONNEL weakness and counters PERSONNEL strengths

These qualities are created through scheming. Scheming concepts is an area of game-planning in which many coaches get lost. The challenge is that the effectiveness of the scheme is dependent on the limiting factors of time and talent. There is only so much time to practice schemed concepts. Schemes also require specific levels of talent to execute the concept properly. Overlooking these factors can quickly make a good game-plan bad.

PASS SCHEME STRATEGIES

We created 3 key categories of schemes that exist in football to help coaches avoid the pitfalls that arise when scheming plays. We call these scheme strategies. We will look at the 3 pass scheme strategies first. The 3 pass scheme strategies that exist in football are FAKE, FLOW, and FLOOD.

FAKE

Fake schemes in the passing game are play action. Play action is used to fake a dual-read defender who has both run and route responsibilities. A Fake scheme can neutralize man-advantage to a side of space. It can also attack a defender who has a positive run accelerator grade. This would be an example of using a personnel strength against a defender. There are many types of play action that can be used to influence a defender. Fake schemes can be as simple as a flash-fake across the quarterback in shotgun all the way to a deep-play action bootleg or run fake from under center.

Here is an example of how using the Fake scheme strategy can neutralize man-advantage.

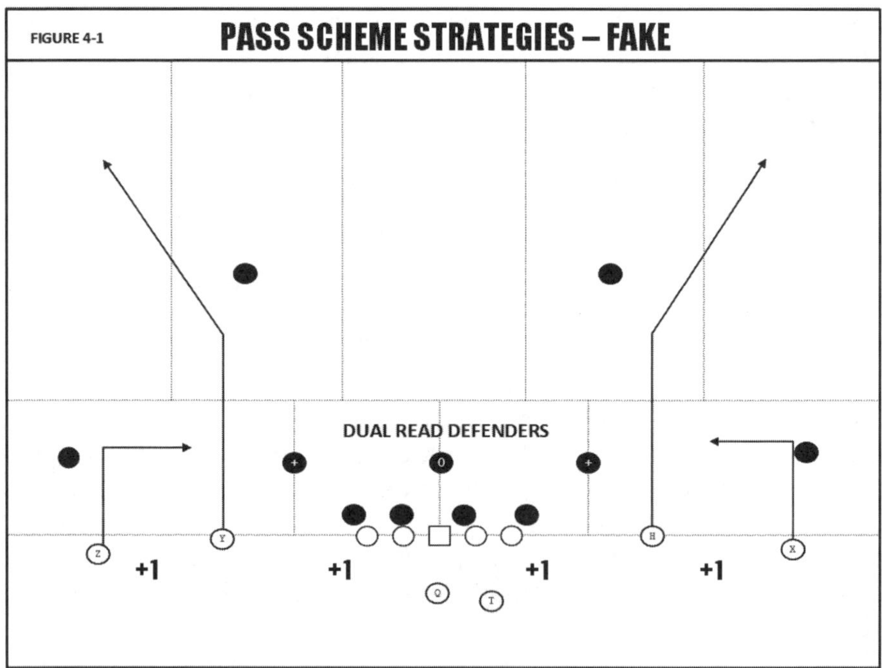

In (FIG. 4-1) the offense is running a mirrored smash concept to attack Cover 2 within a 4-3 defensive alignment. The defense has placed the outside linebackers on the Apex line, pre-snap. This alignment positions the man-advantage count in a +1 favor to each side of run and route space. This favors the defense with 3 defenders over 2 immediate offensive receiver threats that are running the smash concept.

The man-advantage count can be neutralized for a moment in time by incorporating a Fake scheme strategy. The Fake scheme attacks the dual-read defenders on the centerline and makes the man-advantage count in the route space neutral. This helps prevent the apex defenders from using collision to inhibit the stem of the corner route runners. (FIG. 4-2)

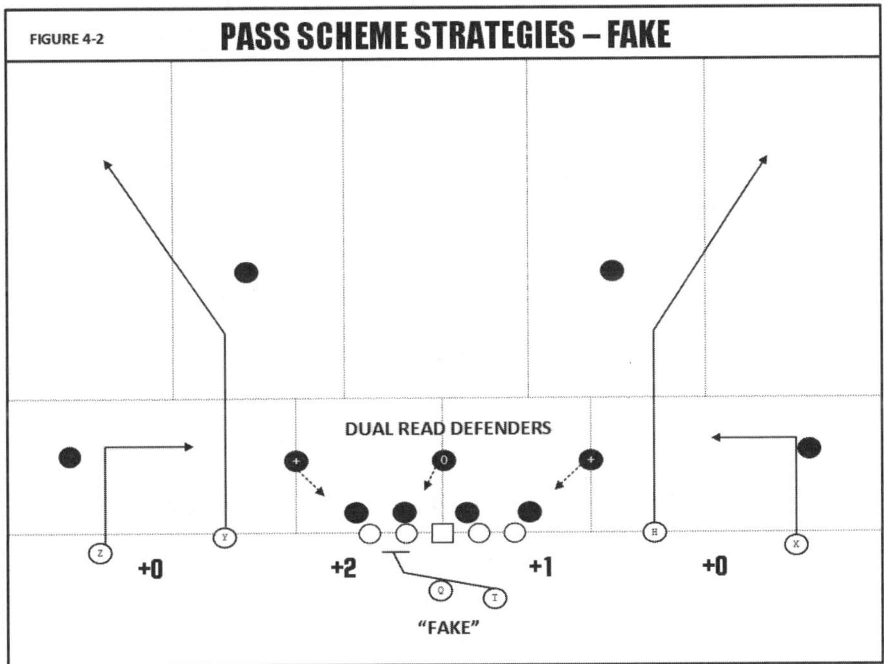

FLOW

Flow is another scheme strategy that can be used in the passing game. There are two styles of Flow schemes in the passing game. They are dependent on the type of coverage used against the offense. Against Zone coverage, the Flow scheme strategy is look-offs by the quarterback. Zone coverage places the eyes of the defenders on the quarterback. Many times, they are reading the quarterback to determine where he is going to throw the ball. This allows the quarterback to use his eyes to force defenders to flow away from where he is going with the ball.

Let's look again at the double-smash concept for an example. (FIG. 4-3)

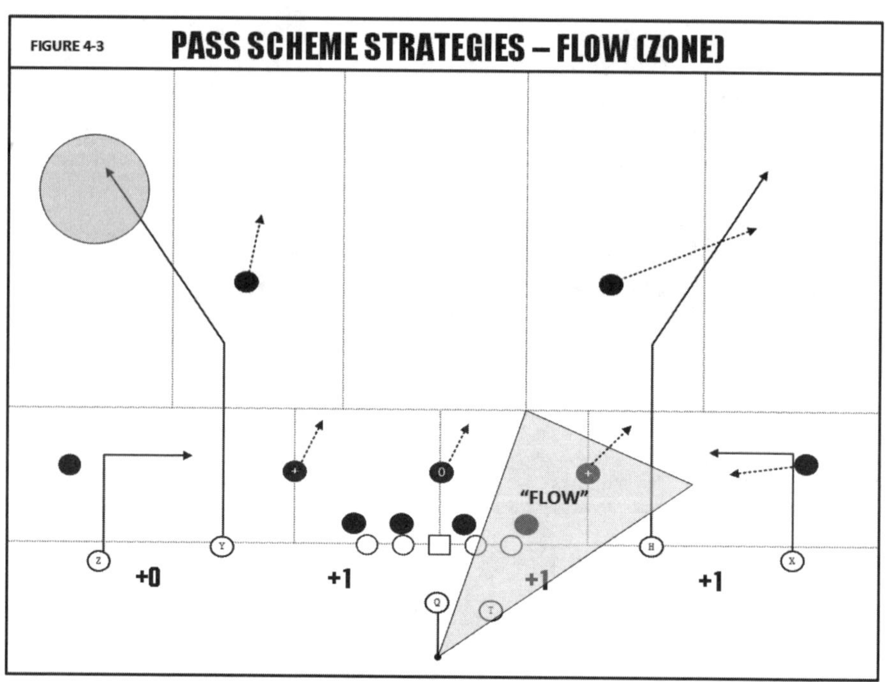
FIGURE 4-3
PASS SCHEME STRATEGIES – FLOW (ZONE)
"FLOW"
Z
Y
H
X
Q
T
+0
+1
+1
+1

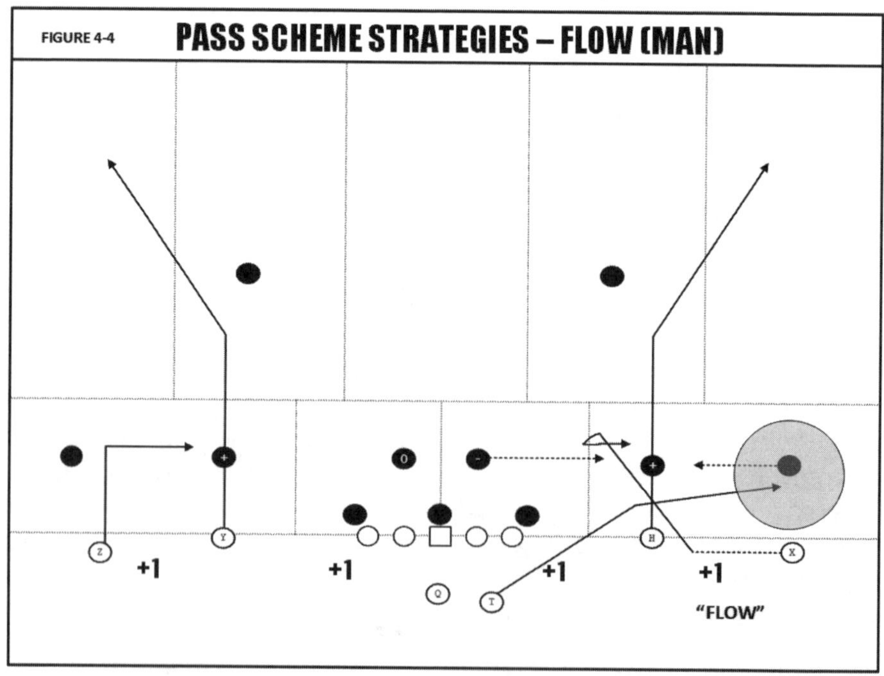
FIGURE 4-4
PASS SCHEME STRATEGIES – FLOW (MAN)
Z
Y
H
X
Q
T
+1
+1
+1
+1
"FLOW"

In zone coverage, the quarterback can use his eyes to look at the smash concept to the right. This creates a flow of defenders who move to that right side of space. For a moment in time, this neutralizes the man-advantage count on the backside smash concept. It can also help to hold the backside safety in a position that can increase the availability of the bubble of space for the backside corner route to attack. The Flow scheme strategy changes in man coverage. In man coverage, defenders are not looking at the eyes of the quarterback. Therefore, look-offs by the quarterback have no effect on the defense.

Flow schemes against man coverage are the intersection of the flow of routes to create space. (FIG. 4-4)

Let's evolve our mirrored smash concept and pretend that the defense is now playing Cover 5 (man under halves) with an Odd Front defensive alignment.

We can use a Flow scheme against this type of man coverage by bringing the routes closer together and using the flow or routes to create picks or rubs. This form of Flow scheme causes defenders to trail and get caught up in the trash of the flow. This type of flow can create bubbles of space for the offense to attack.

FLOOD

The final scheme strategy is Flood. (FIG. 4-5)

The *Flood scheme* is achieved by using one or more routes that attack on or across centerline. They essentially help the offense flood a side of space. Flood schemes can help neutralize man-advantage for a moment in time. The can also provide "hot" routes that attack voids of space that originate against defensive blitzes. Furthermore, flood schemes can help isolate and create bubbles of space against personnel pass accelerators.

The mirrored smash concept can be advanced by using a flood scheme strategy. In this example, the backside corner has been turned into a corner-post route that attacks the centerline. The backside fin route has been converted to a short-motioned Spot route. These two backside routes contain flow strategy properties because they attack the centerline of the formation. This provides a sound "hot" route versus interior

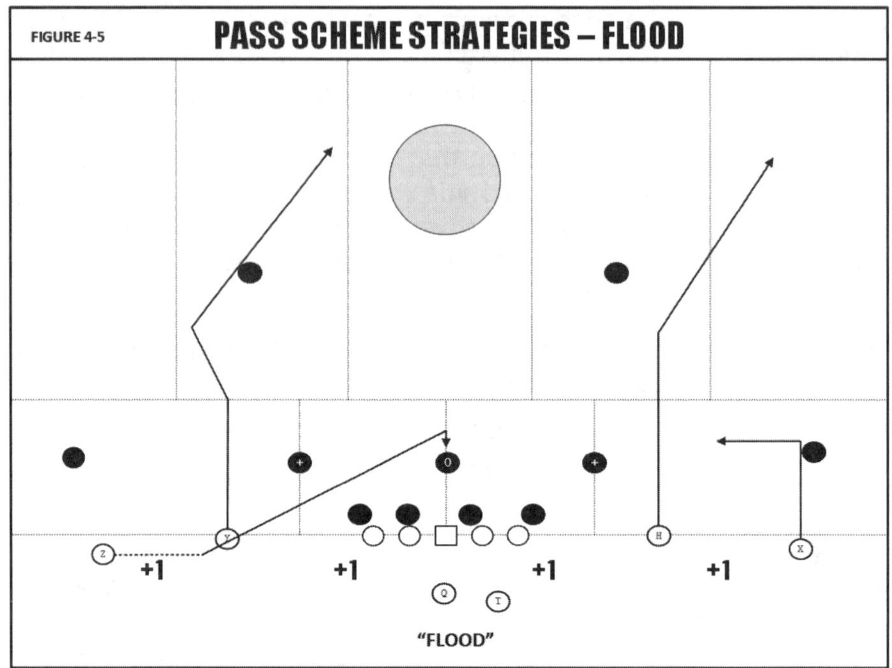

blitzes and also helps to isolate the Corner Post route in a neutral advantage on the backside safety.

ALL WEATHER PASS CONCEPTS – FAKE, FLOW, AND FLOOD

Have you ever watched a professional or college game and identified concepts that every team runs? Teams that consistently run identical concepts must mean they are good, but *why* are they good? Deconstructing good concepts often reveals the secret. The answer is that the best concepts in football contain a combination of fake, flow, and flood scheme strategies. This combination creates the genetic makeup behind the best schemes in football. Many coaches refer to their best concepts as "all weather" plays, meaning that they work against multiple coverage and alignments and personnel accelerators.

If the best plays in football contain a combination of scheme strategies, then it would make sense for us as coaches to look closer at our concepts to ensure that we are maximizing their potential. For example, let's look at our original mirrored smash concept, running mirrored smash plays into the defense's man-advantage favor. If we want to maximize its potential, we need to incorporate fake, flow, and flood scheme strategies within it. (FIG. 4-6)

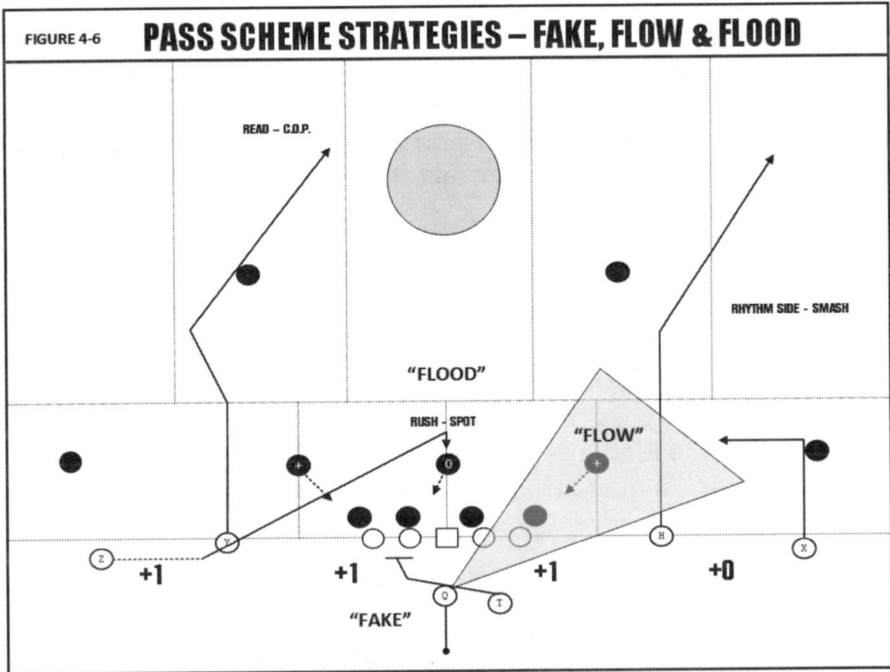

FIGURE 4-6 **PASS SCHEME STRATEGIES – FAKE, FLOW & FLOOD**

In this example, we use a fake flash of play-action to neutralize man-advantage. Next, we use the R4 progression of reading the concept to incorporate the Flow scheme strategy. By rhythming the smash concept, we create a natural flow look-off if the smash is CAPPED. This allows the quarterback to go to the read – Corner Post (C.O.P.) route without staring it down. This helps to create a bubble of space advantage for the C.O.P. route. Finally, we maximize the man-advantage and potential blitz threat by using the flood scheme of taking the C.O.P. and Spot route to attack the centerline.

The scheme strategies of fake, flow and flood provide the offensive weapons necessary to attack or create Bubbles of space. They also neutralize or gain a +1 MAN-ADVANTAGE to a side of space. Furthermore, they attack PERSONNEL weakness and counter PERSONNEL strengths. It is not required that every concept contain fake, flow, and flood scheme strategies. However, a core concept within an offense should contain a combination of scheme strategies to increase its versatility against multiple defensive coverages, alignments and personnel accelerators.

RUN SCHEME STRATEGIES

Game-planning the best runs to use against an opponent is heavily reliant on scheming. The easiest way to advance the football is by running it. Therefore, defenses place a high priority on maintaining a man-advantage in the run box. It is critical that coaches understand how scheme strategies can neutralize the man-advantage count in the run box. The scheme strategies of fake, flow, and flow are still prevalent in the run game.

Fake

Fake schemes in the run game are concepts that place an unblocked defender in a run-pass or run-run conflict. Examples would be draw plays, RPOs, zone read, or option schemes. Fake schemes can manipulate or suspend a man-advantage player for a moment in time. This neutralizes the man-advantage count to a side of space in the offense's favor. (FIG. 4-7)

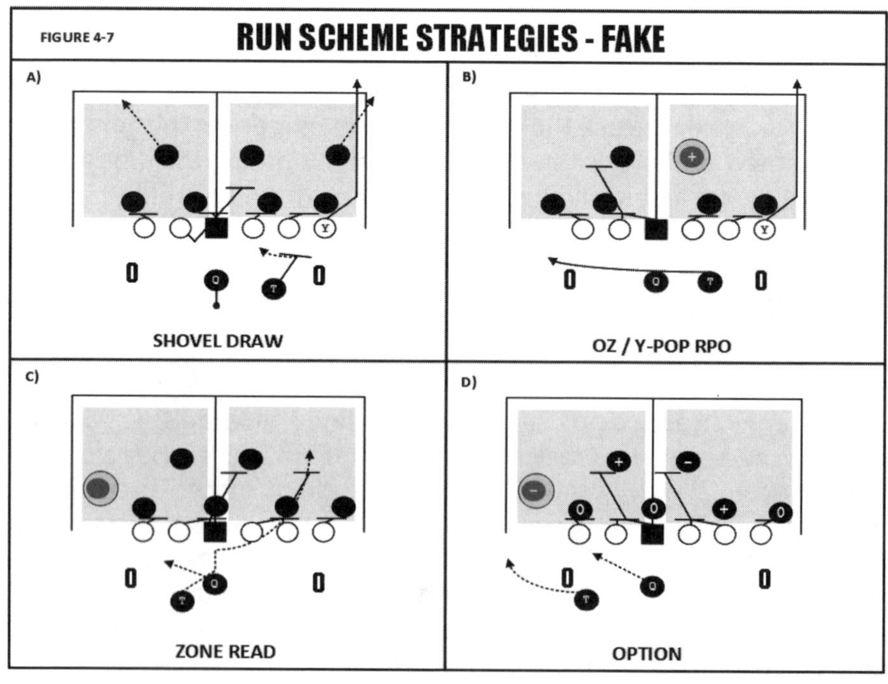

In (DIAGRAM A) an example of using a draw Fake scheme strategy shows how man-advantage is neutralized. Pre-snap, the defense has a +1 man-advantage to each side of run space. The quarterback can gain the man-advantage back by showing a pass drop. The drop along with the pass set action and route by the tight end will influence the linebackers to cover route space instead of run space. The running back will step up to show a pass protecting set, then pivot inside. The quarterback will shovel pass the ball to the running back into a run box that has been neutralized.

Scheme strategies are not just used to neutralize man-advantage. They are also used to attack personnel accelerator threats. In (DIAGRAM B) an example of using an outside zone RPO shows how a positive pursuit player can be attacked by using his pursuit to open route space. The outside zone run of the RPO is given if the pursuit player hesitates to collision or CAP the tight end's release off the line of scrimmage. The pass routes are thrown if the pursuit accelerator moves across the centerline on the mesh of the run.

Another Fake scheme strategy is leaving a defender unblocked and reading him with the quarterback. This is one of the most effective methods to neutralize man-advantage or negate a positive pin or penetration accelerator. In (DIAGRAM C) an example of a zone read concept shows how the man-advantage can be neutralized by reading the backside pin player accelerator.

The final example of a Fake scheme strategy is in (DIAGRAM D). This Fake scheme strategy is used by reading an unblocked defender and placing him in a 2-on-1 run-run conflict between the quarterback and tailback. This is called an option concept and is another effective tool in neutralizing man-advantage and attacking a weak pin accelerator.

FLOW

The next Run scheme strategy is *Flow. Flow schemes* in the run game are misdirection Run schemes or motion that gain a number or leverage advantage. Misdirection and motion can neutralize man-advantage by moving defenders or can cause run game accelerators to hesitate from executing their assignment. They can also place offensive players in a dominant position to UNCAP space or gain a leverage advantage. (FIG. 4-8)

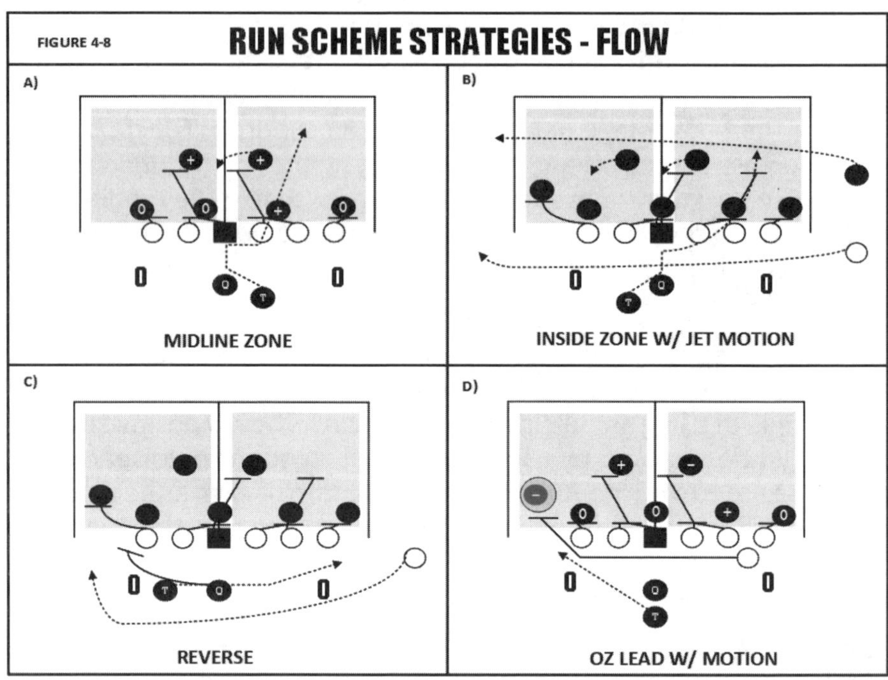

In (DIAGRAM A) an example of using a midline zone Run scheme shows how it can attack a positive pursuit accelerator. The flow of the midline zone scheme causes misdirection by giving the illusion the running back is attacking the front side of the formation. The midline zone is used to set up the backside pursuit play to move over the centerline, thus creating backside UNCAPPED run space.

Motions are another type of Flow scheme strategy. Jet sweep motion is an effective Flow scheme that can influence defenders away from intended run side space. (DIAGRAM B) shows how jet-sweep motion to the left can cause plug-and-pursuit accelerators to flow away from frontside run space on the inside zone handoff by the quarterback.

Another Flow scheme strategy is reverses. A reverse uses the initial flow of the concept in one direction and brings a ball carrier across the centerline to attack run space in the opposite direction. (DIAGRAM C) shows an example of using the flow of outside zone to the right to influence the defense to CAP the right side of run space. Once the defense has been influenced by the flow, the running backhands the ball off to the receiver running to the run space to the left. This flow creates misdirection that can lead to big explosive run plays.

A final example of Flow scheme is pre-snap motion. Motion can neutralize the man-advantage if the defense doesn't adjust. It can also place an offensive player in a dominate leverage position to block a run accelerator. (DIAGRAM D) shows an example of the flow of motion by the full back across the formation neutralizing the man-advantage and placing the full back in a dominate leverage position to block the negative pin player accelerator on outside zone.

FLOOD

The final Run scheme strategy is Flood. Flood schemes in the run game are activated by bringing one or more defenders across the centerline or using a centerline player as a lead blocker to a side of space. These actions can neutralize or create a man-advantage in the offense's favor or place offensive players in dominant positions to block personnel accelerator threats. (FIG. 4-9)

(Fig. 4-9 A) shows an example of the flood scheme strategy within the 1-back power concept. The flood scheme of bringing the backside guard across the centerline provides a leverage-blocking advantage

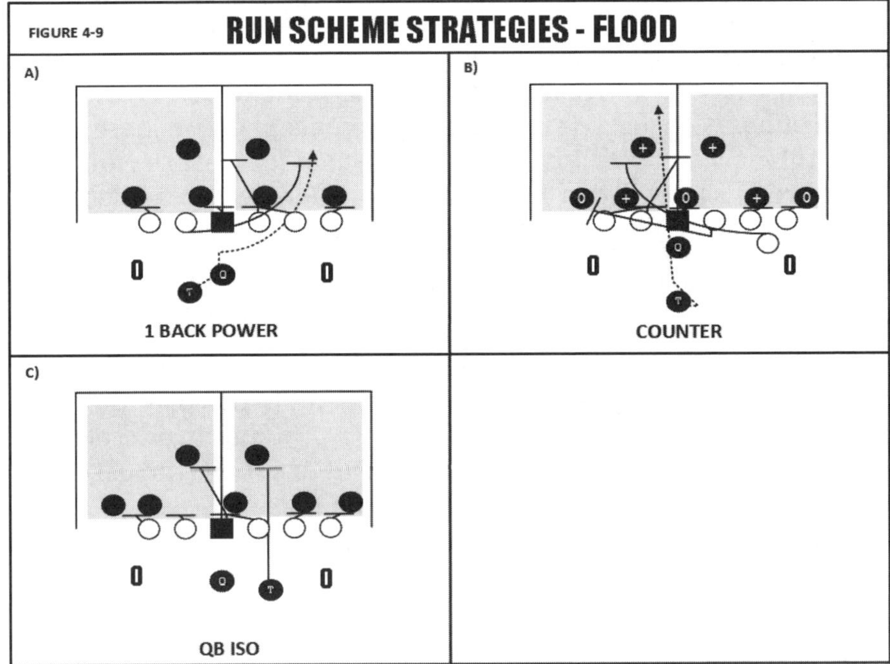

with the frontside double-team on the 3 technique. The pulling guard across the centerline also increases entry point versatility to gain a leverage advantage block on the play-side plug player accelerator.

(Fig. 4-9 B) shows an example of the flood scheme strategy that neutralizes man-advantage by bringing two offensive blockers across the centerline. This flood scheme is called counter. The counter blocking provides two moveable gaps to the play side while gaining a frontside double-team on the penetration accelerator.

(Fig. 4-9 C) shows how the flood scheme strategy can also include using centerline players as lead blockers. For example, a running back is typically not used as a blocker. However, incorporating him as a lead blocker and using the quarterback as the ball carrier "floods" the right side of run space. This neutralizes the man-advantage to the right side of run space and places blockers in dominant leverage positions.

All Weather Run Concepts – Fake, Flow, and Flood

Run concepts can only be maximized by possessing two or more scheme strategy properties. All weather run plays are concepts that incorporate fake, flow, and flood scheme strategies. The need for these scheme strategies helps overcome offensive personnel mismatches. If the offense is the more dominant team, then scheme is less of a priority. An offense can just line up and run any concept they choose. However, this is not a realistic world, especially in post-season play. Therefore, it is a good idea to add Fake, Flow, and Flood scheme strategies into your run plays at the beginning of the season.

This is an example of a weakside counter run play that is effective against man-free coverage with an under front. (Fig. 4-10)

The run accelerator grades are the game-planning indicator to make sure the play will hold up against an opponent. In this play, there is a positive pin player to the backside of the play. This positive accelerator grade can make it difficult for the Y tight end to cut off. The pin player can get on the hip of the second puller and make a tackle for a loss. This takes the coach to the scheme strategies to help overcome the personnel accelerator mismatch.

One of the scheme strategies that can neutralize a positive pin player is the Fake scheme. (FIG. 4-11)

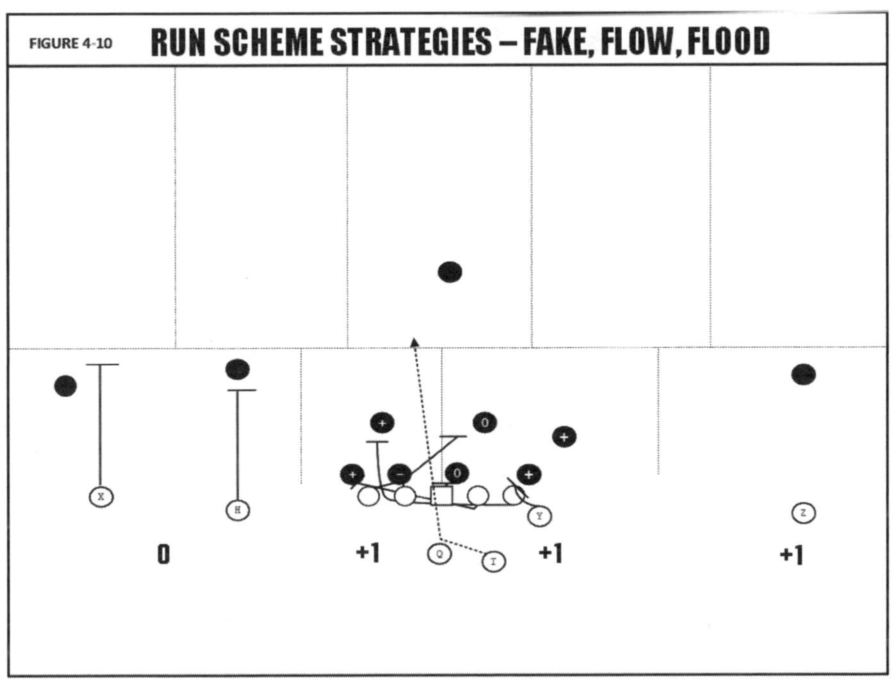
FIGURE 4-10
RUN SCHEME STRATEGIES – FAKE, FLOW, FLOOD
X
H
Y
Z
Q
T
0
+1
+1
+1

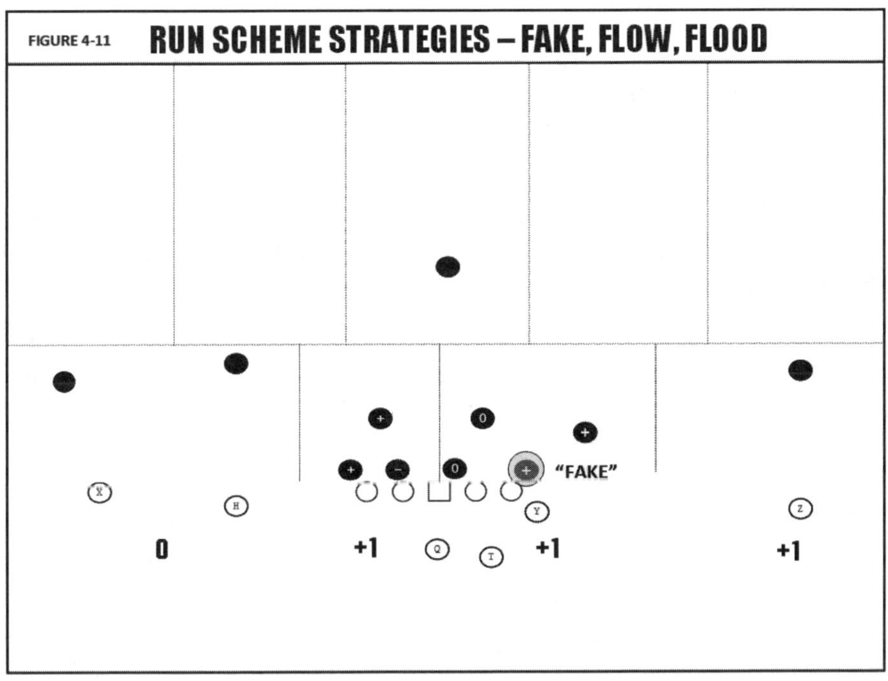
FIGURE 4-11
RUN SCHEME STRATEGIES – FAKE, FLOW, FLOOD
"FAKE"
X
H
Y
Z
Q
T
0
+1
+1
+1

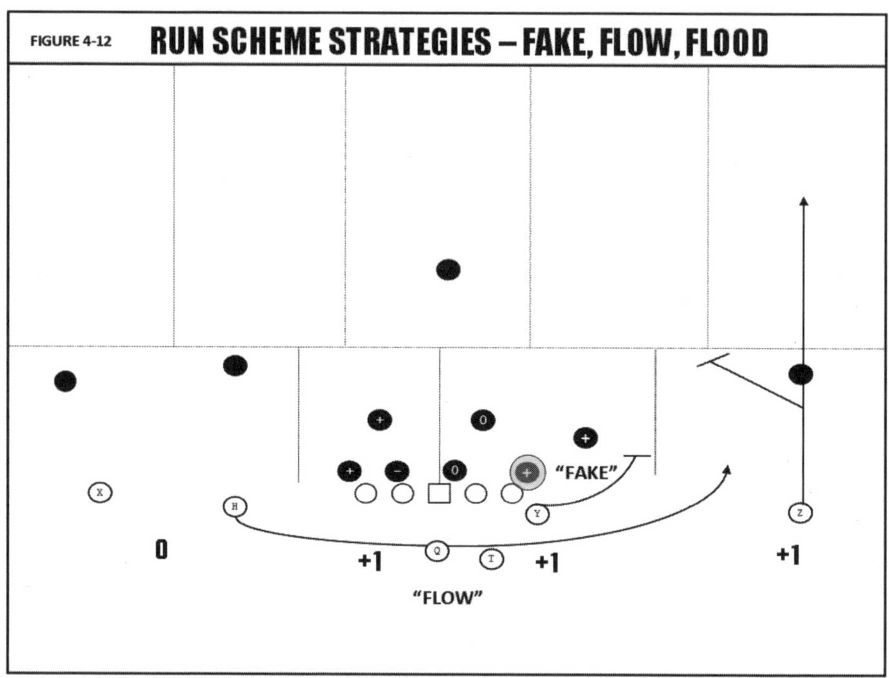

The Fake scheme allows the quarterback to read the pin player causing him to hesitate on the play. Another scheme strategy that can be employed here is using the Flow scheme. (FIG. 4-12)

An example of the Flow scheme would be to use jet sweep motion by the H receiver to further cause hesitation by the backside pin players. The final scheme strategy that can be added to this run concept is the flood scheme. (FIG. 4-13)

A flood scheme can be used to both sides of the formation. The running back can be used as a lead blocker to the right side of run space for the jet sweep motion by the H receiver. The flood scheme can also be used to the left side of run space by bringing the right guard and tackle across the centerline on the counter play.

This run concept has now maximized the stress on the defense by using a fake, flow, and flood scheme strategy. The quarterback will now read the positive pin player and determine whether to give the jet sweep to the right or fake the jet sweep and keep it for the quarterback counter play to the left. This is an example of how to ensure that run

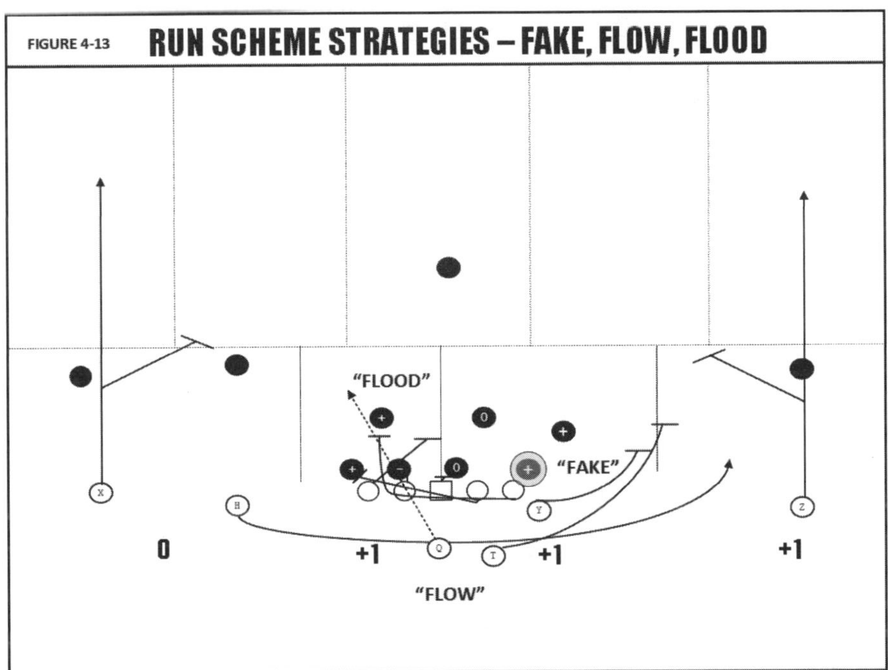

concepts neutralize man-advantage and positive personnel accelerator threats to a side of space.

Fake, flow, and flood schemes strategies to increase concept versatility for both pass and run concepts. The common language and process provide a consistent workflow for coaches to go through when determining what the best plays are to attack an opponent.

CHAPTER 5

STRUCTURAL STRAIN

The 5 Families of Personnel and Formations

STRUCTURAL STRAIN

The 5 Families of Personnel and Formations

The definition of offensive or being on offense is to attack. This requires the ability to dictate the action of an opponent. The single most important trait for an offense to dictate coverage, alignment, and positioning personnel in areas of advantage. This ability originates through personnel and formations. It is critical that a coach understands the strengths and weaknesses that personnel groupings and formations can present to an opponent. The inference engine of R4 reveals the structural strain that personnel and formations create for a defense.

To help streamline this understanding, the inference engine of R4 breaks down personnel and formations into 5 family categories. This allows a coach to accelerate the understanding of the relationships of each personnel family along with the advantages that each formation has within a personnel group. Understanding the relationships of personnel and formations provides the platform to explain the "why" behind a selection of a personnel or formation group within a game-plan.

One of the benefits of R4 is providing coaches and players with the ability to run multiple variations of concepts fluidly through a variety of personnel and formations. R4 is an operating system that can be used to accelerate any offense. Before we can demonstrate this opportunity, we must understand the relationships of personnel and formations.

There are 5 families of personnel and formations in football. The offense can release as many as 5 players downfield on a given play. Personnel is a numerical measure that reflects the action abilities of what these 5 offensive players can do within a formation. The biggest determinate in the personnel families is the number of run gaps presented to the defense. Therefore, the five families of personnel are

FIGURE 5-1	5 PERSONNEL FAMILIES				
5 PERSONNEL FAMILIES	6 GAPS	7 GAPS	8 GAPS	9 GAPS	10 GAPS

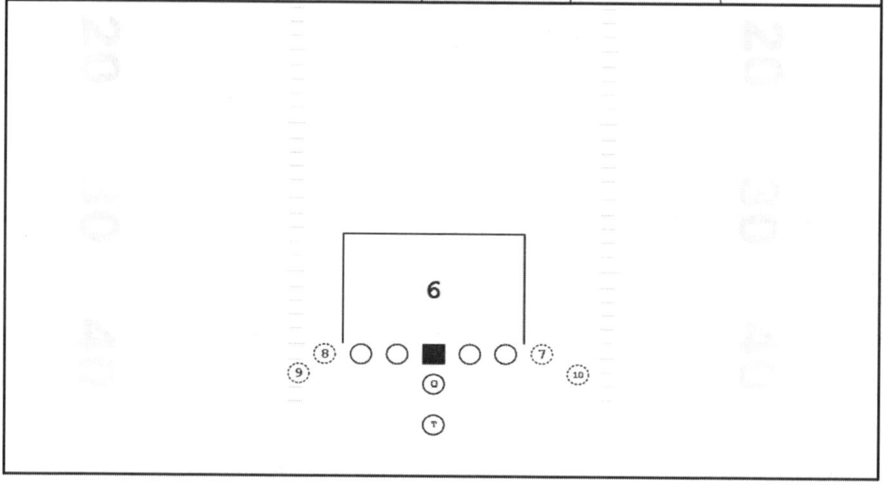

6

8 7 9 10 Q T

categorized by the number of run gaps present within a formation. The 5 families of personnel are 6, 7, 8, 9, and 10 gaps. (FIG. 5-1) Formations determine where these personnel are positioned on the field along with how many gaps are presented to the defense. With 5 offensive linemen always in the game, the baseline number of gaps to defend are 6. Personnel quickly informs the number of gaps that are available for the offense to attack and the defense to defend. The first number of a personnel grouping shows how many running backs are in the game. (FIG. 5-2)

In this example, there is 1. The second number shows how many tight ends are in the game. In this example there is none. We would call this 10-personnel. The number of receivers available can be determined from the 10 Personnel number. In this example, there are 4 detached receivers available because an offense always has 5 moveable threats that make up the formation. Adding a running back or tight ends into the personnel will add gaps to the formation and reduce the number of detached receivers at the same time. This addition and subtraction of gaps are what determines the personnel family an offense is using.

FIGURE 5-2

10 PERSONNEL

5 PERSONNEL FAMILIES	6 GAPS	7 GAPS	8 GAPS	9 GAPS	10 GAPS

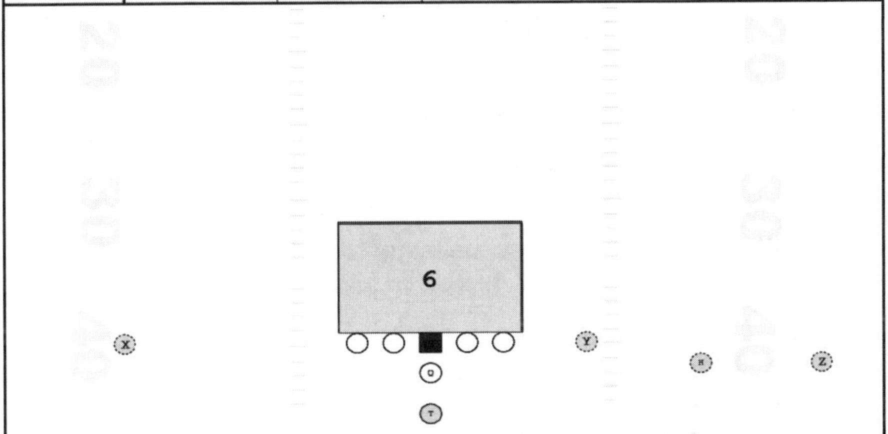

1 (RB) + 0 (TE) > 4 (WR) = 5 MOVEABLE THREATS

FIGURE 5-3

5 FORMATION FAMILIES

5 PERSONNEL FAMILIES	6 GAPS	7 GAPS	8 GAPS	9 GAPS	10 GAPS
5 FORMATION FAMILIES	3 X 1	2 X 2	PRO	SLOT	OVERLOAD

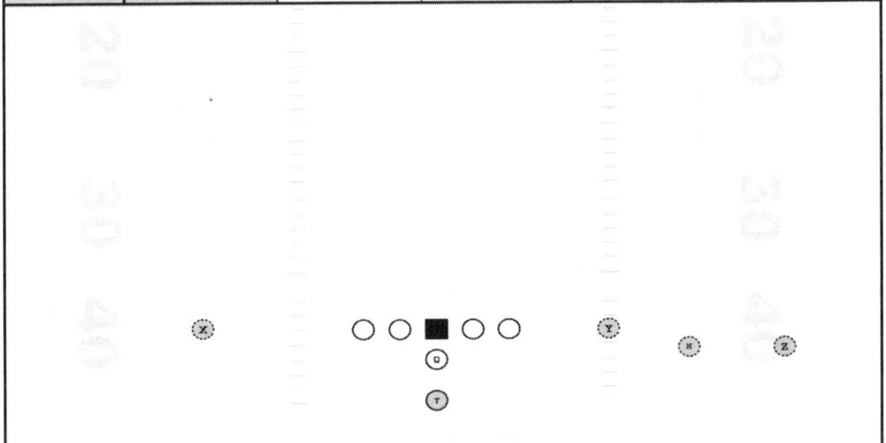

3 X 1 FORMATION

Once we determine the personnel that is in the game, next we must determine how we align personnel in a formation. There are 5 formational families in football. (FIG. 5-3)

1. **3 x 1 Formation** - Unbalanced with 3 receivers positioned to one side of a formation and have a single receiver to the other side of the formation.

2. **2 x 2 Formations** - Balanced formations with 2 receivers to each side of the formation. (FIG. 5-4)

3. **Pro Formation** - Contains 8 gaps with at least 1 moveable gap. (FIG. 5-5)

4. **Slot Formation** - Places the fastest receiver threats to one side with a strong nub tight end or wing set to the backside. (FIG 5-6)

5. **Overload Formations** - This family contains a variety of formations that overload personnel to a side of run or route space that is different than the first 4 families. A Quads Formation here would be a good example. (FIG. 5-7)

10 PERSONNEL 3 X 1 FORMATION

Now that we understand the setup of the 5 personnel and formation families, let's look at the structural strain that different groupings can present to the defense. We'll start with the 6-gap family of personnel. 10 Personnel is made of 1 back and no tight ends. This presents 6 gaps of run space and 4 immediate vertical threats of route space to the defense. The maximum pass pro that can be executed in 10 Personnel is a 6-man protection. (FIG. 5-8)

One of the formations that 10 Personnel can be aligned in is a 3 x 1 formation. The benefit of the 3 x 1 formational family is that it singles up the X wide receiver to a side for a potential 1-on-1 match. Another benefit is that it places 3 fast receivers strong to the field to unbalance the formation. The unbalanced alignment of a 3 x 1 formation provides an easy way for the offense to determine the man-advantage to a side of route space. We refer to this as the Unbalanced 1 CAP / 2 CAP rule. If the boundary safety is to the left of the centerline then the defense has a 2 CAP count to that side. A 2 CAP count to the single side gives

FIGURE 5-4

5 FORMATION FAMILIES

5 PERSONNEL FAMILIES	6 GAPS	7 GAPS	8 GAPS	9 GAPS	10 GAPS
5 FORMATION FAMILIES	3 X 1	2 X 2	PRO	SLOT	OVERLOAD

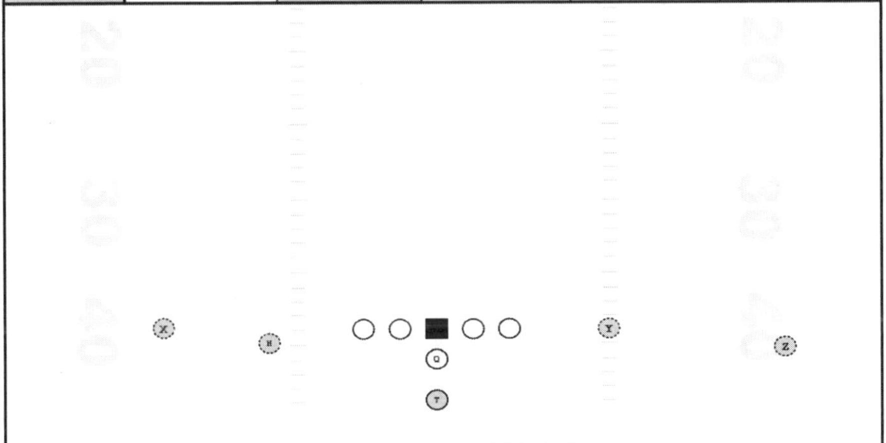

2 X 2 FORMATION

FIGURE 5-5

5 FORMATION FAMILIES

5 PERSONNEL FAMILIES	6 GAPS	7 GAPS	8 GAPS	9 GAPS	10 GAPS
5 FORMATION FAMILIES	3 X 1	2 X 2	PRO	SLOT	OVERLOAD

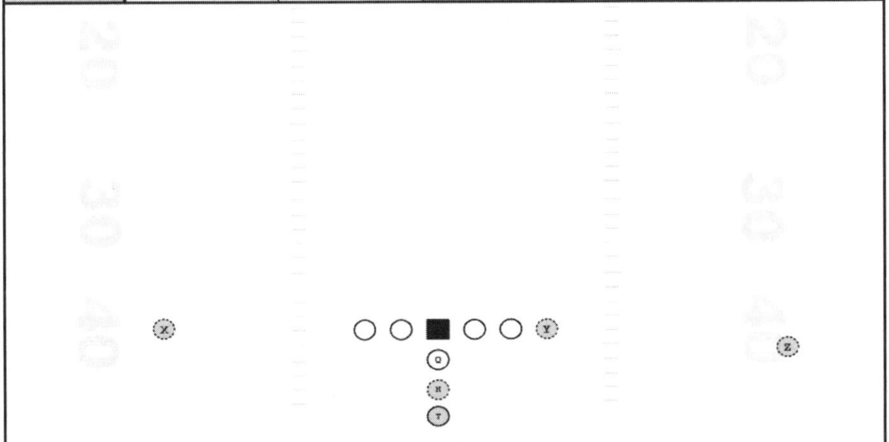

PRO FORMATION

FIGURE 5-6	5 FORMATION FAMILIES				
5 PERSONNEL FAMILIES	6 GAPS	7 GAPS	8 GAPS	9 GAPS	10 GAPS
5 FORMATION FAMILIES	3 X 1	2 X 2	PRO	SLOT	OVERLOAD

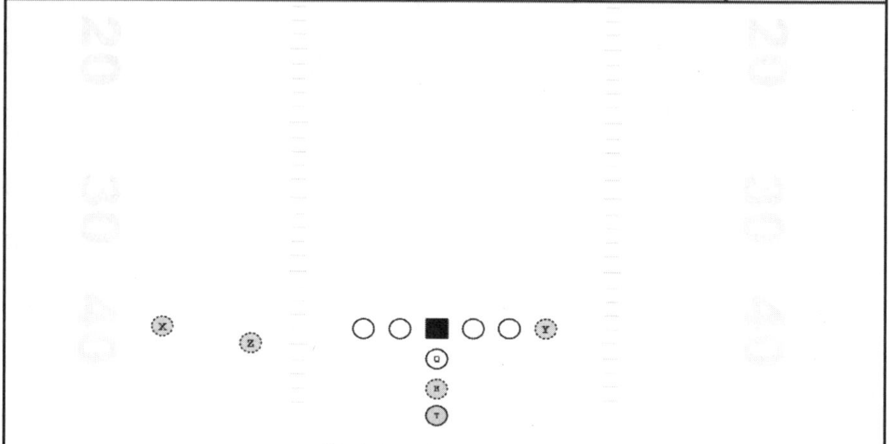

SLOT FORMATION

FIGURE 5-7	5 FORMATION FAMILIES				
5 PERSONNEL FAMILIES	6 GAPS	7 GAPS	8 GAPS	9 GAPS	10 GAPS
5 FORMATION FAMILIES	3 X 1	2 X 2	PRO	SLOT	OVERLOAD

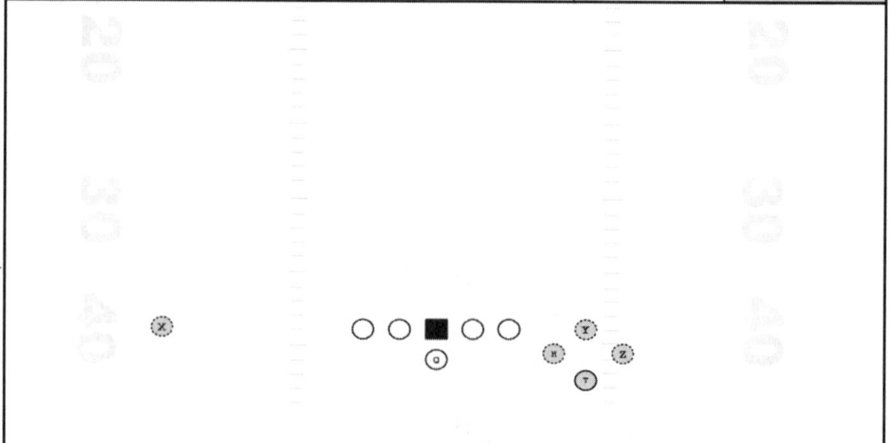

OVERLOAD FORMATION

FIGURE 5-8	10 PERSONNEL 3 X 1 FORMATION				
5 PERSONNEL FAMILIES	6 GAPS	7 GAPS	8 GAPS	9 GAPS	10 GAPS
5 FORMATION FAMILIES	3 X 1	2 X 2	PRO	SLOT	OVERLOAD

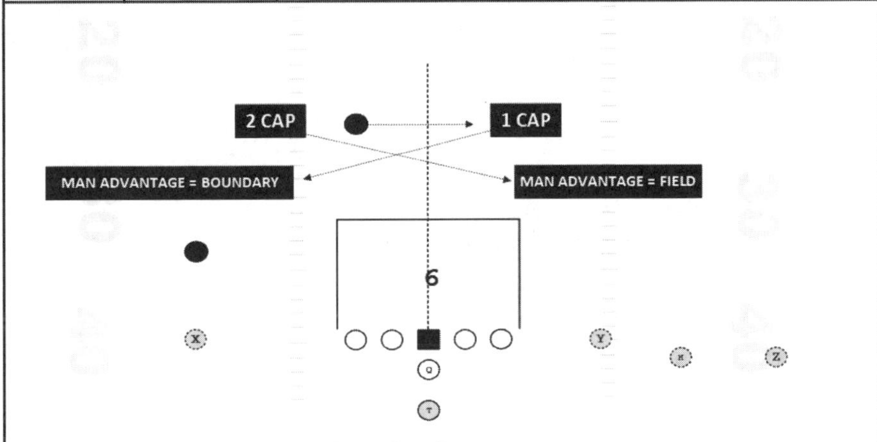

1 (RB) + 0 (TE) > 4 (WR) = 5 MOVEABLE THREATS

the defense the man-advantage to that side of space. However, a 2 CAP count to the single side will give the offense a neutral man-advantage to the trips side of space.

If the boundary safety is to the right of the centerline, then the defense has a 1 CAP count to the single side of space. This gives the offense a neutral advantage to the single side of the formation. The defense, however, will have the man-advantage to the trips side of the formation.

Understanding the 1 CAP / 2 CAP rule in 3 x 1 formations helps coaches and players to quickly determine the man-advantage to a side and, in turn, can accelerate play-call and adjust advantage in their favor.

10 PERSONNEL 3 X 1 FORMATION SUMMARY

STRENGTHS

- 4 IMMEDIATE VERTICAL THREATS
- SINGLE UP BEST WR
- 3 FAST WRs TO OTHER SIDE
- SPREADS DEFENSE OUT TO CREATE SPACE
- 1 CAP / 2 CAP RULE

WEAKNESSES

- SUSCEPTIBLE TO EDGE PRESSURE
- CAN ONLY PASS PROTECT WITH A MAX OF 6 MEN
- REQUIRES DUAL THREAT QB TO NEUTRALIZE MAN-ADVANTAGE

10 PERSONNEL 2 X 2 FORMATION

The other formation that 10 Personnel is most commonly aligned in is a 2 x 2 Formation. (FIG. 5-9) The benefit of a 2 x 2 Formation is that it places 2 fast receivers on each side. This allows for a wider range of route stretches, as well as outside flat tube threats to each side of space. 2 x 2 Formations can force a defense into a more balanced alignment to prevent being outflanked to a side. (Fig. 5-9)

One rule that can limit the effectiveness of 10 Personnel 2 x 2 Formation is when it is used on high school hash marks. Schools that play within the National Federation of State High School Association have hash marks that are 53 feet and 4 inches from the sideline. This limits the amount of space availability into the boundary for 10 Personnel 2 x 2 Formations. This can reduce the structural strain on the defense allowing them to still overplay the field while covering the reduced boundary space with fewer defenders. NCAA rules place the hash marks at 60 feet which increases the space availability into the boundary when the ball is on the hash.

FIGURE 5-9	10 PERSONNEL 2 X 2 FORMATION				
5 PERSONNEL FAMILIES	6 GAPS	7 GAPS	8 GAPS	9 GAPS	10 GAPS
5 FORMATION FAMILIES	3 X 1	2 X 2	PRO	SLOT	OVERLOAD

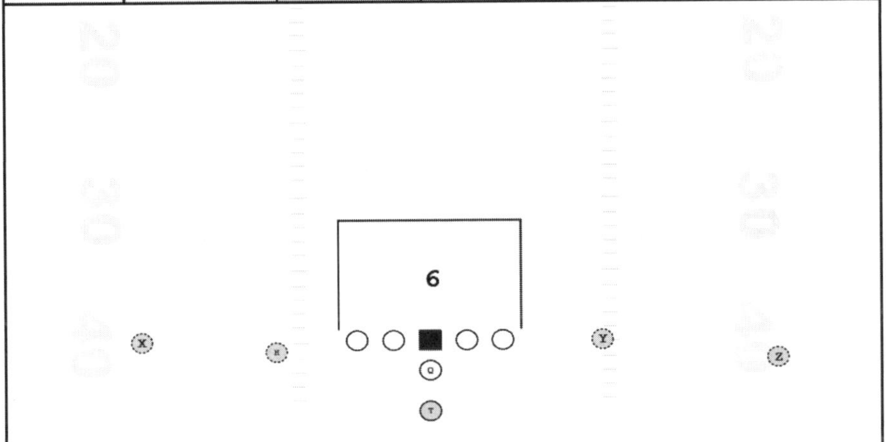

6

X H Y Z Q T

1 (RB) + 0 (TE) > 4 (WR) = 5 MOVEABLE THREATS

10 PERSONNEL 2 X 2 FORMATION SUMMARY

STRENGTHS

- 4 IMMEDIATE VERTICAL THREATS
- INCREASES A WIDER RANGE OF ROUTE STRETCHES
- PROVIDES MULTIPLE OUTSIDE SPACE THREATS TO EACH SIDE
- FORCES THE DEFENSE TO BALANCE BOTH SIDES

WEAKNESSES

- SUSCEPTIBLE TO EDGE PRESSURE
- CAN ONLY PASS PROTECT WITH A MAX OF 6 MEN
- REQUIRES DUAL THREAT QB TO NEUTRALIZE MAN-ADVANTAGE
- LIMITED SPACE TO ATTACK ON HIGH SCHOOL HASHES

11 Personnel 3 x 1 Formation

The next personnel grouping is the **7-gap family.** The 7-gap family is created by adding an additional run gap. One of the personnel groupings in the 7-gap family is 11 Personnel. 11 Personnel is made of 1 back and 1 tight end. (FIG. 5-10)

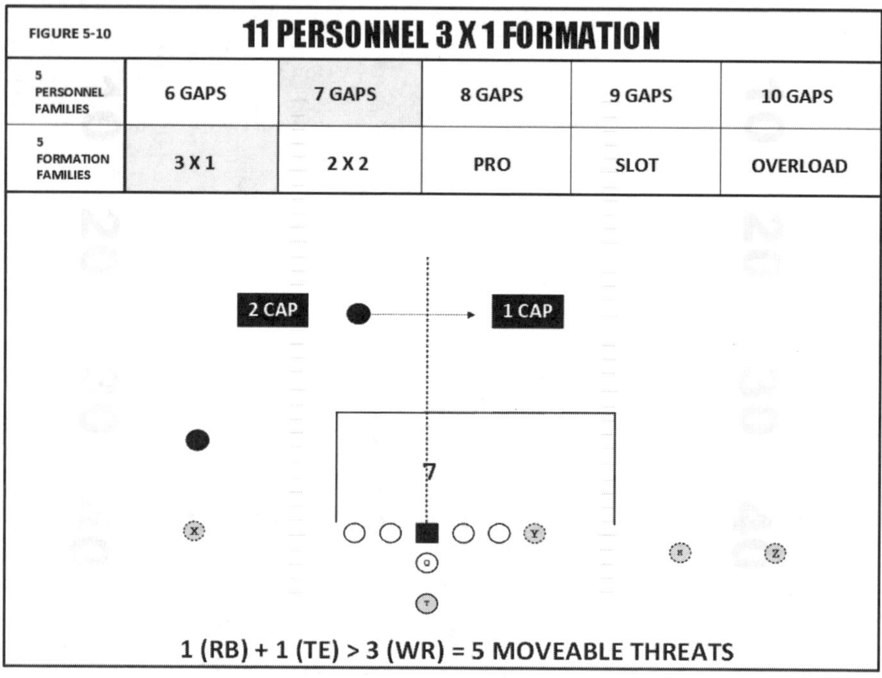

The tight end creates the 7th gap. The addition of a run gap can be used for a variety of benefits. One of the benefits is that the addition gap can be used to dictate defensive strength. This is effective when the defense has a dominant strong side player. The extra run gap can be used to position a dominant defensive player to a specific side of space. Another benefit of an additional gap is that it can be used to help protect immediate edge pressure on a pin player accelerator. Pass protection options can also be maximized with 7-man protection via the extra gap. Furthermore, the offense can still maintain 4 immediate vertical threats with the tight end.

One of the formational families that 11 Personnel can align in is a 3 x 1 formation. The same benefits of single-side match up to one side, along with 3 receiving threats to the other, are still present. The 1 CAP / 2 CAP man-advantage rule still applies, as well.

11 PERSONNEL 3 X 1 FORMATION SUMMARY

STRENGTHS

- 4 IMMEDIATE VERTICAL THREATS
- SINGLE UP BEST WR
- DICTATES DEFENSIVE STRENGTH
- PROTECTS IMMEDIATE EDGE PRESSURE TO A SIDE
- ALLOWS FOR 7-MAN PASS PROTECTION
- 1 CAP / 2 CAP RULE

WEAKNESSES

- 7TH GAP CAN BRING AN EXTRA DEFENDER INTO THE RUN BOX
- ONLY 2 IMMEDIATE OUTSIDE FLAT TUBE THREATS TO A SIDE OF SPACE
- #3 WR (TE) LOSES FREE RELEASE ABILITY, MORE SUSCEPTIBLE TO COLLISION

11 PERSONNEL 2 X 2 FORMATION

The next formation that 11 Personnel can be aligned in is a 2 x 2 Formation. The benefit of the 2 x 2 Formation is that 4 immediate vertical tube threats are present within the formation. The balance of this formation, along with an additional run gap to a side, can help dictate a more consistent defensive alignment or coverage for the offense to attack. (FIG. 5-11)

A 2 x 2 Formation out of 11 Personnel is more favorable for offenses who play on a high school hash mark. A tight end who is placed into the boundary increases the apex line between the outside receiver. This increases the space availability and forces the defense into higher priority space threat to consider. Another benefit is having a run strength opposite of the pass strength with a faster receiver to the field.

FIGURE 5-11	11 PERSONNEL 2 X 2 FORMATION				
5 PERSONNEL FAMILIES	6 GAPS	7 GAPS	8 GAPS	9 GAPS	10 GAPS
5 FORMATION FAMILIES	3 X 1	2 X 2	PRO	SLOT	OVERLOAD

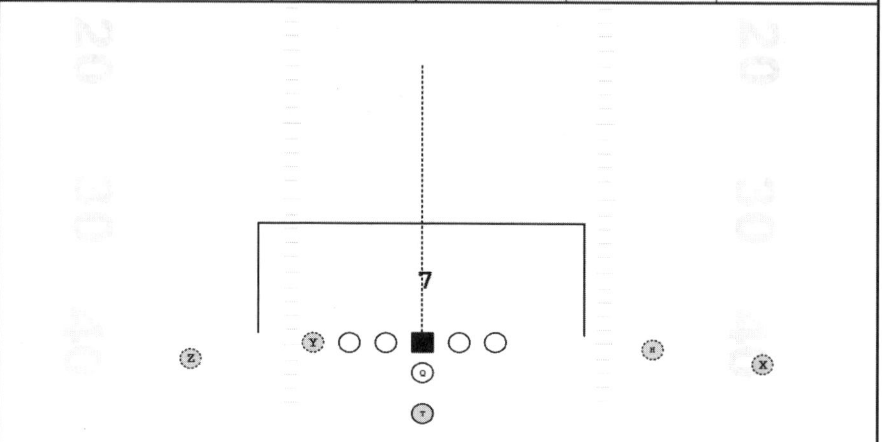

1 (RB) + 1 (TE) > 3 (WR) = 5 MOVEABLE THREATS

11 PERSONNEL 2 X 2 FORMATION SUMMARY

STRENGTHS

- 4 IMMEDIATE VERTICAL THREATS
- DICTATES DEFENSIVE STRENGTH TO A SIDE
- PROVIDES RUN STRENGTH OPPOSITE OF PASS STRENGTH
- FORCES THE DEFENSE TO BALANCE BOTH SIDES
- ALLOWS FOR 7-MAN PASS PROTECTION
- INCREASES SPACE TO BOUNDARY ON HIGH SCHOOL HASH MARKS

WEAKNESSES

- 7TH GAP CAN BRING AN EXTRA DEFENDER INTO THE RUN BOX
- LIMITS IMMEDIATE OUTSIDE FLAT TUBE TO ONLY ONE SIDE
- #2 WR (TE) LOSES FREE RELEASE ABILITY, MORE SUSCEPTIBLE TO COLLISION

11 PERSONNEL SLOT FORMATION

Another formation that 11 Personnel can be aligned in is a Slot Formation. Slot Formations place a tight end in a nub position. A nub position means that the tight end has no eligible wide receiver outside of him. The benefit of Slot Formations is that they place all the fast receivers to a side while maintaining a strong side-run advantage to the opposite side. (FIG. 5-12)

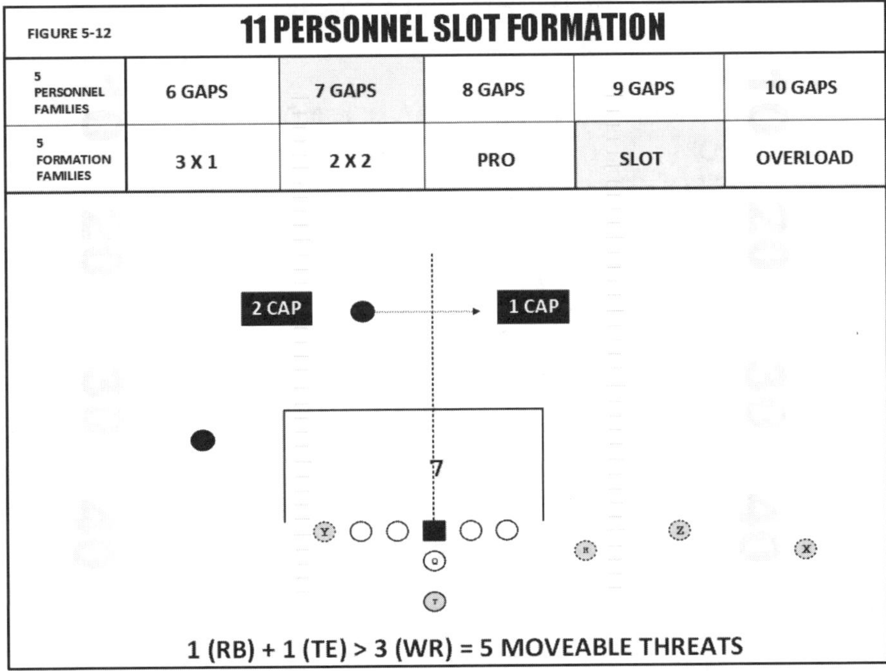

In this personnel grouping, the strong side is created by a nub tight end making 4 gaps of space to be defended. This can dictate a defense to declare strength to a known position for the offense. Slot Formations contains the same 1 CAP / 2 CAP rule properties of the 3 x 1 formations. These formations place a considerable structural strain on defenses. An 11 Personnel Slot Formation still contains 4 immediate vertical threats along with 3 immediate outside flat tube threats to a side.

11 PERSONNEL SLOT FORMATION SUMMARY

STRENGTHS

- 4 IMMEDIATE VERTICAL THREATS
- DICTATES DEFENSIVE STRENGTH
- PROTECTS IMMEDIATE EDGE PRESSURE TO A SIDE
- ALLOWS FOR 7-MAN PASS PROTECTION
- 1 CAP / 2 CAP RULE
- 3 IMMEDIATE OUTSIDE FLAT TUBE THREATS TO A SIDE

WEAKNESSES

- 7TH GAP CAN BRING AN EXTRA DEFENDER INTO THE RUN BOX
- LIMITS ROUTE STRETCH COMBINATIONS TO THE TIGHT END SIDE
- #3 WR (TE) LOSES FREE RELEASE ABILITY, MORE SUSCEPTIBLE TO COLLISION

20 PERSONNEL 3 X 1 FORMATION

Another Personnel grouping that is found in the 7-gap family is 20 Personnel. **20 Personnel** positions two backs in the backfield and no tight ends. The benefit of this personnel grouping is the creation of a moveable gap. A moveable gap allows the offense to move a lead blocker pre- or post-snap and insert the blocker into different gaps. This can present post-snap accelerator issues for the defense. (FIG. 5-13)

One of the formations that 20 Personnel can align in is the **3 x 1 formation family.** This provides a single side WR match to one side, along with maintaining the 1 CAP / 2 CAP rule. The offense maintains two immediate outside flat tube threats to the opposite side.

The downside to having a moveable gap inside the tackle box is that the offense loses the immediate vertical tube threat. Now the offense only has 3 immediate pre-snap vertical threats.

FIGURE 5-13	20 PERSONNEL 3 X 1 FORMATION				
5 PERSONNEL FAMILIES	6 GAPS	7 GAPS	8 GAPS	9 GAPS	10 GAPS
5 FORMATION FAMILIES	3 X 1	2 X 2	PRO	SLOT	OVERLOAD

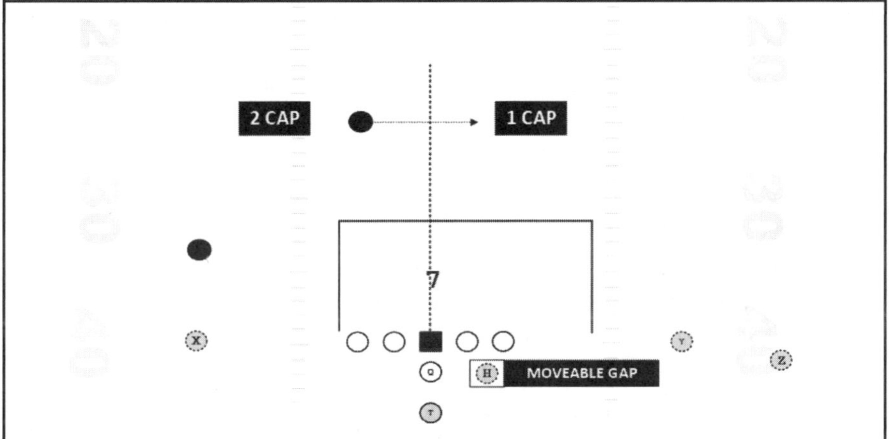

2 CAP
1 CAP
7
X Y Z Q H T
MOVEABLE GAP

2 (RB) + 0 (TE) > 3 (WR) = 5 MOVEABLE THREATS

20 PERSONNEL 3 X 1 FORMATION SUMMARY

STRENGTHS

- PROVIDES A MOVEABLE GAP
- SINGLE UP BEST WR
- DICTATES DEFENSIVE STRENGTH
- PROTECTS IMMEDIATE EDGE PRESSURE TO A SIDE
- ALLOWS FOR 7-MAN PASS PROTECTION
- 1 CAP / 2 CAP RULE

WEAKNESSES

- 7TH GAP CAN BRING AN EXTRA DEFENDER INTO THE RUN BOX
- ONLY PRESENTS 3 IMMEDIATE VERTICAL THREATS
- ONLY 2 IMMEDIATE OUTSIDE FLAT TUBE THREATS TO A SIDE OF SPACE
- #3 WR (H) LOSES FREE RELEASE ABILITY, MORE SUSCEPTIBLE TO COLLISION

20 PERSONNEL 2 X 2 FORMATION

Another formation that 20 Personnel can be aligned in is a **2 x 2 Formation.** (FIG. 5-14)

By aligning the moveable gap on the other side of the formation, pre-snap, the offense can balance the formation and present 2 receiving threats on each side, while still maintaining a moveable post-snap gap. One benefit of balancing a formation with a moveable gap is that it can dictate strength to that side of space, allowing the offense to declare the location of specific defenders.

The moveable gap can provide a leverage advantage against pin players. A moveable gap also sets up space for "bluff" or "chip" action, in which the moveable gap attacks a defender as if he is going to block him, then slips past him on a flat or seam route. These actions are very effective for RPOs and play-action passes.

A downside to the 20 Personnel 2 x 2 Formation is that it only presents 3 immediate vertical threats to the defense. There are only 2 immediate outside flat tube threats to a side of space. The addition of the 7th moveable gap can bring an extra defender into the run box.

FIGURE 5-14 **20 PERSONNEL 2 X 2 FORMATION**

5 PERSONNEL FAMILIES	6 GAPS	7 GAPS	8 GAPS	9 GAPS	10 GAPS
5 FORMATION FAMILIES	3 X 1	2 X 2	PRO	SLOT	OVERLOAD

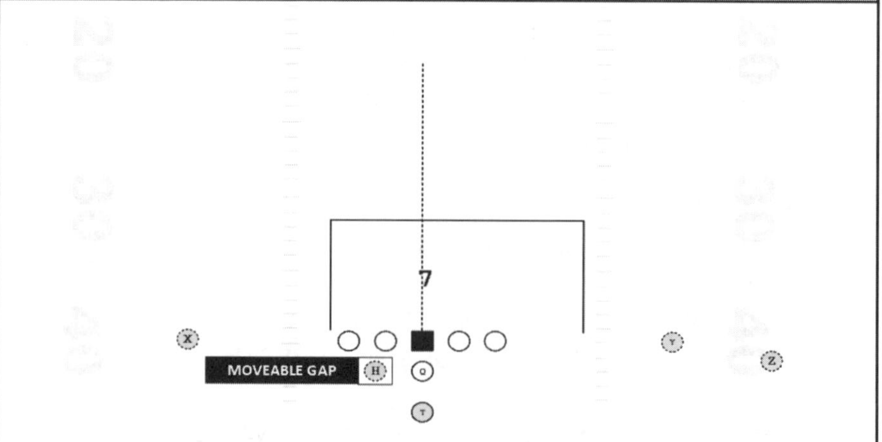

7

X

MOVEABLE GAP H

Q

T

Y

Z

2 (RB) + 0 (TE) > 3 (WR) = 5 MOVEABLE THREATS

20 PERSONNEL 2 X 2 FORMATION SUMMARY

STRENGTHS

- PROVIDES A MOVEABLE GAP
- DICTATES DEFENSIVE STRENGTH TO A SIDE
- PROVIDES RUN STRENGTH OPPOSITE OF PASS STRENGTH
- FORCES THE DEFENSE TO BALANCE BOTH SIDES
- ALLOWS FOR 7-MAN PASS PROTECTION
- INCREASES SPACE TO BOUNDARY ON HIGH SCHOOL HASH MARKS

WEAKNESSES

- 7TH GAP CAN BRING AN EXTRA DEFENDER INTO THE RUN BOX
- LIMITS IMMEDIATE OUTSIDE FLAT TUBE TO ONLY ONE SIDE
- #2 WR (H) LOSES FREE RELEASE ABILITY, MORE SUSCEPTIBLE TO COLLISION

12 PERSONNEL 2 X 2 FORMATION

The next personnel family in football is the **8-gap family.** 12 Personnel is used to create 8 gaps. 12 Personnel contains 1 back and 2 tight ends. The benefit of this personnel is that it creates 2 extra gaps on the line of scrimmage while maintaining 4 immediate vertical threats to the defense. One of the formations that 12 Personnel can align in is a 2 x 2 Formation. The 2 x 2 Formation creates a balanced formation with 1 immediate receiver threat to each side of space. (FIG. 5-15)

This personnel and formation maximize structural strain on the defense. The addition of run gaps within a formation forces defenders into the run box to maintain a man-advantage. This decreases the ability of the defense to CAP vertical tube threats. An offense that contains a personnel pool of at least two tight ends who can run and catch the ball can create an explosive play advantage with these formations.

Another benefit of the 12 Personnel 2 x 2 Formation is that it can provide security to edge pressures and positive pin-player threats for the offense. The positioning of a tight end to each side of the formation

FIGURE 5-15

12 PERSONNEL 2 X 2 FORMATION

5 PERSONNEL FAMILIES	6 GAPS	7 GAPS	8 GAPS	9 GAPS	10 GAPS
5 FORMATION FAMILIES	3 X 1	2 X 2	PRO	SLOT	OVERLOAD

8

Z Y A X Q T

1 (RB) + 2 (TE) > 2 (WR) = 5 MOVEABLE THREATS

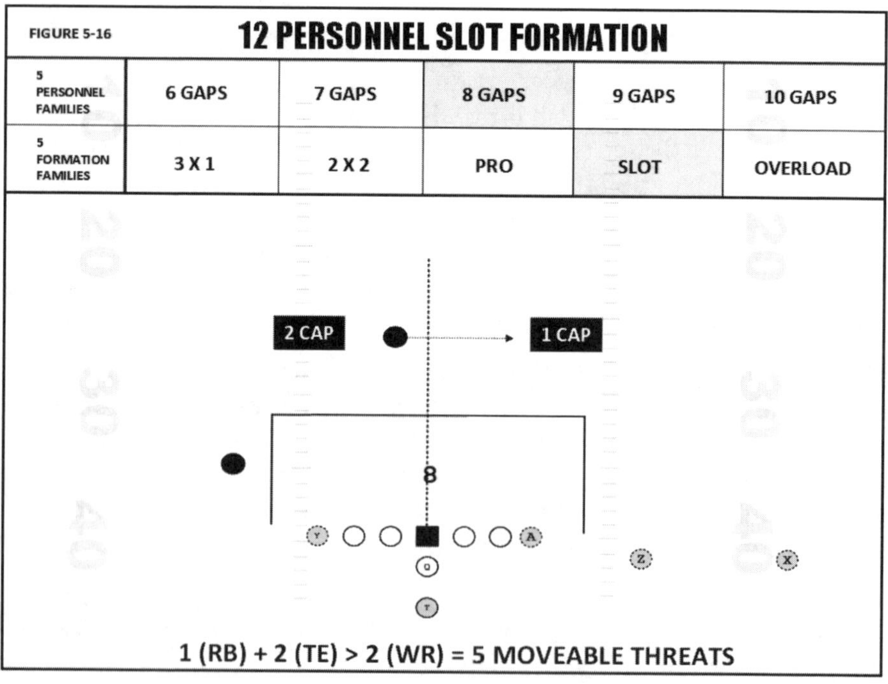

limits defensive pressure and can calm down a defense who uses pressure as an attack weapon. Furthermore, this formation presents that same strength to both sides of run space. This can help an offense dictate defenders to a specific side and allow them to check a run play away from positive defense accelerator threats or coverage adjustments that overload a side of space.

A downside to this formation is that an offensive is limited to only 1 immediate outside flat tube threat to each side. This reduces that ability of an offense to attack the perimeter with screens or RPO route tags.

12 PERSONNEL 2 X 2 FORMATION SUMMARY

STRENGTHS

- PROVIDES A 4-GAP RUN STRENGTH TO BOTH SIDES OF RUN-SPACE
- CREATES MORE UNCAPPED VERTICAL TUBE SPACE
- FORCES THE DEFENSE TO BALANCE BOTH SIDES
- CONTROLS EDGE PRESSURE AND LIMITS BLITZ EFFECTIVENESS
- ALLOWS FOR 8-MAN PASS PROTECTION

WEAKNESSES

- 8TH GAP CAN BRING AN EXTRA DEFENDERS INTO THE RUN BOX
- LIMITS IMMEDIATE OUTSIDE FLAT TUBE THREATS TO BOTH SIDES
- #2 WR (Y & A) LOSES FREE RELEASE ABILITY, MORE SUSCEPTIBLE TO COLLISION

12 PERSONNEL SLOT FORMATION

The other formation that can align in 12 Personnel is a **Slot Formation.** (FIG. 5-16)

The Slot Formation in 12 Personnel maintains 8 gaps and 4 vertical threats but also places the fastest receivers to a side of space while maintaining a strong run side away to the nub. The benefits of 12 Personnel 2 x 2 Formation carry over to this formation but gains additional benefits, as well.

One benefit gained is the unbalanced 1 CAP / 2 CAP rule. The Slot Formation makes it easier for the quarterback to determine where the man-advantage is in the offense's favor. The 12-personnel Slot Formation also generates the ability of an offense to gain 2 immediate outside flat tube threats to a side. This buys back the ability to run perimeter screens and RPO route attachments that are lost in the 2 x 2 Formation.

Furthermore, the offense gains the ability to run 3-man route concepts to the field and use the backside tight end in a 7-man pass protection. The offense can also release the backside tight end to gain man-advantage in route concepts or use him as a vertical tube threat to the backside. This personnel and formation maximize structural strain on the defense.

12 PERSONNEL SLOT FORMATION SUMMARY

STRENGTHS

- PROVIDES A 4-GAP RUN STRENGTH TO BOTH SIDES OF RUN-SPACE
- CREATES MORE UNCAPPED VERTICAL TUBE SPACE
- FORCES THE DEFENSE TO BALANCE BOTH SIDES
- CONTROLS EDGE PRESSURE AND LIMITS BLITZ EFFECTIVENESS
- ALLOWS FOR 8-MAN PASS PROTECTION
- 1 CAP / 2 CAP RULE
- 2 IMMEDIATE OUTSIDE FLAT TUBE THREATS TO A SIDE

WEAKNESSES

- 8TH GAP CAN BRING AN EXTRA DEFENDER INTO THE RUN BOX
- LIMITS IMMEDIATE OUTSIDE FLAT TUBE THREATS TO BOTH SIDES
- #2 WR (Y & A) LOSES FREE RELEASE ABILITY, MORE SUSCEPTIBLE TO COLLISION
- LIMITS ROUTE STRETCH COMBINATIONS TO THE NUB TIGHT END SIDE

21 PERSONNEL PRO FORMATION

Another grouping that can be used in the 8-gap personnel family is **21 Personnel.** One of the formation families that uses 21 Personnel is the Pro formation. Pro formations are made of 2 backs and 1 tight end. The benefit of this formation is that it presents 8 gaps, with one of the gaps being moveable. (FIG. 5-17)

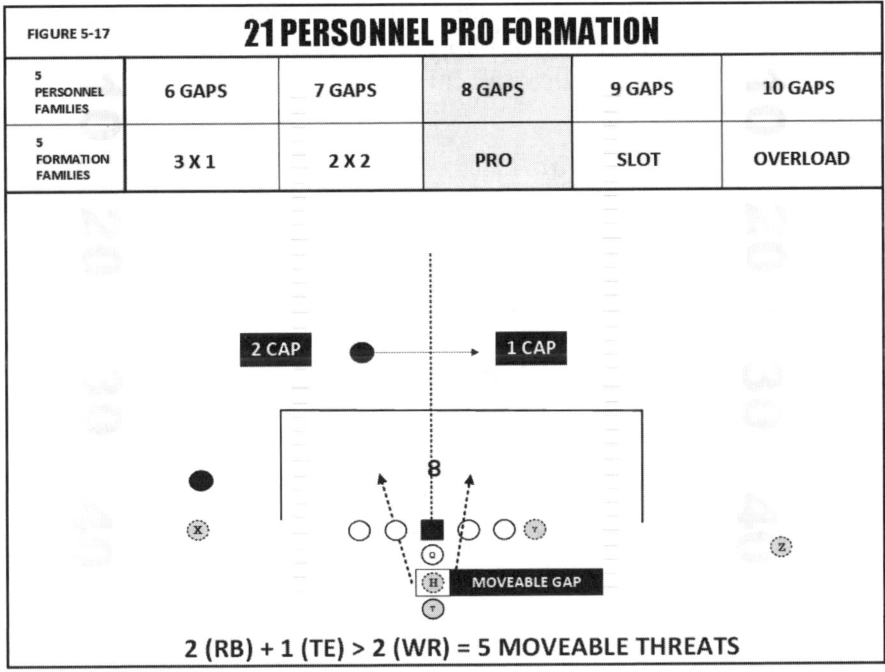

The moveable gap within the Pro formation generates an extreme amount of versatility for the offense. A moveable pre-snap gap that is positioned on the centerline in an I-formation alignment provides a post-snap movement ability to either side of the formation. This allows the offense to create a man-advantage to either side without tipping its hand to the defense.

A Pro formation also singles up a receiver away from the tight end strength for a potential 1-on-1 match. This allows the formation to apply the 1 CAP / 2 CAP man-advantage rule. Another benefit of the Pro formation is that is can provide 7-man pass protection allowing the tight end to release on a route. It can also maximize an 8-man pass protection by leaving the tight end in. Pro formations are also effective play action formations that contain the ability to distribute the tight end and full back out on a variety of routes after a run fake.

A final key advantage of the Pro formation is the ability to transform the strength of the formation by offsetting or motioning the moveable gap. (FIG. 5-18)

The Pro formation can quickly transform into a balanced 2 x 2 or an unbalanced 3 x 1 set by positioning the fullback to either side of the centerline. This provides the Pro formation with shape-shifting abilities that can quickly cause structural and strength declaration issues for the defense.

One of the downsides to the Pro formation is that the offense only has 3 immediate vertical threats. This allows the defense to load the box to gain a man-advantage in run space. The offense also only has 2 immediate outside flat tube threats to each side of space. This eliminates versatility with perimeter screens and RPO attachment options.

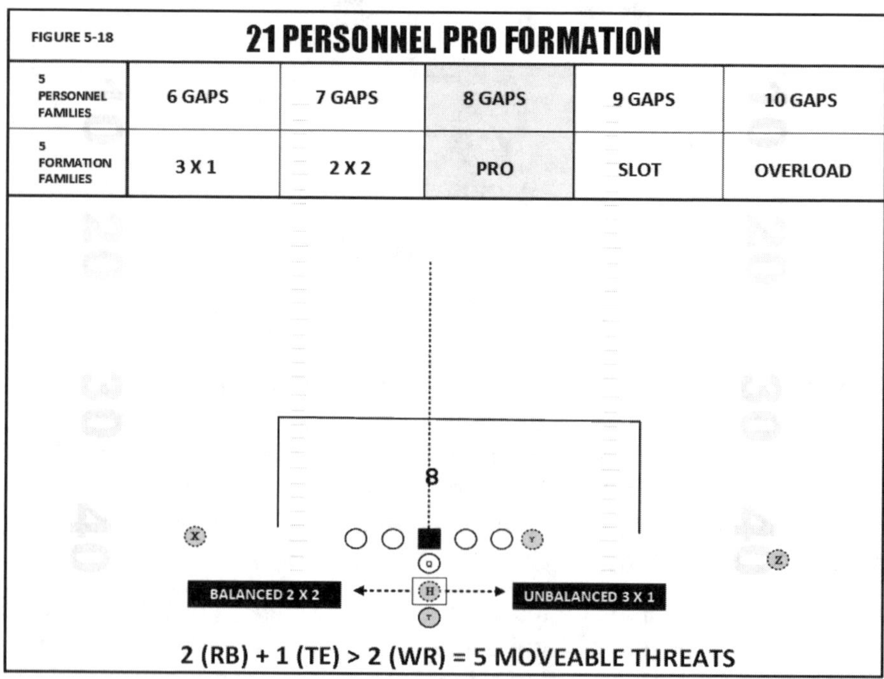

21 PERSONNEL PRO FORMATION SUMMARY

STRENGTHS

- PROVIDES A 4-GAP RUN STRENGTH TO A SIDE
- CREATES MORE UNCAPPED VERTICAL TUBE SPACE
- FULLBACK ON THE CENTERLINE CREATES MAN-ADVANTAGE OPTION TO BOTH SIDES
- FULLBACK POSITIONING CAN QUICKLY BALANCE OR UN BALANCE FORMATION
- ALLOWS FOR 8-MAN PASS PROTECTION
- 1 CAP / 2 CAP RULE

WEAKNESSES

- 8TH GAP CAN BRING AN EXTRA DEFENDERS INTO THE RUN BOX
- LIMITS IMMEDIATE OUTSIDE FLAT TUBE THREATS TO BOTH SIDES
- WR (Y & H) LOSES FREE RELEASE ABILITY, MORE SUSCEPTIBLE TO COLLISION
- ROUTE CONCEPTS LIMITED MOSTLY TO PLAY ACTION

21 PERSONNEL PRO SLOT FORMATION

21 Personnel can be aligned in a Pro Slot Formation. A Pro Slot Formation puts the best receivers on the same side of space. The Pro Slot Formation allows the offense to regain the immediate outside flat tube threats to a side. This provides the ability to add a variety of perimeter screens and RPO route attachments back into the formation. (FIG. 5-19)

The nub tight end side of a Pro Slot Formation presents a strong side of 4 gaps of run space. This can be used to dictate the positioning of defenders to a side of space. The nub alignment also applies the 1 CAP / 2 CAP man-advantage rule.

The movable gap allows the offense to maintain the same advantages that are found in the Pro formation. The fullback who is aligned on the centerline can be used as a man-advantage player to both sides of run space.

FIGURE 5-19	21 PERSONNEL PRO SLOT FORMATION				
5 PERSONNEL FAMILIES	6 GAPS	7 GAPS	8 GAPS	9 GAPS	10 GAPS
5 FORMATION FAMILIES	3 X 1	2 X 2	PRO	SLOT	OVERLOAD

2 CAP

1 CAP

8

Y

Q

H

T

MOVEABLE GAP

Z

X

2 (RB) + 1 (TE) > 2 (WR) = 5 MOVEABLE THREATS

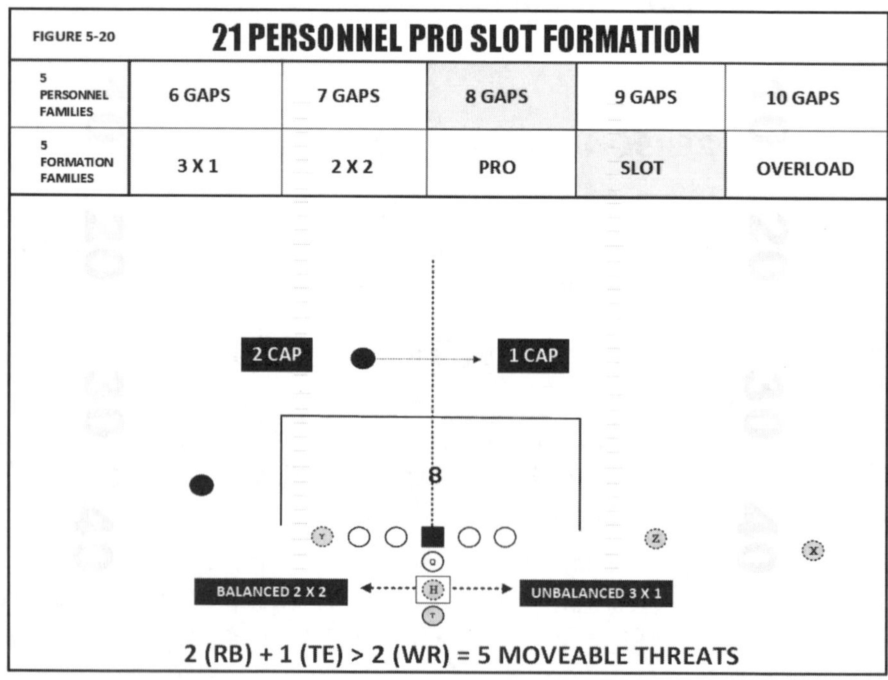

FIGURE 5-20	21 PERSONNEL PRO SLOT FORMATION				
5 PERSONNEL FAMILIES	6 GAPS	7 GAPS	8 GAPS	9 GAPS	10 GAPS
5 FORMATION FAMILIES	3 X 1	2 X 2	PRO	SLOT	OVERLOAD

The position or motion of the moveable gap within a Slot Formation also allows the offense to quickly convert into a balanced 2 x 2 or unbalanced 3 x 1 formation. (FIG. 5-20)

The 21 Personnel grouping and Pro Slot Formation increases some of the deficiencies that were lacking in the Pro formation. However, there are still some downsides to the Slot Formation.

One downside is that the immediate route space threats are only to one side. This can allow the defense to place pass strength defenders to a side and overload the run strength side with better run accelerators. Another issue is the nub tight end side has a limited number of route stretches that it stresses on the defense.

21 PERSONNEL PRO SLOT FORMATION SUMMARY

STRENGTHS

- PROVIDES A 4-GAP RUN STRENGTH TO A SIDE
- FULLBACK ON THE CENTERLINE CREATES MAN-ADVANTAGE OPTION TO BOTH SIDES
- FULLBACK POSITIONING CAN QUICKLY BALANCE OR UNBALANCE FORMATION
- ALLOWS FOR 8-MAN PASS PROTECTION
- 1 CAP / 2 CAP RULE
- 2 IMMEDIATE OUTSIDE FLAT TUBE THREATS TO A SIDE

WEAKNESSES

- 8TH GAP CAN BRING AN EXTRA DEFENDERS INTO THE RUN BOX
- LIMITS IMMEDIATE OUTSIDE FLAT TUBE THREATS TO BOTH SIDES
- WR (Y & H) LOSES FREE RELEASE ABILITY, MORE SUSCEPTIBLE TO COLLISION
- LIMITS ROUTE STRETCH COMBINATIONS TO THE NUB TIGHT END SIDE

FIGURE 5-20

21 PERSONNEL PRO SLOT FORMATION

5 PERSONNEL FAMILIES	6 GAPS	7 GAPS	8 GAPS	9 GAPS	10 GAPS
5 FORMATION FAMILIES	3 X 1	2 X 2	PRO	SLOT	OVERLOAD

2 CAP

1 CAP

BALANCED 2 X 2

UNBALANCED 3 X 1

2 (RB) + 1 (TE) > 2 (WR) = 5 MOVEABLE THREATS

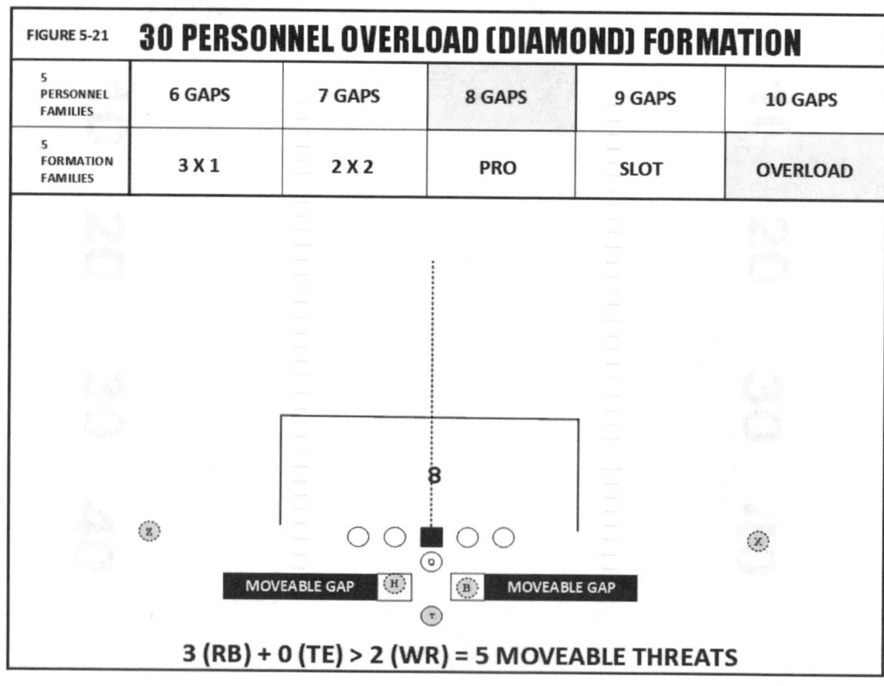

FIGURE 5-21

30 PERSONNEL OVERLOAD (DIAMOND) FORMATION

5 PERSONNEL FAMILIES	6 GAPS	7 GAPS	8 GAPS	9 GAPS	10 GAPS
5 FORMATION FAMILIES	3 X 1	2 X 2	PRO	SLOT	OVERLOAD

3 (RB) + 0 (TE) > 2 (WR) = 5 MOVEABLE THREATS

30 PERSONNEL OVERLOAD (DIAMOND) FORMATION

Another personnel grouping that may be employed in the 8-gap family is **30 Personnel.** 30 Personnel is made of 3 running backs and no tight ends. (FIG. 5-21)

The benefit of 30 Personnel is that it creates 8-gaps, with 2 of them being moveable. This puts an extreme amount of post-snap stress on the run box of the defense. The formational family that this 30 Personnel is aligned to is the **Overload Family.** The Overload Family is any formation that has an unbalanced distribution of players who are different than the first 4 families. This particular formation is often referred to as the **Diamond Formation.**

The Diamond Formation is considered an Overload Formation when all three running backs are aligned within the tackles. This alignment places moveable gaps in proximity to the centerline. A multiple movement threat that can quickly occur over the centerline pre-snap or post-snap presents a variety of post-snap man-advantage issues for the defense. These force the defense to treat this formation as a specialized family.

The downside to the Diamond Formation is that it only has 1 immediate vertical threat to each side of space. This limits the perimeter screen and RPO attachment options that can be used with run plays. Another issue is that the formation only presents 2 immediate vertical tube threats. The running backs alignment inside the tackles reduces the vertical attack ability by increasing the collision accelerator threat. This allows the defense to stack the run box with a man-advantage count to each side of space, making it more difficult to run the ball.

This requires the offense to use the duel-moveable gap movement ability to scheme man-advantage back in the offense's favor.

30 PERSONNEL OVERLOAD (DIAMOND) FORMATION SUMMARY

STRENGTHS

- PROVIDES A 4-GAP RUN STRENGTH TO BOTH SIDES OF RUN-SPACE
- CREATES MORE UNCAPPED VERTICAL TUBE SPACE
- FORCES THE DEFENSE TO BALANCE BOTH SIDES
- CONTROLS EDGE PRESSURE AND LIMITS BLITZ EFFECTIVENESS
- ALLOWS FOR 8-MAN PASS PROTECTION
- MULTIPLE MOVEABLE GAPS INCREASE MAN-ADVANTAGE FAVOR

WEAKNESSES

- 8TH GAP CAN BRING AN EXTRA DEFENDERS INTO THE RUN BOX
- LIMITS IMMEDIATE OUTSIDE FLAT TUBE THREATS TO BOTH SIDES
- RB (H & B) LOSES FREE RELEASE ABILITY, MORE SUSCEPTIBLE TO COLLISION

22 PERSONNEL SLOT (TIGHT) FORMATION

The next personnel family is the **9-gap family.** One of the personnel groups that presents 9-gaps to the defense is 22 Personnel. 22 Personnel is made of 2 backs and 2 tight ends. A common formation that is used with 22 Personnel is a Slot variation that we call **Tight Formation.** (FIG. 5-22)

The benefit of the Tight Formation with 22 Personnel is that it creates 9-gaps, with 1 of them being moveable while maintaining 3 immediate vertical threats.

The Tight Formation singles the best receiver to a side of space to create 1-on-1 match ups. This receiver is lined up off the line of scrimmage, which permits him pre-snap motion. This can be used to create leverage advantages for blocking. This can also provide the ability to open this receiver for Flow scheme strategies with jet sweep action.

FIGURE 5-22 **22 PERSONNEL SLOT (TIGHT) FORMATION**

5 PERSONNEL FAMILIES	6 GAPS	7 GAPS	8 GAPS	9 GAPS	10 GAPS
5 FORMATION FAMILIES	3 X 1	2 X 2	PRO	SLOT	OVERLOAD

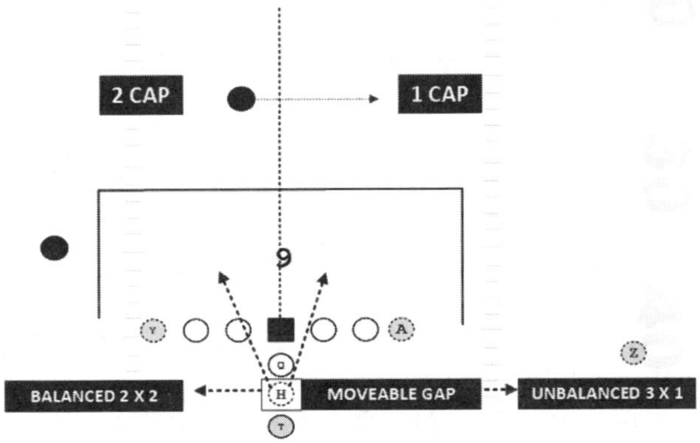

2 CAP

1 CAP

9

Y A Q H T Z

BALANCED 2 X 2

MOVEABLE GAP

UNBALANCED 3 X 1

2 (RB) + 2 (TE) > 1 (WR) = 5 MOVEABLE THREATS

The Tight Formation places a tight end on each side of run space to create 4 run gaps to each side. Another benefit of the Tight Formation is that it contains the benefit of a moveable gap with the full back. This moveable gap provides the same attack alignments that were discussed with the Pro and Slot Formation used with 21 Personnel.

This allows the Tight Formation to easily become a balanced 2 x 2 Formation or an unbalanced 3 x 1 Formation by moving the movable gap across the centerline, pre- or post-snap. The Tight Formation also provides the unbalanced 1 CAP / 2 CAP man-advantage rule. The addition of two tight ends and a full back can dictate extra defenders in the run box, which creates more UNCAPPED vertical tube space. This can improve explosive play opportunity if the offensive personnel pool contains athletic tight ends who can run and catch. Furthermore, the formation can provide a maximum of 9-man pass protection that can increase space and time for the single-side receiver to create UNCAPPED space vertically downfield.

The downside to this formation is that pass concepts are reduced primarily to play action. The formation only presents 1 immediate outside space threat in the flat tube to a side of space. This limits the perimeter screen and RPO route attachment options within the formation. The offense must also possess a personnel advantage to run the ball out of this formation since the defense will generally maintain the man-advantage to both sides of run space.

22 PERSONNEL SLOT (TIGHT) FORMATION SUMMARY

STRENGTHS

- PROVIDES A 4-GAP RUN STRENGTH TO BOTH SIDES OF RUN-SPACE
- CREATES MORE UNCAPPED VERTICAL TUBE SPACE
- CONTROLS EDGE PRESSURE AND LIMITS BLITZ EFFECTIVENESS
- FULLBACK ON THE CENTERLINE CREATES MAN-ADVANTAGE OPTION TO BOTH SIDES
- FULLBACK POSITIONING CAN QUICKLY BALANCE OR UNBALANCE FORMATION
- ALLOWS FOR 9-MAN PASS PROTECTION
- SINGLE UP BEST RECEIVER FOR 1-ON-1 MATCHUPS
- SINGLE-SIDE RECEIVER IS OFF L.O.S. ALLOWING MOTION AND JET SWEEP ACTION
- 1 CAP / 2 CAP RULE

WEAKNESSES

- 9TH GAP CAN BRING AN EXTRA DEFENDER INTO THE RUN BOX
- LIMITS IMMEDIATE OUTSIDE FLAT TUBE THREATS TO BOTH SIDES
- WR (Y, A & H) LOSES FREE RELEASE ABILITY, MORE SUSCEPTIBLE TO COLLISION
- LIMITS ROUTE STRETCH COMBINATIONS TO THE NUB TIGHT END SIDE
- PASS CONCEPTS ARE LIMITED TO PRIMARILY PLAY ACTION
- REQUIRES OFFENSIVE PERSONNEL ADVANTAGE TO OVERCOME MAN-ADVANTAGE IN RUN BOX

31 PERSONNEL OVERLOAD (STRONG DIAMOND) FORMATION

Another personnel grouping that can be used in the 9-gap family is 31 Personnel. **31 Personnel** is made up of 3 backs and 1 tight end. 31 Personnel is most commonly used in creating a strong Diamond Formation. (FIG. 5-23)

The benefit of 31 Personnel in a strong Diamond Formation is that it maintains 9 gaps of run space with 2 of the gaps being moveable.

The positioning of the dual-moveable gaps inside the tackles creates a multiple man-advantage threat to the defense. This dual threat on the centerline places the strong Diamond Formation in the Overload Family of formations. The defense must account for this formation differently than others.

The major benefit of the strong Diamond Formation over the Tight Formation is the dual-moveable gap threat. However, the downside is that the single-side receiver is locked on the line of scrimmage. The receiver loses the pre-snap motion ability.

FIGURE 5-23 **31 PERSONNEL OVERLOAD (STRONG DIAMOND) FORMATION**

5 PERSONNEL FAMILIES	6 GAPS	7 GAPS	8 GAPS	9 GAPS	10 GAPS
5 FORMATION FAMILIES	3 X 1	2 X 2	PRO	SLOT	OVERLOAD

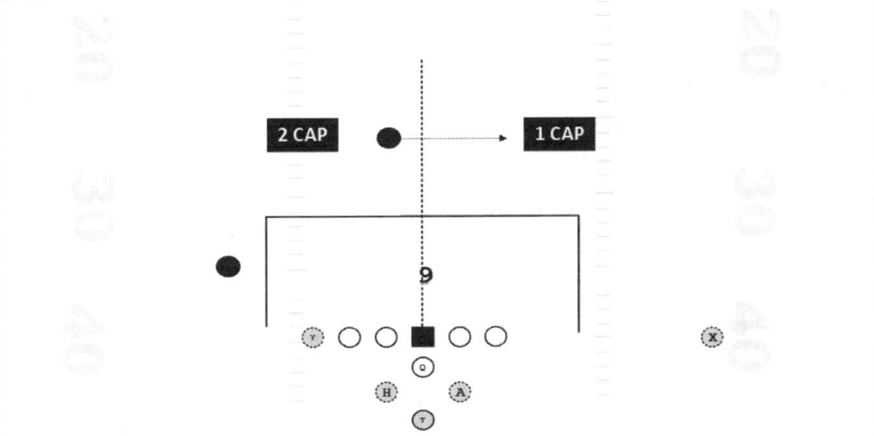

2 CAP
1 CAP
9
Y
X
Q
H
A
T

3 (RB) + 1 (TE) > 1 (WR) = 5 MOVEABLE THREATS

31 PERSONNEL OVERLOAD (STRONG DIAMOND) FORMATION

STRENGTHS

- PROVIDES A 5-GAP RUN STRENGTH TO A SIDE OF SPACE
- CREATES MORE UNCAPPED VERTICAL TUBE SPACE
- MOVEABLE GAPS INCREASE MAN-ADVANTAGE FAVOR
- ALLOWS FOR 9-MAN PASS PROTECTION
- SINGLE UP BEST RECEIVER FOR 1-ON-1 MATCHUPS
- 1 CAP / 2 CAP RULE

WEAKNESSES

- 9TH GAP CAN BRING AN EXTRA DEFENDER INTO THE RUN BOX
- LIMITS IMMEDIATE OUTSIDE FLAT TUBE THREATS TO BOTH SIDES
- SINGLE SIDE RECEIVER CANNOT MOTION PRE-SNAP
- WR (Y, A, and H) LOSES FREE RELEASE ABILITY, MORE SUSCEPTIBLE TO COLLISION
- LIMITS ROUTE STRETCH COMBINATIONS TO THE NUB TIGHT END SIDE
- PASS CONCEPTS ARE LIMITED TO PRIMARILY PLAY ACTION
- REQUIRES OFFENSIVE PERSONNEL ADVANTAGE TO OVERCOME MAN-ADVANTAGE IN RUN BOX

THE OVERLOAD FORMATION FAMILY

The remaining formations to cover are all placed in the Overload Formation family. We have previously discussed some of the qualities that place a formation in the Overload Family. However, we want to clearly define the characteristics that make an Overload Formation. Overload Formations contain qualities that are outside the norm of the other Formation families. They contain properties that place an extreme amount of structural strain on defenses. The key components that classify a formation as an Overload are:

- Formations that contain 3 running backs in the backfield
- Formations with no backs in the backfield
- Formations with 4 eligible receivers to a side
- Formations that move an offensive tackle over to the other side a.k.a. (heavy sets)

32 PERSONNEL OVERLOAD (DOUBLE WING) FORMATION

The first Overload Formation is the Double Wing Formation. The Double Wing Formation is commonly run out of 32 Personnel that is in the 10-gap family. (FIG. 5-24)

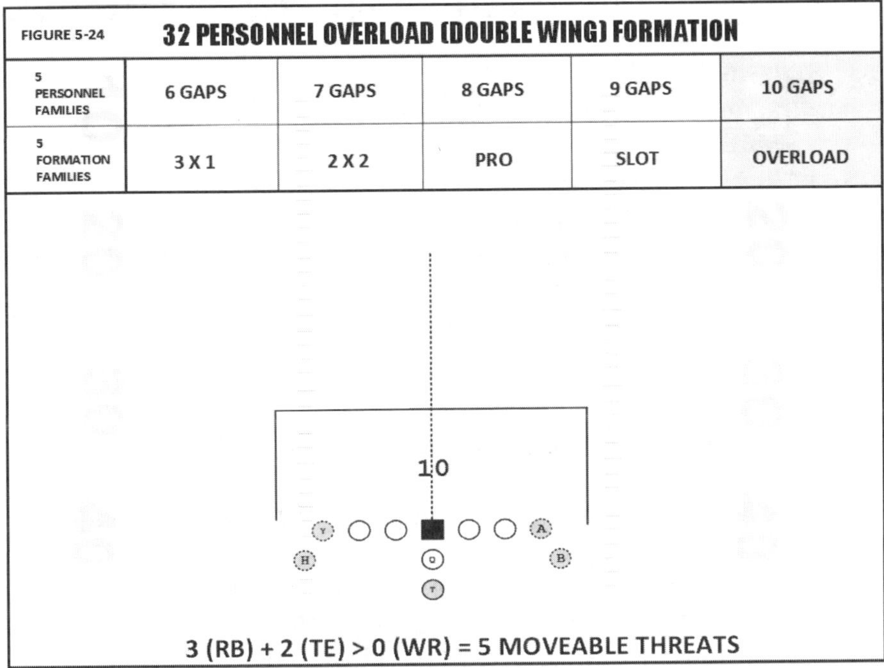
FIGURE 5-24 **32 PERSONNEL OVERLOAD (DOUBLE WING) FORMATION**

5 PERSONNEL FAMILIES	6 GAPS	7 GAPS	8 GAPS	9 GAPS	10 GAPS
5 FORMATION FAMILIES	3 X 1	2 X 2	PRO	SLOT	OVERLOAD

3 (RB) + 2 (TE) > 0 (WR) = 5 MOVEABLE THREATS

There are 3 backs and 2 tight ends in 32 Personnel. The benefit of this personnel is that it presents 10 gaps of run space to the defense with 2 moveable gaps. A total of 4 immediate vertical threats are present If the backs are placed outside the tight ends in a wing alignment. This places a heavy structural strain on the defense. Another benefit is the misdirection that can take place with the running backs and quarterbacks. There are a variety of pre-snap motions and fakes that can be used to neutralize the man-advantage count to each side of space.

The downside to this formation occurs in the passing game. The most effective pass concepts are primarily play-actions. There are no immediate outside flat tube threats to either side. 32 Personnel is often limited in the route running ability needed to execute intermediate pass route concepts. When this occurs, the defense can flood the run box space and attack aggressively to stop the run.

The offense that uses a Double Wing Formation must counter these deficiencies by using the quarterback as a run threat. A quarterback who is used as a run threat is a man-advantage player for the offense and can add an additional run gap to each side of space.

32 PERSONNEL OVERLOAD (DOUBLE WING) FORMATION

STRENGTHS

- PROVIDES A 5-GAP RUN STRENGTH TO EACH SIDE OF SPACE
- CREATES MORE UNCAPPED VERTICAL TUBE SPACE
- 4 IMMEDIATE VERTICAL THREATS
- MOVEABLE GAPS INCREASE MAN-ADVANTAGE FAVOR
- FORCES THE DEFENSE TO BALANCE BOTH SIDES OF SPACE
- INCREASES MISDIRECTION ABILITY

WEAKNESSES

- 10TH GAP CAN BRING ALL 11 DEFENDERS INTO THE RUN BOX
- NO IMMEDIATE OUTSIDE FLAT TUBE THREATS TO BOTH SIDES
- ALL WR (Y, A, H & B) LOSES FREE RELEASE ABILITY, MORE SUSCEPTIBLE TO COLLISION
- PASS CONCEPTS ARE LIMITED TO PRIMARILY PLAY ACTION
- REQUIRES OFFENSIVE PERSONNEL ADVANTAGE TO OVERCOME MAN-ADVANTAGE IN RUN BOX
- QB MUST BE A RUN THREAT

32 PERSONNEL OVERLOAD (SINGLE WING) FORMATION

The next Overload Formation that 32 Personnel can align in is the single wing formation. The Single Wing Formation is within the 10-gap personnel family. This formation is like the Double Wing Formation but increases versatility by bringing the offensive tackle over in a heavy-set alignment. (FIG. 5-25)

This heavy-set along with the positioning of the running backs create 7 run gaps to the strong side and 3 run gaps to the weak side of the formation. This unbalanced formation allows the offense to use the 1

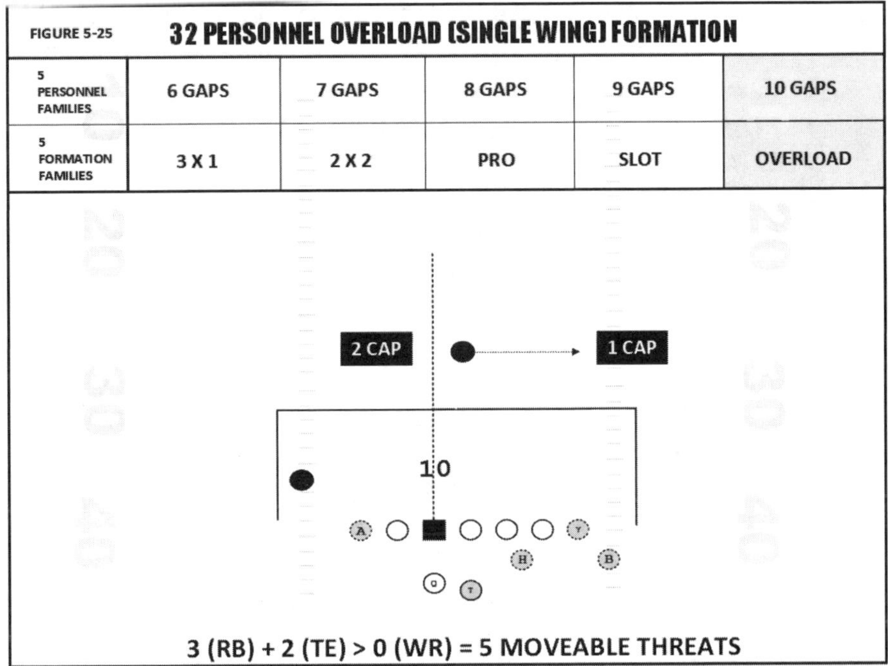

CAP / 2 CAP rule. Structural strain is placed on the defense by having multiple moveable gaps to neutralize man-advantage. Furthermore, additional pressure is placed on the defense when the quarterback is used as a run threat. The single wing maximizes misdirection with a variety of pre- and post-snap motions.

The downside to the Single Wing Formation is that there are no immediate outside flat tube threats to either side of space. The offense only has 3 immediate vertical tube threats. This limits the pass concepts that can be incorporated within the formation. Play action is the primary pass concept that can be implemented with this formation.

32 PERSONNEL OVERLOAD (SINGLE WING) FORMATION

STRENGTHS

- PROVIDES A 7-GAP RUN STRENGTH TO A SIDE OF SPACE
- DICTATES STRENGTH OF DEFENDERS
- CREATES MORE UNCAPPED VERTICAL TUBE SPACE
- MOVEABLE GAPS INCREASE MAN-ADVANTAGE FAVOR
- FORCES THE DEFENSE TO UNBALANCE
- INCREASES MISDIRECTION ABILITY

WEAKNESSES

- 10TH GAP CAN BRING ALL 11 DEFENDERS INTO THE RUN BOX
- NO IMMEDIATE OUTSIDE FLAT TUBE THREATS TO BOTH SIDES
- ALL WR (Y, A, H & B) LOSES FREE RELEASE ABILITY, MORE SUSCEPTIBLE TO COLLISION
- PASS CONCEPTS ARE LIMITED TO PRIMARILY PLAY ACTION
- REQUIRES OFFENSIVE PERSONNEL ADVANTAGE TO OVERCOME MAN-ADVANTAGE IN RUN BOX
- QB MUST BE A RUN THREAT

00 PERSONNEL OVERLOAD (EMPTY) FORMATION

The next Overload Formation is the empty formation. The empty formation is typically run out of 00 Personnel. 00 Personnel contains 0 backs and 0 tight ends. (FIG. 5-26)

There are 5 wide receivers present in this formation. Three receivers are positioned to one side and two receivers to the other side. The empty formation presents 6 gaps of run space. The problem with the run space availability is that there are no backs in the backfield to attack it. This requires the quarterback to be a run threat in order to attack run space out of the empty formation.

A quarterback who is used as a runner creates a +1 man-advantage player for the offense. This increases the structural strain on the defense, making this formation part of the Overload Family. The benefit of this formation is that it presents 5 immediate vertical tube threats. This positions an immediate vertical threat to occupy all 5 vertical tubes. There are also 3 immediate outside flat tube threats to a side, along with 2 immediate outside flat tube threats on the other side.

FIGURE 5-26	00 PERSONNEL OVERLOAD (EMPTY) FORMATION				
5 PERSONNEL FAMILIES	6 GAPS	7 GAPS	8 GAPS	9 GAPS	10 GAPS
5 FORMATION FAMILIES	3 X 1	2 X 2	PRO	SLOT	OVERLOAD

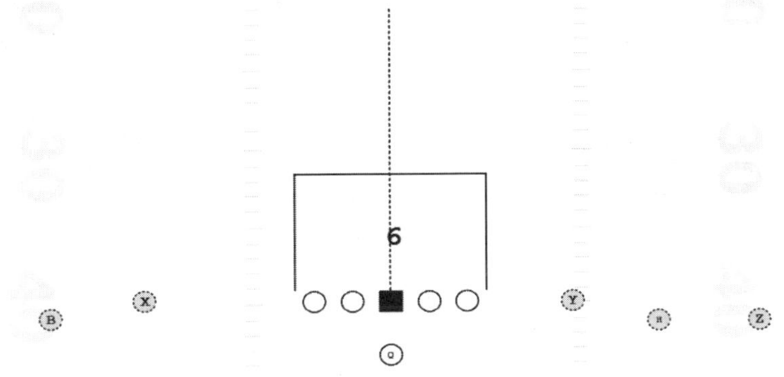

6

B X Y H Z Q

0 (RB) + 0 (TE) > 5 (WR) = 5 MOVEABLE THREATS

The downside to this formation is that the quarterback must be a run threat to maximize the structural strain on the defense. Pass protection is another issue. No backs in the backfield allow for only 5-man pass protection. This limits that amount of time to attack and create space through concepts.

00 PERSONNEL OVERLOAD (EMPTY) FORMATION

STRENGTHS

- PROVIDES A 5 IMMEDIATE VERTICAL TUBE THREATS
- PROVIDES 3 IMMEDIATE OUTSIDE FLAT TUBE THREATS TO A SIDE
- PROVIDES 2 IMMEDIATE OUTSIDE FLAT TUBE THREATS TO A SIDE
- FORCES DEFENSE TO EXPAND OUTSIDE THE RUN BOX

WEAKNESSES

- ALLOWS ONLY 5-MAN PROTECTION
- QB MUST BE A RUN THREAT TO ATTACK RUN-SPACE
- QB MUST BE DURABLE AND ILLUSIVE

00 PERSONNEL OVERLOAD (QUADS) FORMATION

The next Overload Formation is the Quads Formation. The Quads Formation is also typically run out of 00 Personnel. (FIG. 5-27)

This formation is like the empty formation but places four receivers to a side of space and only 1 receiver away. The added benefits of this alignment are that the offense can now single up its best receiver to a side. This also permits the use of the 1 CAP / 2CAP rule to determine man-advantage.

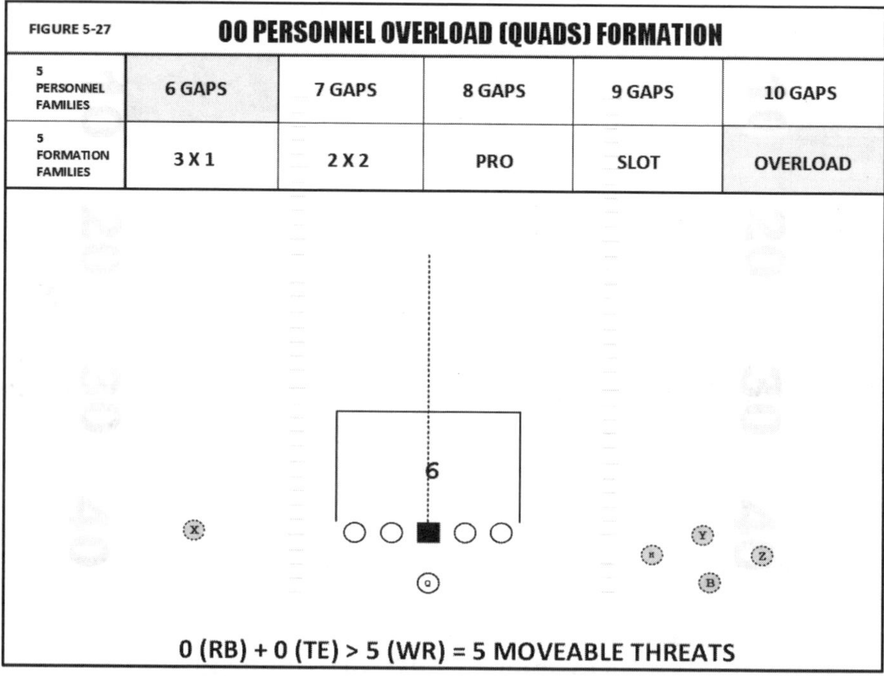

FIGURE 5-27 **00 PERSONNEL OVERLOAD (QUADS) FORMATION**

5 PERSONNEL FAMILIES	6 GAPS	7 GAPS	8 GAPS	9 GAPS	10 GAPS
5 FORMATION FAMILIES	3 X 1	2 X 2	PRO	SLOT	OVERLOAD

The positioning of four receivers to a side of space forces the defense to overload coverage to maintain a man-advantage. This overload requires the defense to neutralize man-advantage in the run box or to the single side route space.

The downsides to this formation are the same that were covered with the empty formation. Another downside is that your single side receiver must be a matchup advantage against the opponent. Otherwise, the defense can man him up and push coverage to the quads side to account for the overload.

00 PERSONNEL OVERLOAD (QUADS) FORMATION

STRENGTHS

- PROVIDES A 5 IMMEDIATE VERTICAL TUBE THREATS
- PROVIDES 4 IMMEDIATE OUTSIDE FLAT TUBE THREATS TO A SIDE
- SINGLES UP BEST RECEIVER FOR 1-ON-1 MATCHUPS TO A SIDE
- 1 CAP / 2 CAP RULE
- FORCES DEFENSE TO EXPAND OUTSIDE THE RUN BOX

WEAKNESSES

- ALLOWS ONLY 5-MAN PROTECTION
- QB MUST BE A RUN THREAT TO ATTACK RUN-SPACE
- QB MUST BE DURABLE AND ILLUSIVE
- SINGLE SIDE RECEIVER MUST BE A MATCH UP ISSUE FOR OPPONENT

11 Personnel Overload (Heavy Trey) Formation

The next Overload Formation is in the 7-gap personnel family. This is called a Heavy Trey Formation. Heavy Trey is placed in the Overload Family because the offensive tackle is aligned to the opposite side of the formation. This creates a heavy unbalanced set with three big offensive linemen along with three immediate eligible receivers to the same side of space. (FIG. 5-28)

The weak side of the formation contains a 2-man surface with the nub tight end and guard to that side of space. The benefits of this formation begin with creating confusion on the strength of the formation. Many defenses declare strength to the tight end side. The heavy-set changes this strength by moving the tackle over to the opposite side of the tight end. A defense can be caught off guard and declare strength to the tight end not realizing that the offensive tackle has moved to the other side.

This requires the defense to shift the front strength away from the tight end. This is done with coverage and front adjustments. However, the tight end is an eligible receiver and there are 3 immediate route space

FIGURE 5-28	11 PERSONNEL OVERLOAD (HEAVY TREY) FORMATION				
5 PERSONNEL FAMILIES	6 GAPS	7 GAPS	8 GAPS	9 GAPS	10 GAPS
5 FORMATION FAMILIES	3 X 1	2 X 2	PRO	SLOT	OVERLOAD

2 CAP

1 CAP

7

1 (RB) + 1 (TE) > 3 (WR) = 5 MOVEABLE THREATS

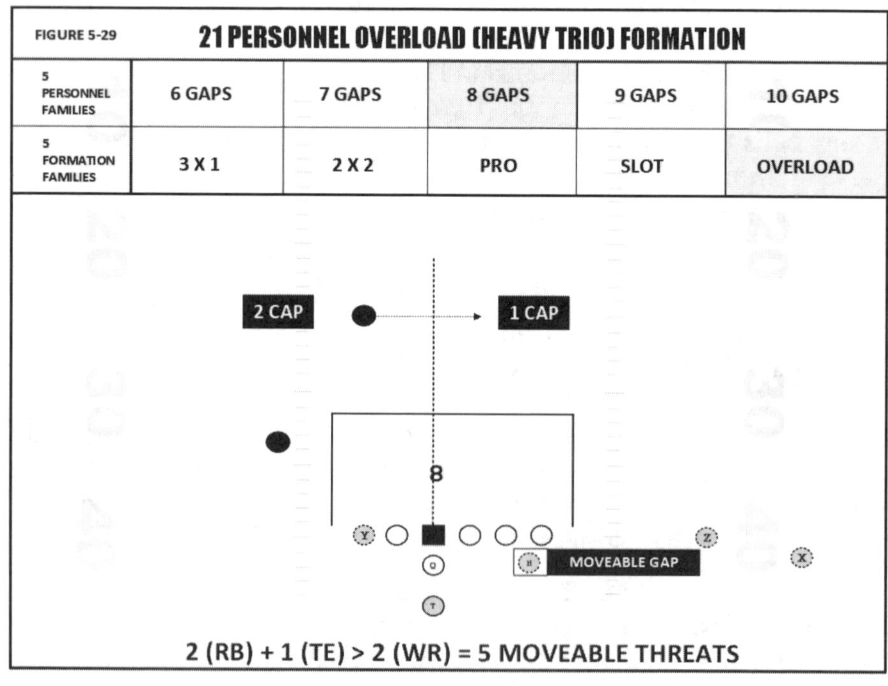

FIGURE 5-29	21 PERSONNEL OVERLOAD (HEAVY TRIO) FORMATION				
5 PERSONNEL FAMILIES	6 GAPS	7 GAPS	8 GAPS	9 GAPS	10 GAPS
5 FORMATION FAMILIES	3 X 1	2 X 2	PRO	SLOT	OVERLOAD

2 (RB) + 1 (TE) > 2 (WR) = 5 MOVEABLE THREATS

threats on the other side. These threats to each side of space make it more difficult for the defense to account for the heavy run strength set.

The downside to this formation is that the tight end is to the short side. The loss of the tackle to that side creates a short edge for the pass rush if the tight end is released on a route. Furthermore, a tight end that cannot be used as an immediate route threat allows the defense to overload the opposite side of space. This requires the quarterback to be a run threat or the use of a receiver in a jet sweep scheme to present a weakside attack threat within the formation.

11 PERSONNEL OVERLOAD (HEAVY TREY) FORMATION SUMMARY

STRENGTHS

- CREATES 4 RUN GAPS TO A SIDE OF SPACE
- PROVIDES 4 IMMEDIATE VERTICAL TUBE THREATS
- PROVIDES 3 IMMEDIATE OUTSIDE FLAT TUBE THREATS TO A SIDE
- DICTATES DEFENSIVE STRENGTH
- 1 CAP / 2 CAP RULE
- ALLOWS FOR 7-MAN PASS PROTECTION
- FORCES DEFENSE TO EXPAND OUTSIDE THE RUN BOX

WEAKNESSES

- SHORT EDGE TO TIGHT END SIDE INCREASES PASS RUSH PRESSURE
- TE MUST BE A ROUTE-SPACE THREAT
- QB MUST BE A RUN THREAT TO ATTACK WEAKSIDE RUN-SPACE

21 Personnel Overload (Heavy Trio) Formation

The last Overload Formation covered is the Heavy Trio Formation. The Heavy Trio Formation is in the 8-gap family and typically run out of a 21 Personnel grouping. This formation maintains many of the advantages of the Heavy Trey Formation. (FIG. 5-29)

However, one of the added benefits is the addition of the moveable gap. This moveable gap presents multiple entry point options for the formation. It also provides pass protection answers to the weak side of the formation. Another benefit of the moveable gap is that it can quickly create a balanced formation with pre- or post-snap motion.

The downside to this formation is that it only has 3 immediate vertical tube threats and 2 immediate outside flat tube threats to a side. This allows the defense to load the run box space and maintain a man-advantage.

21 PERSONNEL OVERLOAD (HEAVY TRIO) FORMATION

STRENGTHS

- CREATES 5 RUN GAPS TO A SIDE OF SPACE
- 2 IMMEDIATE FLAT TUBE THREATS TO A SIDE
- MOVEABLE GAPS INCREASE MAN-ADVANTAGE FAVOR
- DICTATES DEFENSIVE STRENGTH
- 1 CAP / 2 CAP RULE
- ALLOWS FOR 8-MAN PASS PROTECTION

WEAKNESSES

- SHORT EDGE TO TIGHT END SIDE INCREASES PASS RUSH PRESSURE
- TE MUST BE A ROUTE-SPACE THREAT
- ONLY 3 IMMEDIATE VERTICAL TUBE THREATS

USING PERSONNEL TO MAKE FLUID FORMATIONS

The one constant that can be expected every year is that the personnel a coach uses to create formations will change. Therefore, personnel does not dictate the formations that can be used. The numbering system is just a reference point to communicate who is in the game and responsible for creating the formation that is called.

Personnel families are categorized by the number of run gaps that the defense must defend. Defending the run box is the highest priority of the defense, and the personnel used is a key indicator on the strengths and alignments of their positions. Not all personnel groupings are specific to the personnel gap families. For instance, let's say we are in 11 Personnel but have 2 of those receivers who are big and physical enough to play tight end and full back.

In this case, we can use that same 11 Personnel in Pro and Slot Formations in which we would normally only use 12 and 21 Personnel. While this is a rarity, the bigger, faster and stronger my 5 movable threats, the more formations I can align to and find success. The better the offensive skill personnel, the more formational versatility that an offense can create.

Even so, having personnel who lack in size, strength and speed ability doesn't mean a coach can't still use deficient personnel in positions to create a formation. Offensive position alignments within a formation can still trigger specific coverage and front calls no matter what personnel is making the formation. For instance, a receiver with only one arm placed to the single side of a 3 x 1 formation has a great chance the defense will still cover him.

This is an example of how particular personnel can change alignments to create formations that typically use specific personnel. (FIG. 5-30)

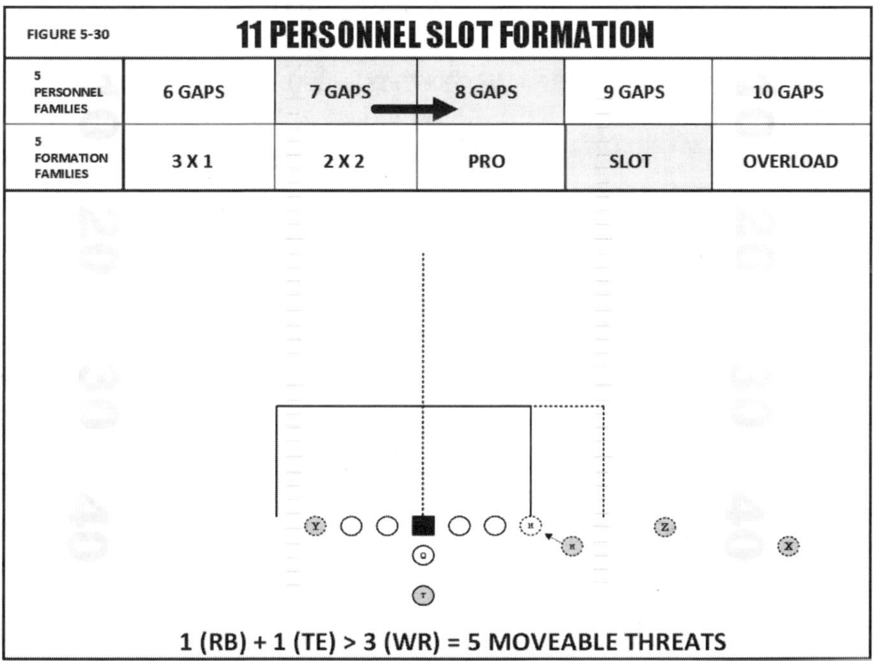

Each year an offense may only have the players to run one personnel grouping. Let's say it's 11 Personnel. The Slot Formation is a primary 11 Personnel formation. However, In the game-planning process, a staff may determine that it needs to gain the advantages of a 12 Personnel Slot Formation. There is no reason that the H receiver cannot line up in a tight end split to create the structural strain of a 12 Personnel Slot Formation.

This H receiver may not be able to carry out the blocks required to neutralize a positive pin player accelerator, however, his alignment may trigger specific coverage and front checks that a 12 Personnel Slot Formation would. This alignment within 11 Personnel shows how a formation can transition from a 7-gap family into an 8-gap family without changing personnel.

Another example is shown in (FIG. 5-31).

The offense is still limited to only using 11 Personnel. However, the H receiver may gain advantages of a 21 Personnel Slot Formation by lining up as a fullback. This could allow the offense to use different fake, flow, and flood scheme strategies to create an explosive play advantage for a dominant offensive player.

This makes a case for the necessity of an offense to have terminology for all the personnel and formation families listed. A coach may be privy to specific personnel and formations for the offensive schemes that he feels comfortable each year. However, a coach can increase offensive scheme versatility within game-planning by already having these formations built within his playbook.

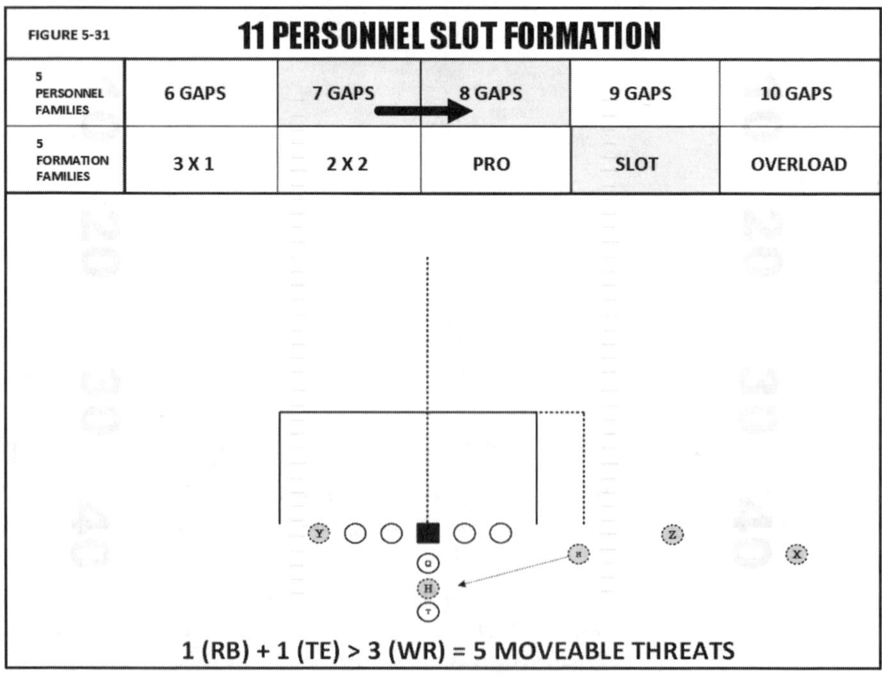

CHAPTER 6

STORYBOARDING
The R4 Progression Platforms

STORYBOARDING

The R4 Progression Platforms

In my first years as a quarterback coach, I was also in charge of game-planning the passing game concepts for an upcoming opponent. Each week I would watch hours of film and extract information to determine what pass plays would work best. At the end of the day on Sunday, I would give my list of plays to the offensive coordinator. Throughout the week I would script the pass plays from the game-plan list for each practice.

The challenge was that most of the run game-plan was built out of formations and personnel that was different than the passing game-plan. My perceptions of space availability and how to attack it was different from the offensive coordinator who was constructing the run game-plan. We were game-planning from two different perspectives. The problem was that we didn't have an interface and inference engine to bridge the disconnect.

Walt Disney understood this dilemma, as well, during the development and production of motion pictures in the 1930s. A story could be easily written on paper by an individual. However, bringing the story to life in a motion picture required a team of people working together in detail under strict time constraints. Illustrators in charge of bringing different parts of the story to life struggled with connecting the pieces together into a production that flowed smoothly.

The Disney studio created a method to accelerate this undertaking called storyboarding. Storyboards are illustrations displayed in a sequence that provide users with a plan and pre-visual of scenes to create a motion picture. Storyboards organized key parts of the story in patterns that allowed everyone in the studio to see the overall picture. This process provided the ability to evaluate key scenes and ensured that the integrity of the story comes across to the user. Storyboards became the engine that powered the production of motion pictures.

As a coach, I needed a system that sequenced plays like a storyboard. The HALO and CAP interface tools provided a process to create the "best" scenes for the game-plan story. These interface tools accelerated the ability to create the "best" play for a given situation. However, the most difficult part of game-planning is linking the "best" plays together into a fluid pattern that adapts to changing events within a game. The R4 inference engine provided the storyboard solution.

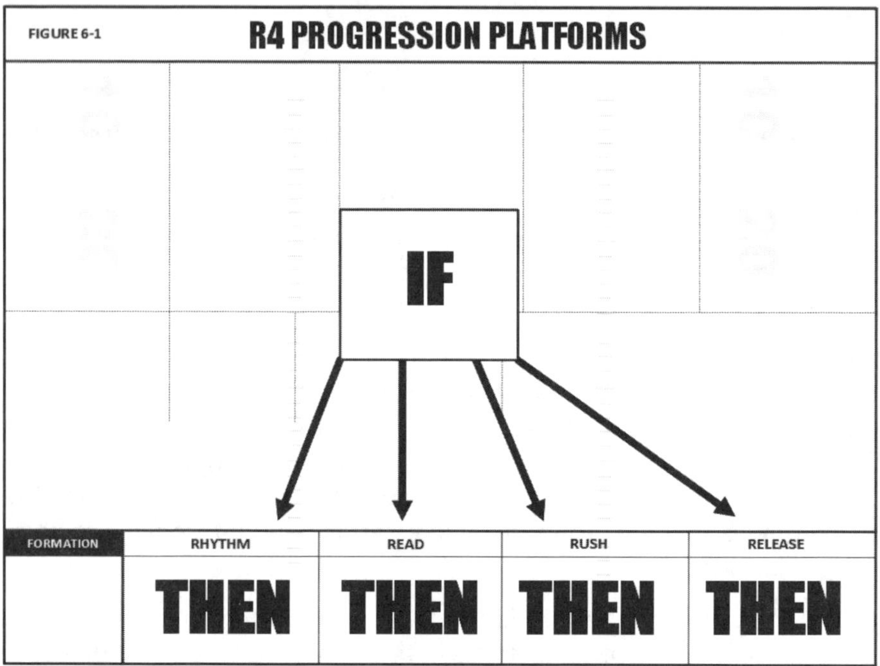

The R4 inference engine is a reasoning process that asks the right questions to accelerate the "best" answers for a given situation. (FIG. 6-1) The process is built through an IF/THEN decision-making workflow. The primary tool of the inference engine is the R4 progression platforms. The R4 progression platforms are a football formation storyboard that organizes the "best" plays into a sequence. This sequence is built upon four primary platforms of situational needs and scenarios that occur within a game. They are Rhythm, Read, Rush, and Release.

RHYTHM PLAYS

The first situational family of plays is called Rhythm plays. Rhythm plays are the primary plays that will work best against a specific defensive look. Rhythm plays are concepts that have been constructed through the interface of the CAP game-planning process.

C – Rhythm plays attack bubbles of space
A – Rhythm plays scheme bubbles of space by neutralizing the man-advantage.
P – Rhythm plays capitalize on personnel weakness along with countering personnel strengths.

Rhythm plays begin the IF/THEN storyboard of the R4 inference engine. **IF** an offensive formation and personnel group A is covered, aligned, and played with defensive personnel B **THEN** space is attacked by rhythm concept C.

Rhythm plays are complementary concepts that establish a foothold for the play-caller. These plays provide the baseline that all other plays within a formation are called from. This allows the play-caller to survey the scene and determine the next "best" play to call. Rhythm plays must be run a minimum of 3-6 times per game to set up the compliments that will be schemed off them. These plays are best used on base downs like 1st and 10 that gain a minimum of 4 yds and keep the offense in Rhythm to convert a series of downs.

Here is an example of how a Rhythm play is determined in a game-plan. (FIG. 6-2)

It begins by selecting a formation and personnel grouping. The coach should begin the process by selecting the formation and personnel that gives them the most consistent defensive coverage and alignment (front). In this look, the defense is playing split field coverage. We call this Cover 40. They are playing Cover 0 on the X receiver and tight end. They are playing Cover 4 to the field over the H and Z receiver. The defense is using an Odd front alignment. The quick end is playing a 4i technique and the strong end is playing a 4 technique.

Let's say the coach uses an R.P.O. as the Rhythm play. The R.P.O. increases space advantage versatility. This is done by attaching an arrow screen to the inside zone run. The arrow screen attacks the bubble in the outside space to the field. The inside zone schemes a bubble of space in the run box to the left by using the FLOW of the running back and the FLOOD of the center to neutralize the man-advantage. This concept should gain a minimum of 4 yards if this defensive look remains consistent and the offense can neutralize the positive personnel accelerators in the run box.

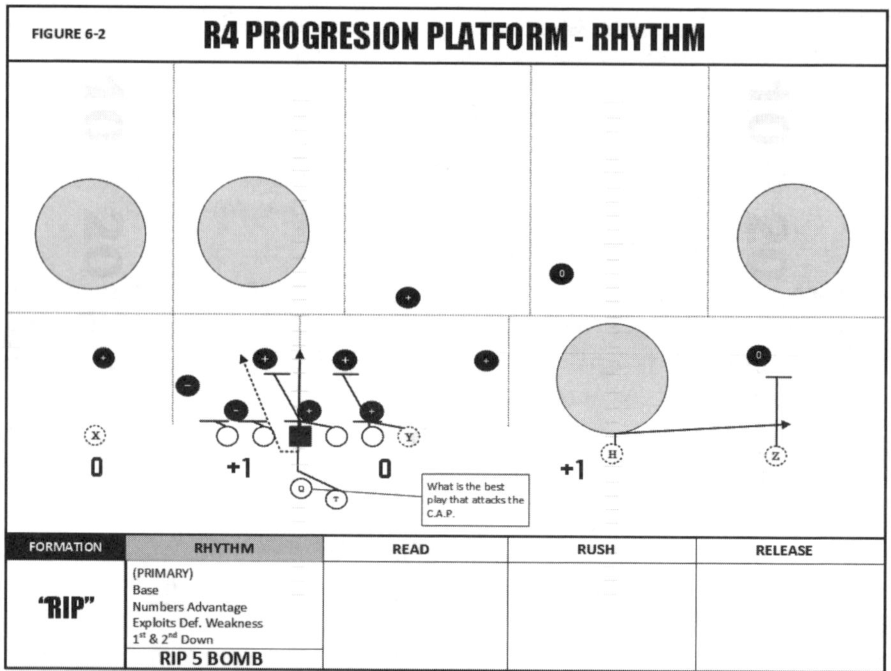

However, there are a variety of factors that can inhibit the success of this play. The defense can adjust the coverage, front, or CAP the run and route space with personnel accelerator actions that defeat the scheme. These factors require ancillary plays that answer these issues. This takes us to the Read phase of the play-calling progression.

READ PLAYS

The next family of plays is Read plays. Read plays are the next "best" play that attacks the highest priority threat to the Rhythm play. Read plays require the most discipline for a coach when game-planning. It is impossible to have constraint plays that protect every possible issue that can occur within a game. As a result, coaches fall into the trap of scripting numerous constraints to answer everything that could go wrong in a game. This results in hours of wasted game-planning time. It also accounts for confusion and extra practice reps on plays that will never be called in a game. Grandmaster chess players understand this dilemma.

In chess, an expert could know every possible move that an opponent could make on a given turn. However, it is impossible to predict with any certainty which exact move in the myriad of choices that the opponent will make. An expert will avoid overthinking and wasted practice time by assessing the highest priority threat on a given situation. This ranking process accelerates the best counter move to make. A football coach must implement this same strategy when selecting the Read play.

The CAP interface provides a coach with the process to determine the highest priority threat that will eliminate a Rhythm play. A coach can then use this information to rank the highest threat to the Rhythm play and game-plan the "best" Read play to protect it. A Read play attacks one or more of these three defensive weapons.

- **C** – Read plays attack the most anticipated Coverage adjustment
- **A** – Read plays attack the most anticipated Alignment (Front) adjustment
- **P** – Read plays attack the most anticipated post-snap personnel movement or mismatch

Read plays continue the IF/THEN storyboard of the R4 inference engine. **IF** an offensive formation and personnel group A is countered with a coverage, alignment, or defensive personnel movement B **THEN** space is attacked by Read Concept C.

Read plays provide the best answer to the 2nd and 3rd down situations in which defenses adjust. Establishing a Read play to counter a coverage or alignment adjustment is simple for most coaches. The real challenge comes when determining the "best" Read play to counter post-snap personnel reactions and mismatches. Personnel is usually the highest priority threat to a Rhythm play. Therefore, most Read plays are driven by personnel accelerators. A coach must obtain the ability to process defensive accelerator actions quickly. (FIG. 6-3)

Here is an example of how a Read play is determined in a game-plan. The Rhythm play was a weakside inside zone R.P.O. concept. The defense can change the coverage, alignment, or rely on a post-snap personnel movement or mismatch to eliminate the Rhythm play. The coach must determine which of these three weapons presents the highest priority threat to the Rhythm play. In this situation, we are

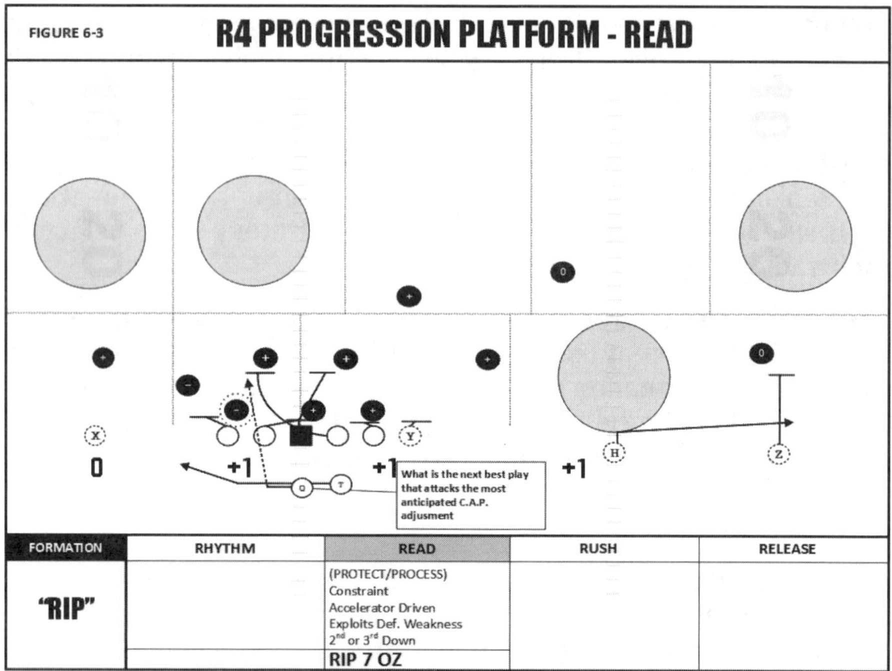

going to say that the positive penetrators, plug, and pursuit players present the biggest threat to the Rhythm play.

A coach needs an insurance plan to attack these positive defensive accelerators. The offense game-plans a 1-back power read concept to use as the Read play. This concept can help neutralize a positive penetrating nose guard with a double-team that works back to the backside pursuit player. The backside pulling guard provides a better - surface block on the play-side plug player. This run concept combines all three Run scheme strategies into the same play. The 4i is left unblocked and read by the quarterback on the FAKE. The quarterback is also used as a run threat off the centerline. This FLOW with the running backing neutralizes the defensive man-advantage. The FLOOD of the pulling guard creates a leverage block advantage on the plug player.

RUSH PLAYS

The next family of plays is Rush plays. Rush plays are concepts called when the offense is at a number disadvantage to a side of space. Rush plays protect the offense from movements and blitzes in areas that the defense intends to overload. Rush plays provide further constraints to the defense to keep the Rhythm play optimal. Rush plays are any down plays and have a high probability of execution in Red Zone and Blitz situations.

C – Rush plays attack the most anticipated Coverage pressure adjustment

A – Rush plays attack the most anticipated Alignment (Front) pressure adjustment

P – Rush plays attack the most anticipated personnel blitz or pressure adjustment

Rush plays continue the IF/THEN storyboard of the R4 inference engine. **IF** an offensive formation and personnel group A is pressured with a coverage, alignment, or defensive personnel movement B **THEN** space is attacked by rush concept C.

The most common defensive maneuver that takes away the rhythm and read run is an overload of numbers. Therefore, Rush plays are commonly play-action passes, R.P.O. man beating attachments, or screens. Protection adjustments are also considered here, as well. This is used to counter cover 0 / 1 Man blitzes. Also, that pressure does not always have to be a blitz. A defensive call can drop 8 defenders into coverage. This overloads numbers and creates pressure in the route space. This would be a situation when a draw play would be effective.

Here is an example of a game-planned Rush play. (FIG. 6-4)

The anticipated pressure was a boundary corner blitz. The defense must rotate coverage to the boundary, as well as to protect the secondary corner blitz. They play Cover 3 behind the pressure. This was a defensive answer to overload numbers in the rhythm and Read play run space. One play constraint that would take advantage of this overload would be to run a naked bootleg concept off the same weakside run action. This bootleg variation provides multiple rush route options along with an over drag by the X receiver that attacks the bubble of space in the field seam tube.

RELEASE PLAYS

The last family of plays is Release plays. Release plays are personnel-driven plays that use the best offensive players to scheme explosive plays. Release plays are set up by the Rhythm play. The establishment

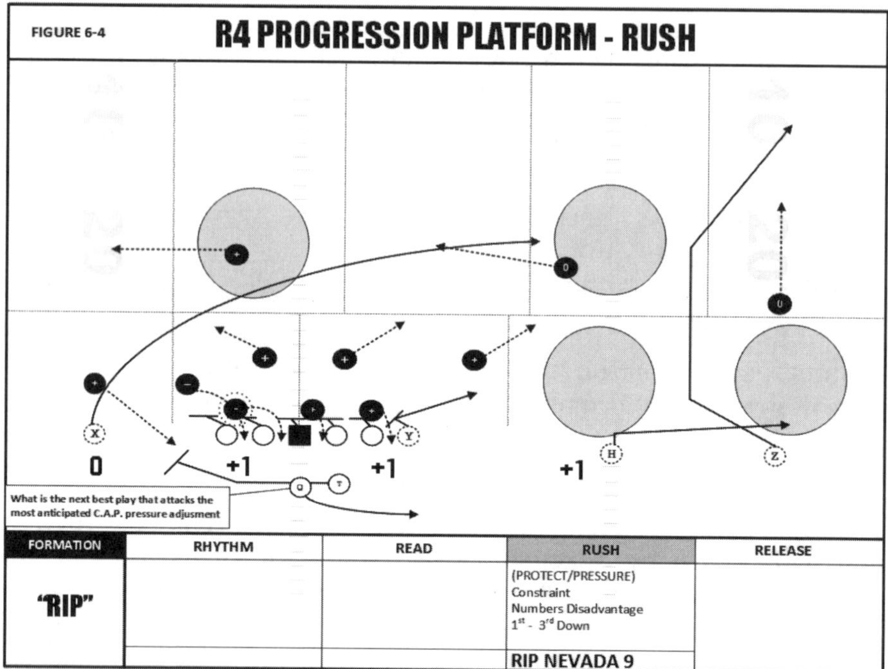

of the Rhythm play within a game will force specific countermoves by the defense. The offense can use these anticipated counter moves to position their best player in a position to attack the adjustment weakness. Double-move routes, reverses, and many other gadget concepts are common Release plays.

- **C** – Release plays attack the most anticipated Coverage adjustment mismatch
- **A** – Release plays attack the most anticipated Alignment (Front) adjustment mismatch
- **P** – Release plays attack the most anticipated personnel movement mismatch

Release plays finalize or transition the IF/THEN storyboard of the R4 inference engine. **IF** an offensive formation and personnel group A has a mismatch with a coverage, alignment, or defensive personnel movement B **THEN** space is attacked by Release Concept C.

Release plays do not always have to be an explosive countermove-constraint play off the Rhythm play. Release plays can use shifts or motions of a player(s) to gain a CAP advantage on the base Rhythm play.

Release plays can also be used as a transition to another formational grid on your play sheet.

Here is an example of a game-planned Release play. (FIG. 6-5)

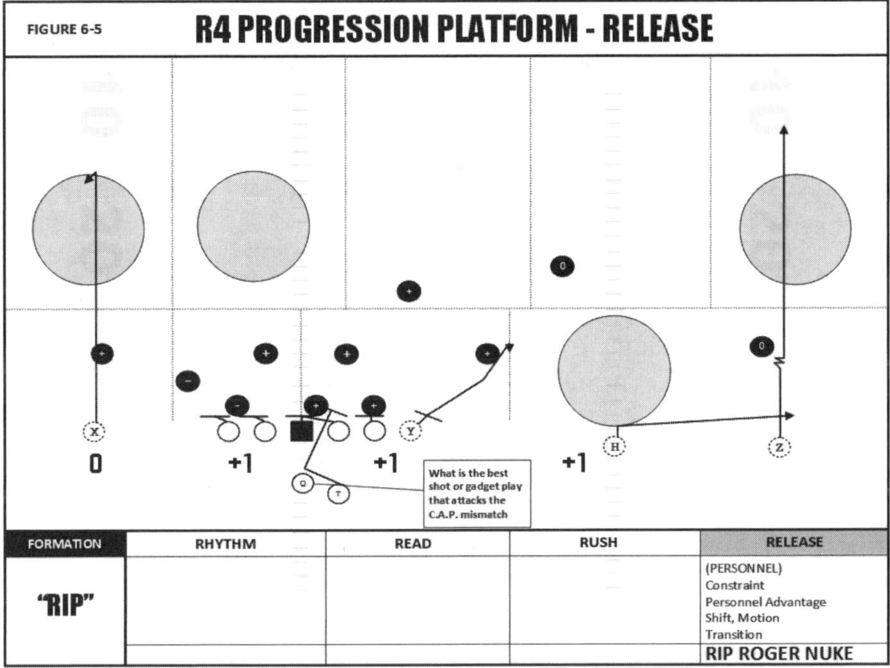

The Rhythm play was an inside zone R.P.O. concept. The field cornerback will have to defeat the stalk block by the Z receiver to inhibit the arrow screen. The offense can use this anticipated action to position its best receiver at the Z position. The Release play used is a stalk-and-go route built off the arrow screen. This concept is called Nuke. The offense will use a 7-man check Release play action protection to simulate the Rhythm play.

TELLING THE STORY OF "OPEN"

I desperately needed this process in my first game-plan meeting as an offensive coordinator. I knew internally what I wanted to do in the game. However, I didn't possess the tools necessary to paint a picture of the plan. I was left with notes and scribbles of plays that I liked, along with a stack of more of the same from the other coaches on the staff.

I spent the rest of the night trying to force the conglomeration of ideas together like a 1000-piece puzzle.

I did not look forward to Monday of a game-plan week. The offense had a 20-minute team meeting before practice to cover the game-plan. It was my job to present the game-plan and instill confidence in the team. This was a challenge for me because I understood the difference between presenting and storytelling. In my first game-planning meeting I was presenting. Presenting is like watching a documentary. It's a boring presentation of information. Players are falling asleep and coaches are in the back talking to each other. There is no flow and connection. What I needed was a story.

Storytelling is the oldest method of information transport in human history. The human brain is hardwired for story. Stories pack information in a pattern using plot and character frames of reference to convey information in a form that can easily be communicated and recalled. Stories can bring information to life in the brain.

Similarly, the R4 progression creates a storyboard process that brings a game-plan story to life.

The HALO and CAP interface tools overlaid on a formation create storyboards that allow coaches and players to plan and pre-visualize "what is open." The Rhythm, Read, Rush, and Release sequence ask the right questions to generate the best solutions for each scene. The inference engine drives the decision to move the game-plan story forward through an IF/THEN decision-making process.

Now game-plan and team meetings are no longer mundane. Players and coaches follow the flow of the game-plan story. Everyone is viewing the reality of space through the same lens. The R4 progression provides guardrails that keep the coaches on track and prevent the game-plan from going into the ditch.

Furthermore, the R4 progression helps develop an intuitive ability to accelerate play-call decisions under pressure. (FIG. 6-6)

Like the power of story, the R4 progression platforms give the coach the ability to forward chain events in an order of priority. Forward chaining is the ability to process information using inference rules to extract even more information until the best solution is reached. This allows the coach to play out both expected and unexpected scenarios that occur in a game, in order. This mental progression of playing the

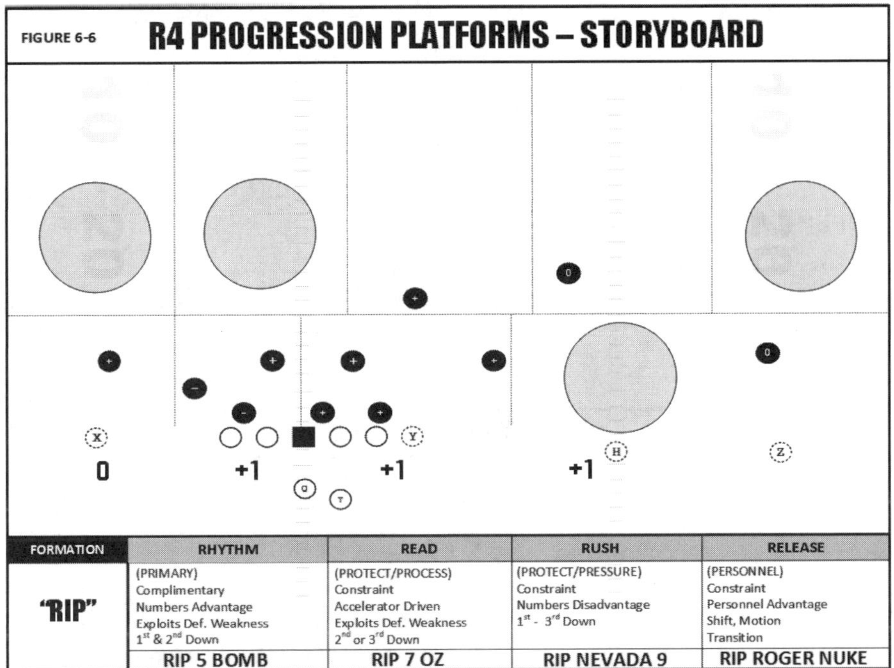

FORMATION	RHYTHM	READ	RUSH	RELEASE
"RIP"	(PRIMARY) Complimentary Numbers Advantage Exploits Def. Weakness 1st & 2nd Down	(PROTECT/PROCESS) Constraint Accelerator Driven Exploits Def. Weakness 2nd or 3rd Down	(PROTECT/PRESSURE) Constraint Numbers Disadvantage 1st - 3rd Down	(PERSONNEL) Constraint Personnel Advantage Shift, Motion Transition
	RIP 5 BOMB	RIP 7 OZ	RIP NEVADA 9	RIP ROGER NUKE

story out in the mind opens the door for intuitive recall in the game, when pressure is the highest.

This ability is further enhanced because the coach is no longer alone in the process. The R4 progression brings all the coaches and players together. operating from the same frames of reference. They can now understand the story, as well as the play-caller. This allows the play-caller to share consciousness with others. Every brain on a team can link together to create a supercomputer. This increases confidence and feedback through shared intelligence on plays as they occur within the game.

Another benefit of the R4 progression is that it also provides the users with the ability to backward chain as well. Backward chaining is the ability to prove a solution in the absence of clear evidence or data. This occurs frequently in game-planning when there is not enough information to conclude how the defense will defend a formation or situation. This also occurs in games when a play breaks down. The R4 progression provides the process for coaches and players to work backward through the progression, from a defensive perspective. This allows the users to search for the inference rules until they find an IF/THEN clause that matches the desired goal or play result. (Fig. 6-7)

Forward and backward chaining is a key element in achieving mastery in a domain. It is one of the foundational components that make up an expert system. This trait is found in grandmaster chess players and experts in game theory. The R4 progression is the cipher that cracks the code on achieving this ability. When a coach can tell the story of "open" forwards and backward, he is placed on the fast-track to becoming an expert.

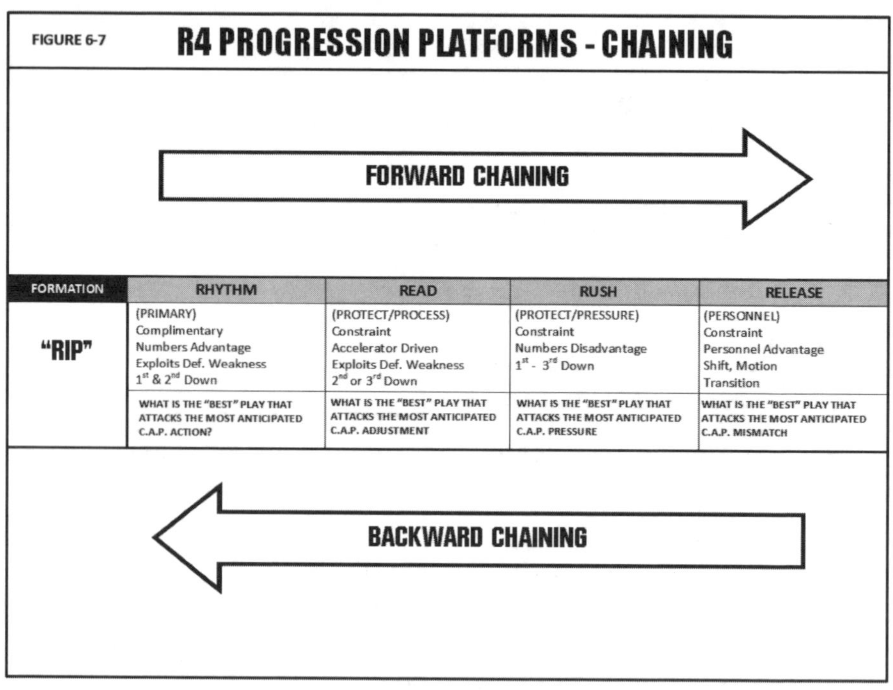

FORMATION	RHYTHM	READ	RUSH	RELEASE
"RIP"	(PRIMARY) Complimentary Numbers Advantage Exploits Def. Weakness 1st & 2nd Down	(PROTECT/PROCESS) Constraint Accelerator Driven Exploits Def. Weakness 2nd or 3rd Down	(PROTECT/PRESSURE) Constraint Numbers Disadvantage 1st - 3rd Down	(PERSONNEL) Constraint Personnel Advantage Shift, Motion Transition
	WHAT IS THE "BEST" PLAY THAT ATTACKS THE MOST ANTICIPATED C.A.P. ACTION?	WHAT IS THE "BEST" PLAY THAT ATTACKS THE MOST ANTICIPATED C.A.P. ADJUSTMENT	WHAT IS THE "BEST" PLAY THAT ATTACKS THE MOST ANTICIPATED C.A.P. PRESSURE	WHAT IS THE "BEST" PLAY THAT ATTACKS THE MOST ANTICIPATED C.A.P. MISMATCH

CHAPTER 7

CHOOSE YOUR OWN ADVENTURE

The R4 Grid

CHOOSE YOUR OWN ADVENTURE

The R4 Grid

Most offensive game-plans and play-calls are built around a series of opening plays. Coaches may differ on the number of plays they script to call at the opening of a game; the goal is to call the best plays against the most anticipated looks and gather information. In my first year as an offensive coordinator, I enjoyed calling the opening 10-15 plays in the game. This opening script usually was executed well after hours of film study and practice in the previous week. However, there were many times that the defense came out in something entirely unexpected. This threw me off-script as I scrambled through the play-call sheet to find plays that answered the defensive adjustments.

It was in these moments that I struggled the most to match the reality of what was occurring on the field to what was printed on the play-call sheet. I was stuck on a page of printed plays instead of reading the reality of what was occurring in real-time. This was when I was at my worst as a play-caller. The problem was that I didn't know how to combat this common problem that usually showed up in the biggest game with the most pressure.

I felt like I was trying to read a story on paper instead of being in the real story on the field. Most fictional books are written in this manner. A third-person point of view places the reader on the outside looking into what is occurring. Third-person stories require the reader to attempt to relate to the main character's point of view.

In the late 1970s, a new opportunity presented itself to readers. Edward Packard created a new type of story that thrust the reader into the middle of the story. The Choose Your Own Adventure series became one of the most popular series of children's books in the 1980s and 1990s, selling more than 250 million copies. These books were written from a second-person point of view. This made the reader the main character in the book. These stories further advanced the user experience by providing the reader with different choice options that lead to different endings within the book.

All of a sudden, the reader had the power to control the story. If danger presented itself, the reader could choose the best solution to overcome the situation. Each time the book was read, a new story developed, keeping the book relevant. I remembered reading the books as a kid and they reminded me of the play-calling process. The game-plan was not like a traditional story that could be predicted and read from beginning to end in a consistent pattern. Each game was full of unexpected twists and turns that required decision-making under pressure. My game-plans were not built for the reality of the game. I needed a method that allowed me to build a game-plan in the format of the *Choose Your Own Adventure* books. This began the development of the R4 grid.

THE R4 GRID

The R4 grid is 16-box framework used to provide a process of solutions for a formation against an opponent. The grid is built upon the four progression platforms of the Rhythm, Read, Rush, and Release sequence that was covered in the last chapter. The grid advances the option of plays to call within a formation. (FIG. 7-1)

The R4 sequence of plays that were covered in the last chapter were built in a storyboard that began by attacking the weak side of the Rip formation. What if the defense came out in a different coverage and alignment (front) that made the weakside run space less optimal? The naked bootleg concept was the Rush play that attacked an overload of numbers to the weakside run space. This concept may work once or twice, but it is not an effective Rhythm play.

This is where the R4 grid provides the answer to unanticipated defensive adjustments. If the defense chooses to overload the weakside run space, then the offense may gain an advantage to the strongside run space. The R4 grid adds further play-call options that allow the play-caller to attack every part of the field in a Rhythm, Read, Rush, Release sequence. These options are organized into four additional categories. They are Strong Run, Weak Run, 3-Step, and 5-Step concept categories.

FIGURE 7-1

THE R4 GRID

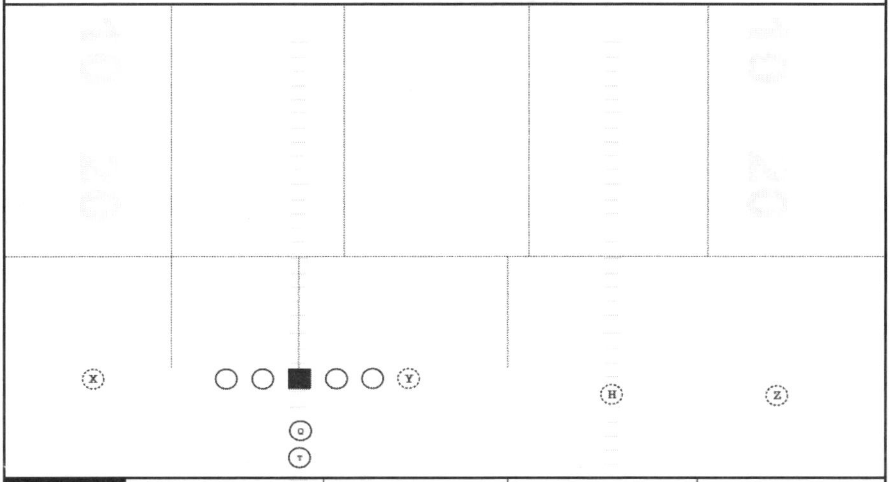

X O O ■ O O Y H Z
Q
T

FORMATION	RHYTHM	READ	RUSH	RELEASE
STRONG RUN				
WEAK RUN				
3 STEP				
5 STEP				

STRONG RUN / RHYTHM

The Strong Run category begins with the best Rhythm play that attacks the strong side run space. (FIG. 7-2)

The remainder of the Read, Rush, and Release storyboard progression can be filled in once the strong rhythm run play is determined. The Strong Run play is selected based on the CAP of the defense.

This is a continuation of the Rip formation used in the previous chapter. The defense is playing Cover 40. They are aligned in an odd front that is shaded strong. We call this Kings Strong in our terminology. There are five positive defensive personnel accelerators to the strong side of the formation. (FIG. 7-3)

A 1-back power concept variation is selected as the rhythm run strong. This provides two double-teams on the positive penetrators. The tackle is the puller to allow the backside guard to secure the 4i technique. The backside tackle will pull for the first pin or plug threat to the right side of run space. The backside safety is playing man on the tight end. This brings a potential extra defender into the man-advantage count. The running back will be responsible for this extra defender.

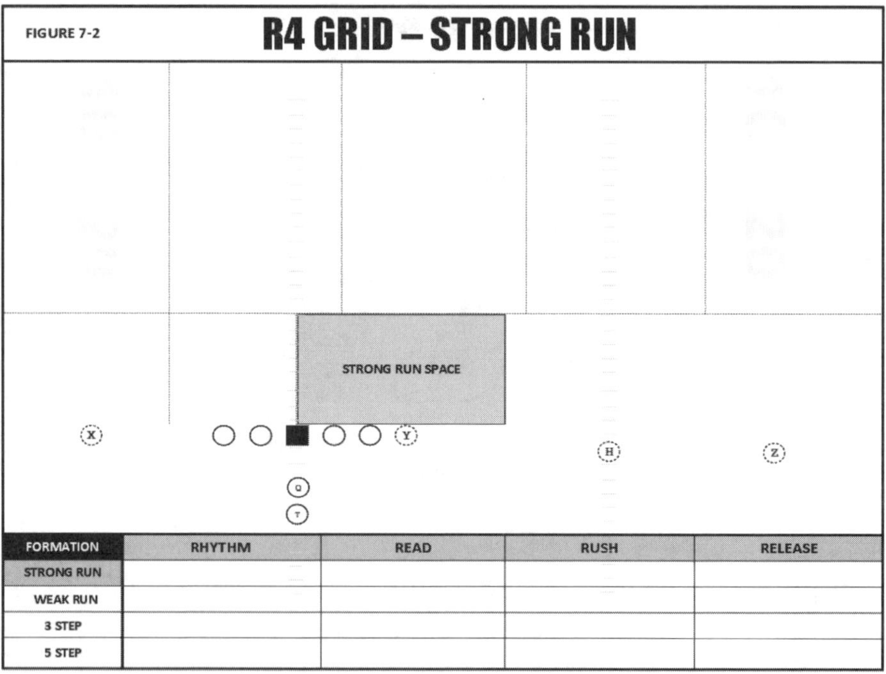
FIGURE 7-2
R4 GRID – STRONG RUN
STRONG RUN SPACE
X
Y
H
Z
Q
T
FORMATION
RHYTHM
READ
RUSH
RELEASE
STRONG RUN
WEAK RUN
3 STEP
5 STEP

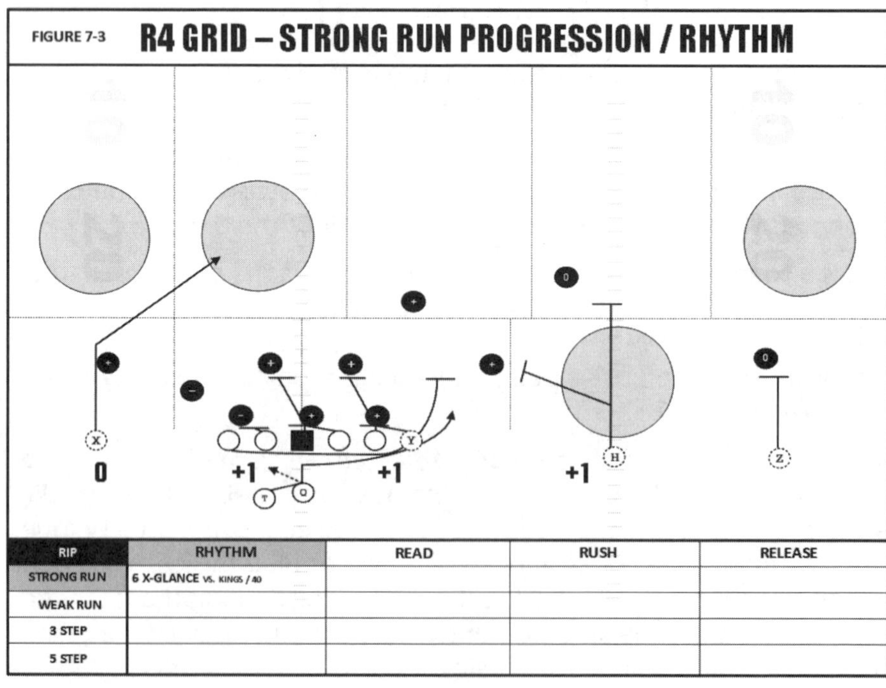
FIGURE 7-3
R4 GRID – STRONG RUN PROGRESSION / RHYTHM
X
Y
H
Z
T
Q
0
+1
+1
+1
RIP
RHYTHM
READ
RUSH
RELEASE
STRONG RUN
6 X-GLANCE vs. KINGS / 40
WEAK RUN
3 STEP
5 STEP

This is a difficult look to run into it the H receiver cannot handle the positive pin player. This play may require the weak side run to be successful to force a coverage change to even-up the run box numbers. This rhythm run becomes an R.P.O. option by attaching a backside glance to the play. This allows the boundary bubbles to the weak side to be attacked if the X receiver can uncap the route space. The FAKE, FLOW, and FLOOD scheme strategies within this play make it a viable rhythm concept against this defensive look.

STRONG RUN - READ

The next play to game-plan in the Strong Run category is the Read play. The Read play is the best play that attacks the most anticipated defensive CAP adjustment. The highest priority threat to the Rhythm Strong Run is the potential overload of positive personnel accelerators to the right side of run space. If the Rhythm play cannot handle this alignment and personnel, then the offense must scheme a man-advantage play. (FIG. 7-4)

FIGURE 7-4 **R4 GRID – STRONG RUN PROGRESSION / READ**

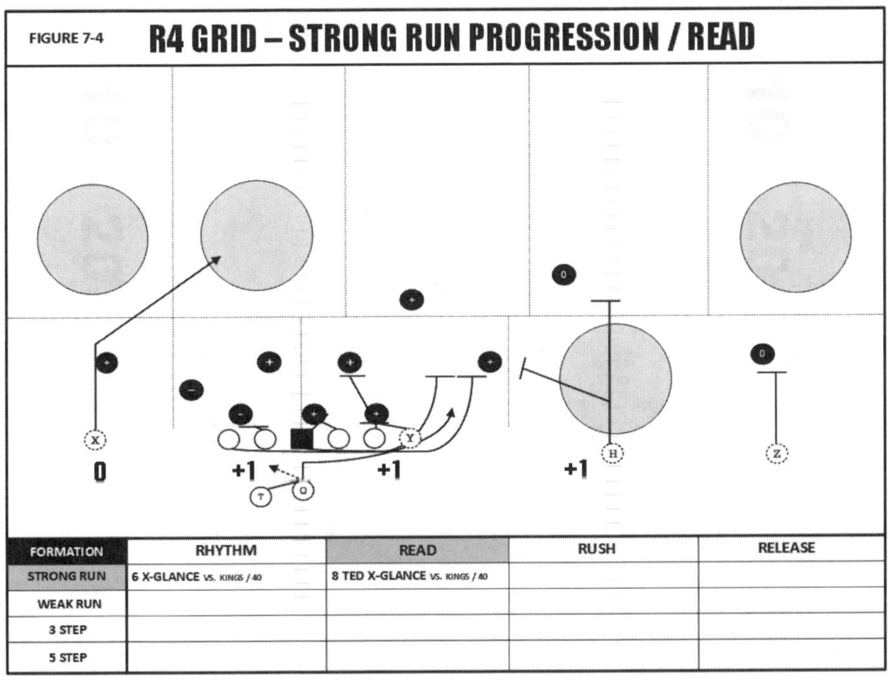

FORMATION	RHYTHM	READ	RUSH	RELEASE
STRONG RUN	6 X-GLANCE vs. KINGS / 40	8 TED X-GLANCE vs. KINGS / 40		
WEAK RUN				
3 STEP				
5 STEP				

The play that was selected here is a pin-and-pull scheme that FLOODS a side of space by pulling the center. The center becomes an additional man-advantage player that can help neutralize the count. The benefit of this scheme is that it still provides a good down-block angle on the positive nose guard while maintaining a double-team on the 4 technique. The quarterback must hold the backside pursuit-and-pin players with the run and route threat within the R.P.O.

STRONG RUN / RUSH

The next play to game-plan in the Strong Run category is the Rush play. The Rush play is the best play that attacks the most anticipated CAP pressure. (FIG. 7-5)

In this game-plan, the defense has shown the tendency to bring dual exterior pressure with Cover 0 played behind it. We call this a Dagger Wham blitz. Cover 0 blitzes create a numbers disadvantage for the offense. This also opens an additional bubble of space above the Hard

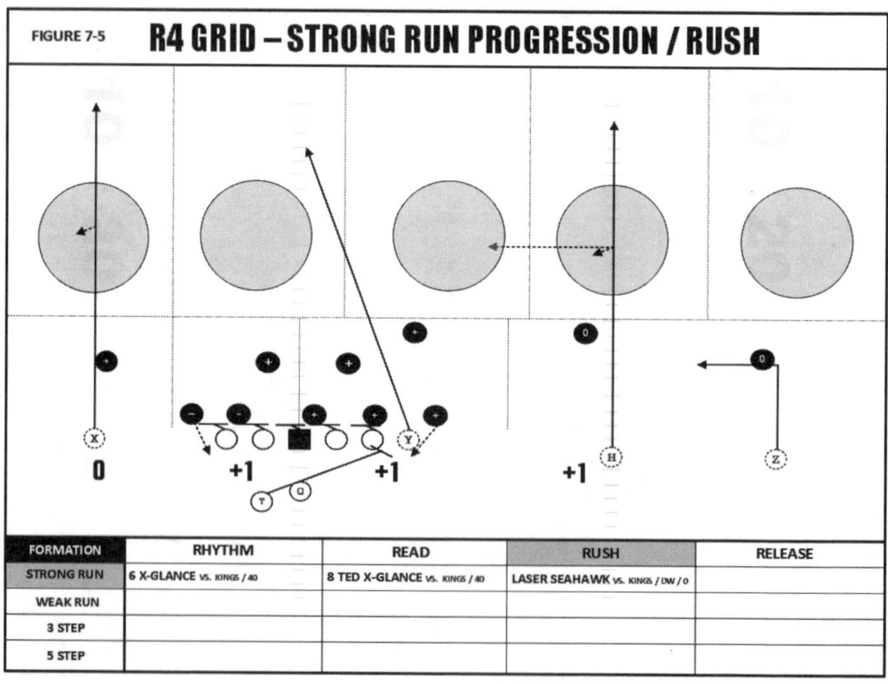

FIGURE 7-5 R4 GRID – STRONG RUN PROGRESSION / RUSH

FORMATION	RHYTHM	READ	RUSH	RELEASE
STRONG RUN	6 X-GLANCE vs. KINGS / 40	8 TED X-GLANCE vs. KINGS / 40	LASER SEAHAWK vs. KINGS / DW / 0	
WEAK RUN				
3 STEP				
5 STEP				

Deck. A 6-man slide protection along with a seam read concept is game-planned to attack this situation. The best mismatch is the H receiver on a neutral field safety.

STRONG RUN / RELEASE

The final play to game-plan in the Strong Run category is the Release play. The Release play is the best trick-or-tag play that is set up off the Rhythm play. One of the biggest threats that would eliminate the strong side rhythm run is an aggressive action by the backside pursuit player. (FIG. 7-6)

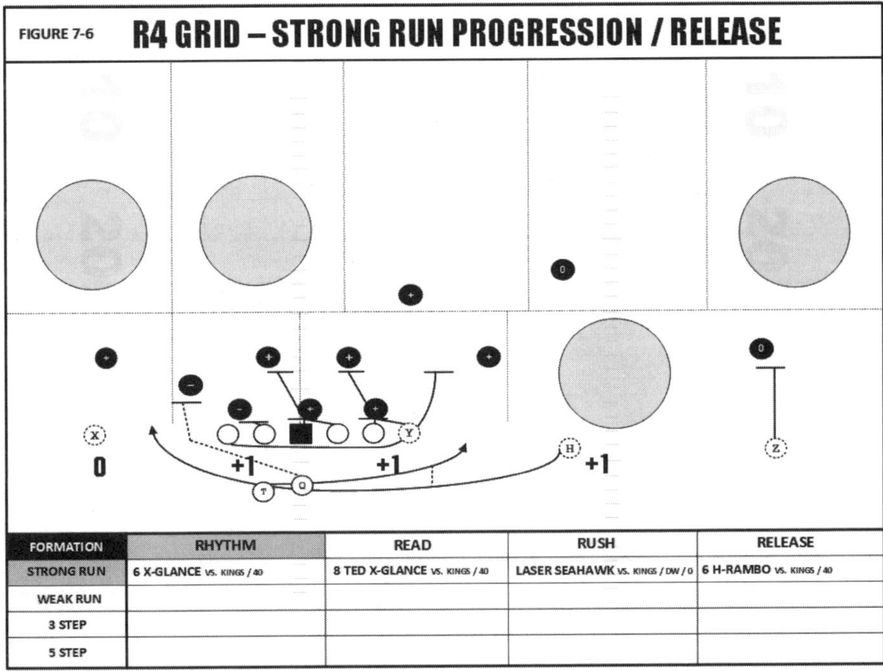

FORMATION	RHYTHM	READ	RUSH	RELEASE
STRONG RUN	6 X-GLANCE vs. KINGS / 40	8 TED X-GLANCE vs. KINGS / 40	LASER SEAHAWK vs. KINGS / DW / 0	6 H-RAMBO vs. KINGS / 40
WEAK RUN				
3 STEP				
5 STEP				

Therefore, a reverse concept is game-planned as the Release play. The offensive line will run the rhythm Run scheme. The tailback will take the handoff and pitch the ball to the H receiver on the reverse. The quarterback becomes the man-advantage block on the backside to generate an explosive play.

This is an example of how to fill in a Strong Run R4 progression platform storyboard.

FIGURE 7-7

R4 GRID – WEAK RUN

WEAK RUN SPACE

X Y H Z Q T

FORMATION	RHYTHM	READ	RUSH	RELEASE
STRONG RUN				
WEAK RUN				
3 STEP				
5 STEP				

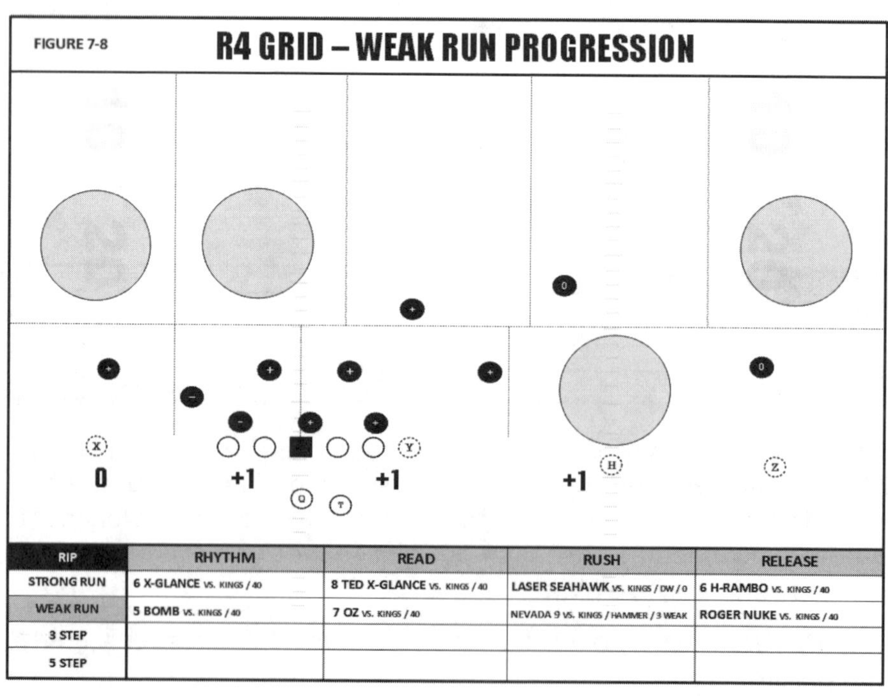

FIGURE 7-8

R4 GRID – WEAK RUN PROGRESSION

RIP	RHYTHM	READ	RUSH	RELEASE
STRONG RUN	6 X-GLANCE VS. KINGS / 40	8 TED X-GLANCE VS. KINGS / 40	LASER SEAHAWK VS. KINGS / DW / 0	6 H-RAMBO VS. KINGS / 40
WEAK RUN	5 BOMB VS. KINGS / 40	7 OZ VS. KINGS / 40	NEVADA 9 VS. KINGS / HAMMER / 3 WEAK	ROGER NUKE VS. KINGS / 40
3 STEP				
5 STEP				

WEAK RUN – RHYTHM, READ, RUSH, RELEASE

The next sequence to game-plan is the Weak Run category. This category contains concepts that are designed to attack the weak side run space. (FIG. 7-7)

The Read, Rush, and Release plays in the sequence possess constraint plays based on defensive CAP adjustment.

This sequence was already game-planned in the previous chapter and can be reviewed there. The weak side concepts have been transferred into the grid here. (FIG. 7-8)

3 STEP PASS / RHYTHM

The next sequence to game-plan is the 3-step Pass category. The 3-step Pass category begins with the best Rhythm play that attacks the 3-step route space under the Hard Deck. 3-step concepts can still possess routes that attack vertical space. However, their core route stretches are created to attack horizontal space under the Hard Deck. (FIG. 7-9)

FIGURE 7-9

R4 GRID – 3 STEP

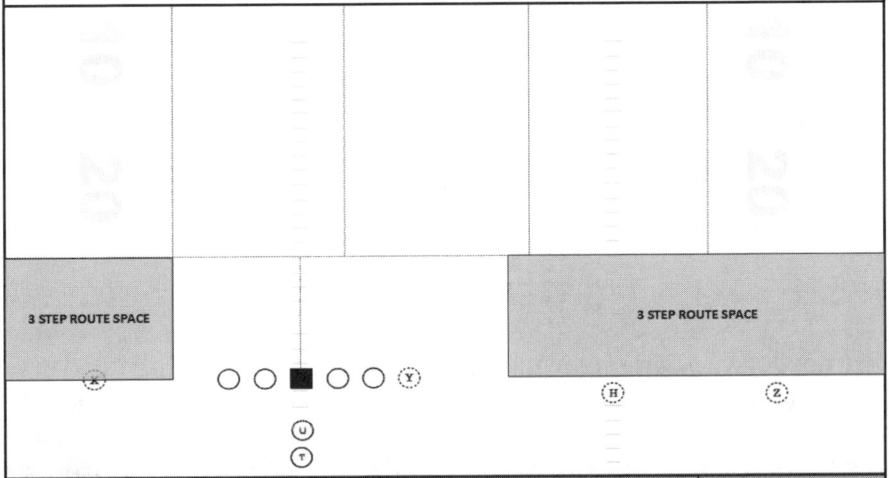

3 STEP ROUTE SPACE

3 STEP ROUTE SPACE

X Y H Z U T

FORMATION	RHYTHM	READ	RUSH	RELEASE
STRONG RUN				
WEAK RUN				
3 STEP				
5 STEP				

The ancillary Read, Rush, and Release plays can be selected once the 3-step Rhythm play is determined.

The Y-stick concept is selected as the Rhythm 3-step Pass. (FIG. 7-10)

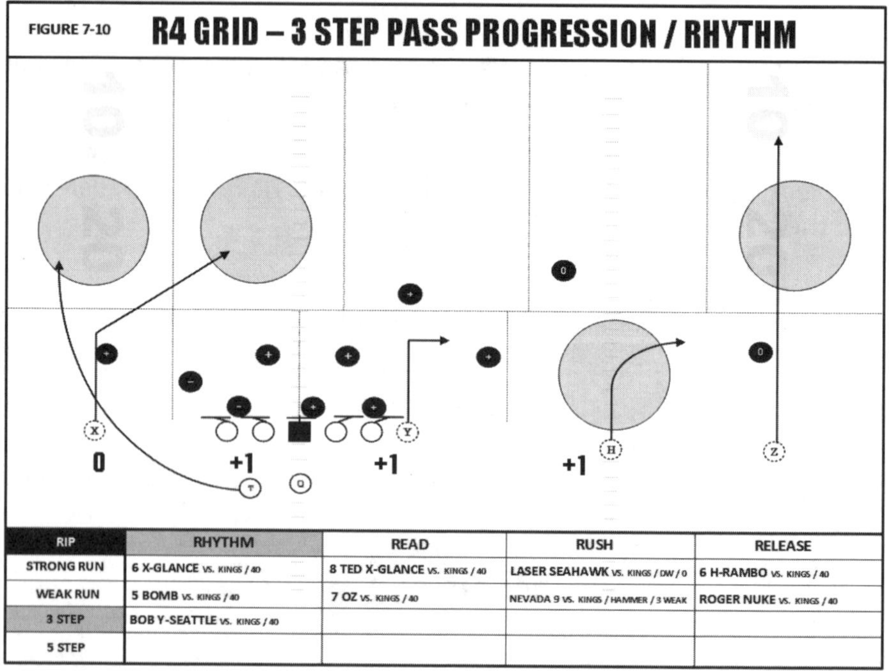

RIP	RHYTHM	READ	RUSH	RELEASE
STRONG RUN	6 X-GLANCE vs. KINGS / 40	8 TED X-GLANCE vs. KINGS / 40	LASER SEAHAWK vs. KINGS / DW / 0	6 H-RAMBO vs. KINGS / 40
WEAK RUN	5 BOMB vs. KINGS / 40	7 OZ vs. KINGS / 40	NEVADA 9 vs. KINGS / HAMMER / 3 WEAK	ROGER NUKE vs. KINGS / 40
3 STEP	BOB Y-SEATTLE vs. KINGS / 40			
5 STEP				

This concept provides the ability for the quarterback to attack multiple bubbles of space against the Cover 40. The stick and quick-out to the field present quick "hot" route throws against pressure, while allowing the Slant-Wheel combo to develop to the boundary side of route space.

3 STEP PASS / READ

The next play to game-plan in the **3-step Pass** category is the Read play. The Read play is the best play that attacks the most anticipated CAP adjustment by the defense. The highest priority threat to the rhythm 3-step Y-stick concept is a coverage adjustment by the defense. The defense has shown to play some Cover 7 Stubbie. This creates a 2 CAP man-advantage to the boundary side of route space. This allows the defense to CAP the Slant-Wheel combination on the Y-stick concept. (FIG. 7-11)

FIGURE 7-11 **R4 GRID – 3 STEP PASS PROGRESSION / READ**

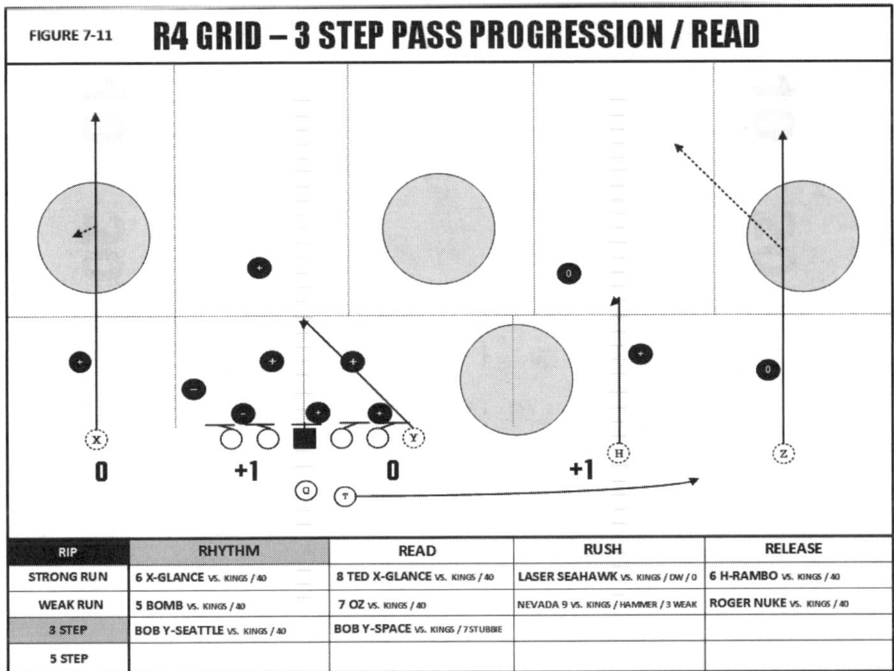

RIP	RHYTHM	READ	RUSH	RELEASE
STRONG RUN	6 X-GLANCE VS. KINGS / 40	8 TED X-GLANCE VS. KINGS / 40	LASER SEAHAWK VS. KINGS / DW / 0	6 H-RAMBO VS. KINGS / 40
WEAK RUN	5 BOMB VS. KINGS / 40	7 OZ VS. KINGS / 40	NEVADA 9 VS. KINGS / HAMMER / 3 WEAK	ROGER NUKE VS. KINGS / 40
3 STEP	BOB Y-SEATTLE VS. KINGS / 40	BOB Y-SPACE VS. KINGS / 7 STUBBIE		
5 STEP				

This coverage adjustment creates an opportunity to scheme a man-advantage play to the field. A 4-man field spacing concept is game-planned here. This spacing concept provides a rhythm "hot" throw with the Spot route by the Y receiver. It also creates a 2-on-1 stretch that attacks the bubble in the outside field flat tube with the Sit and Swing route.

3 STEP PASS / RUSH

The next play to game-plan in the 3-step category is the Rush play. The Rush play is the best play that attacks the most anticipated CAP pressure by the defense. The Cover 0 Dagger Wham pressure is the highest priority threat shown by the defense. (FIG. 7-12)

A play that can neutralize this numbers disadvantage is an S.P.O. This stands for Screen Pass Option. These concepts provide the quarterback with an easy chain-moving throw to the field while setting up the running back screen to the boundary.

FIGURE 7-12

R4 GRID – 3 STEP PASS PROGRESSION / RUSH

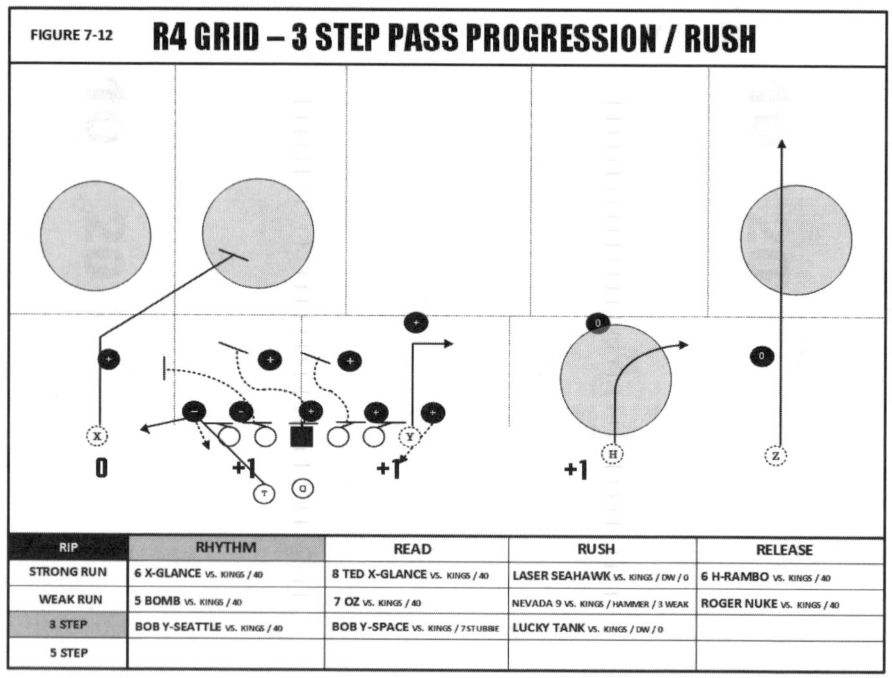

RIP	RHYTHM	READ	RUSH	RELEASE
STRONG RUN	6 X-GLANCE vs. KINGS / 40	8 TED X-GLANCE vs. KINGS / 40	LASER SEAHAWK vs. KINGS / DW / 0	6 H-RAMBO vs. KINGS / 40
WEAK RUN	5 BOMB vs. KINGS / 40	7 OZ vs. KINGS / 40	NEVADA 9 vs. KINGS / HAMMER / 3 WEAK	ROGER NUKE vs. KINGS / 40
3 STEP	BOB Y-SEATTLE vs. KINGS / 40	BOB Y-SPACE vs. KINGS / 7 STUBBIE	LUCKY TANK vs. KINGS / DW / 0	
5 STEP				

FIGURE 7-13

R4 GRID – 3 STEP PASS PROGRESSION / RELEASE

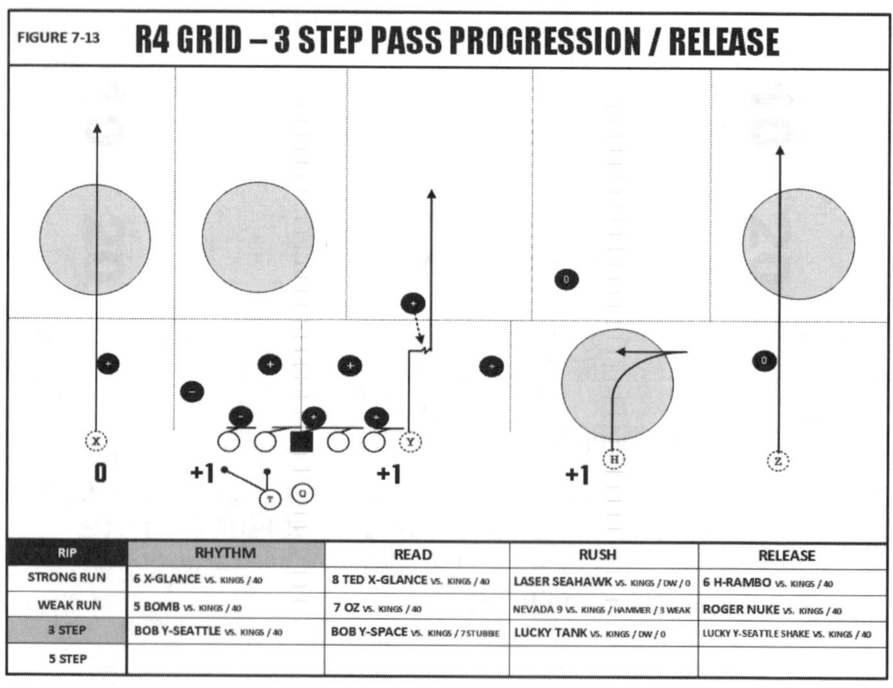

RIP	RHYTHM	READ	RUSH	RELEASE
STRONG RUN	6 X-GLANCE vs. KINGS / 40	8 TED X-GLANCE vs. KINGS / 40	LASER SEAHAWK vs. KINGS / DW / 0	6 H-RAMBO vs. KINGS / 40
WEAK RUN	5 BOMB vs. KINGS / 40	7 OZ vs. KINGS / 40	NEVADA 9 vs. KINGS / HAMMER / 3 WEAK	ROGER NUKE vs. KINGS / 40
3 STEP	BOB Y-SEATTLE vs. KINGS / 40	BOB Y-SPACE vs. KINGS / 7 STUBBIE	LUCKY TANK vs. KINGS / DW / 0	LUCKY Y-SEATTLE SHAKE vs. KINGS / 40
5 STEP				

3 STEP PASS / RELEASE

The final play to game-plan in the 3-step pass category is the Release play. The Release play is the trick-or-tag play that is set up off the Rhythm play. One of the most dangerous threats to the rhythm Y-stick concept is the boundary safety that is manned up on the tight end. (FIG. 7-13)

A counter to attack an aggressive safety on a stick route is the stick-and-go. This is called a Shake route. A Shake tag is used with the Y-stick concept as the Release play. This play will be called when the safety starts to become aggressive at capping the Stick route.

This is an example of how to fill in a 3-step pass progression storyboard.

5 STEP PASS / RHYTHM

The final sequence to game-plan is the 5-step Pass category. (FIG. 7-14)

The 5-step Pass category begins with the best Rhythm play that attacks the 5-step route space above the Hard Deck. 5-step concepts can still

FIGURE 7-14

R4 GRID – 5 STEP PROGRESSION

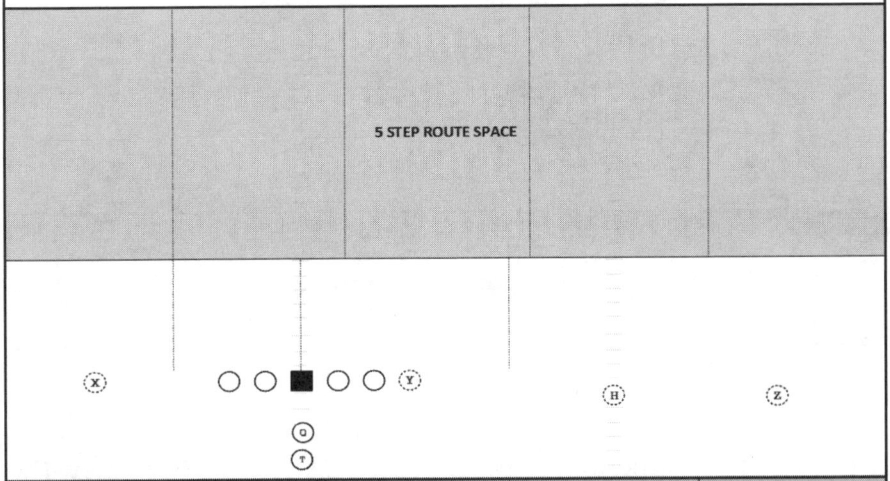

5 STEP ROUTE SPACE

X Y H Z Q T

FORMATION	RHYTHM	READ	RUSH	RELEASE
STRONG RUN				
WEAK RUN				
3 STEP				
5 STEP				

possess routes that attack horizontal space below the Hard Deck. However, their core route stretches are created to attack vertical space above the Hard Deck.

The ancillary Read, Rush, and Release plays can be selected once the 5-step Rhythm play is determined.

A boundary smash variation is selected as the Rhythm 5-step play. (FIG. 7-15)

This concept provides the quarterback with a glance route to the field that can attack a post-snap bubble created by the safety manned-up on the tight end. This allows time for the boundary smash concept to develop.

FIGURE 7-15 **R4 GRID – 5 STEP PASS PROGRESSION / RHYTHM**

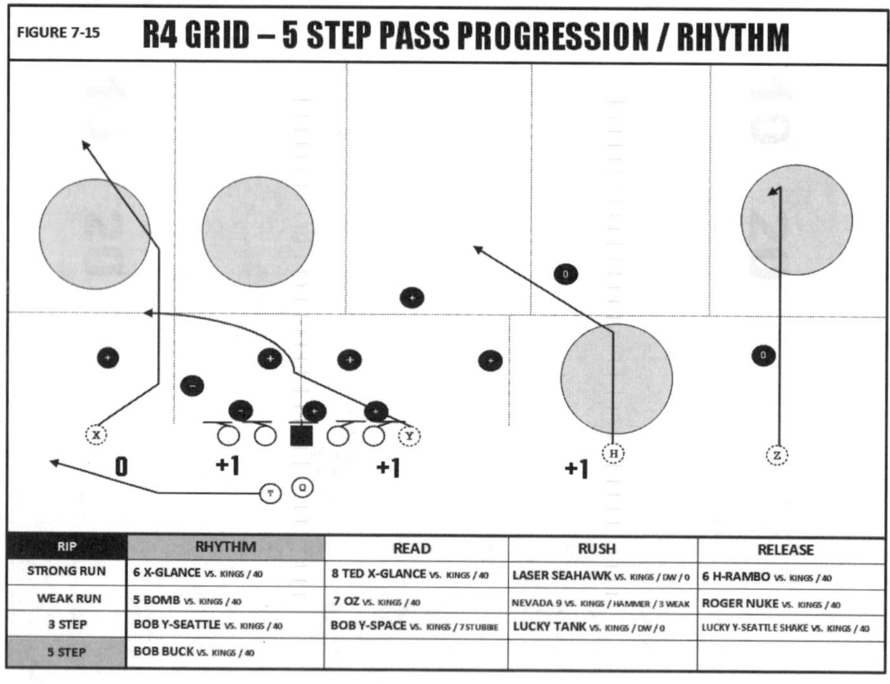

RIP	RHYTHM	READ	RUSH	RELEASE
STRONG RUN	6 X-GLANCE vs. KINGS / 40	8 TED X-GLANCE vs. KINGS / 40	LASER SEAHAWK vs. KINGS / DW / 0	6 H-RAMBO vs. KINGS / 40
WEAK RUN	5 BOMB vs. KINGS / 40	7 OZ vs. KINGS / 40	NEVADA 9 vs. KINGS / HAMMER / 3 WEAK	ROGER NUKE vs. KINGS / 40
3 STEP	BOB Y-SEATTLE vs. KINGS / 40	BOB Y-SPACE vs. KINGS / 7 STUBBIE	LUCKY TANK vs. KINGS / DW / 0	LUCKY Y-SEATTLE SHAKE vs. KINGS / 40
5 STEP	BOB BUCK vs. KINGS / 40			

5 STEP PASS / READ

The next play to game-plan in the 5-step category is the Read play. The Read play is the best play that attacks the most anticipated CAP adjustment by the defense. The highest priority threat to the Rhythm 5-step concept is a coverage adjustment that the defense has been shown to play. (FIG. 7-16)

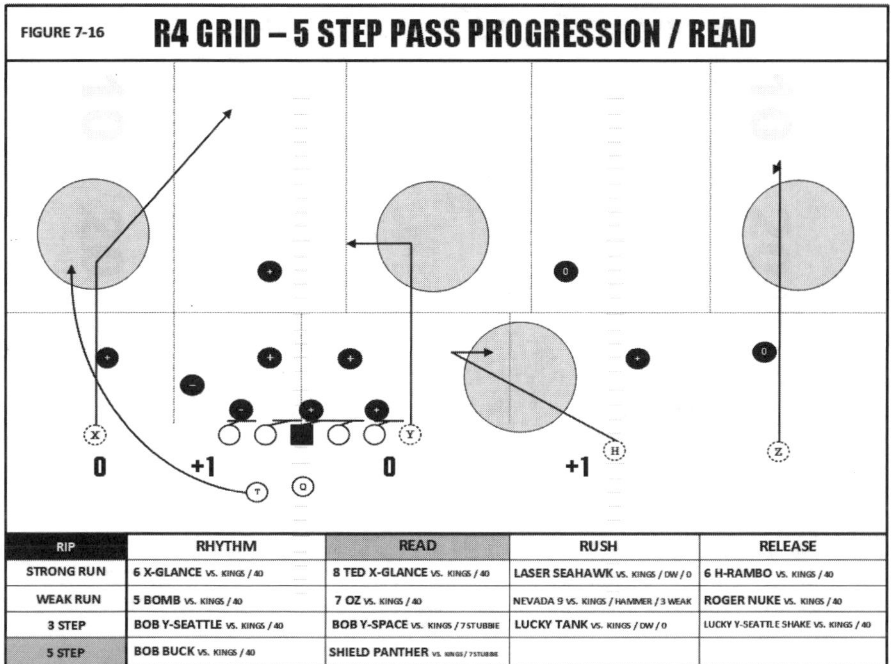

RIP	RHYTHM	READ	RUSH	RELEASE
STRONG RUN	6 X-GLANCE VS. KINGS / 40	8 TED X-GLANCE VS. KINGS / 40	LASER SEAHAWK VS. KINGS / DW / 0	6 H-RAMBO VS. KINGS / 40
WEAK RUN	5 BOMB VS. KINGS / 40	7 OZ VS. KINGS / 40	NEVADA 9 VS. KINGS / HAMMER / 3 WEAK	ROGER NUKE VS. KINGS / 40
3 STEP	BOB Y-SEATTLE VS. KINGS / 40	BOB Y-SPACE VS. KINGS / 7 STUBBIE	LUCKY TANK VS. KINGS / DW / 0	LUCKY Y-SEATTLE SHAKE VS. KINGS / 40
5 STEP	BOB BUCK VS. KINGS / 40	SHIELD PANTHER VS. KINGS / 7 STUBBIE		

This is Cover 7 Stubbie. As previously mentioned, this coverage positions 2 capping defenders to the boundary side of route space. This coverage creates additional bubbles of space to the field. An interior Levels concept off the Post-Wheel combo is game-planned here. The Post-Wheel occupies the 2 CAP positions within Cover 7 and allows the Dig and Pivot routes to the field to develop.

5 STEP PASS / RUSH

The next play to game-plan in the 5-step category is the Rush play. The Rush play is the best play that attacks the most anticipated CAP pressure by the defense. It is important to remember that pressure does not always mean the defense is playing man coverage and bringing a blitz. A zone drop quarters coverage is another example of pressure. The overload of defenders into route space reduces the bubbles to throw into. (FIG. 7-17)

A running back draw play is game-planned for this variation of pressure. The offense will give a 4-vertical pass concept look while releasing linemen downfield. The quarterback will show pass, then hand the ball off to the running back on this play.

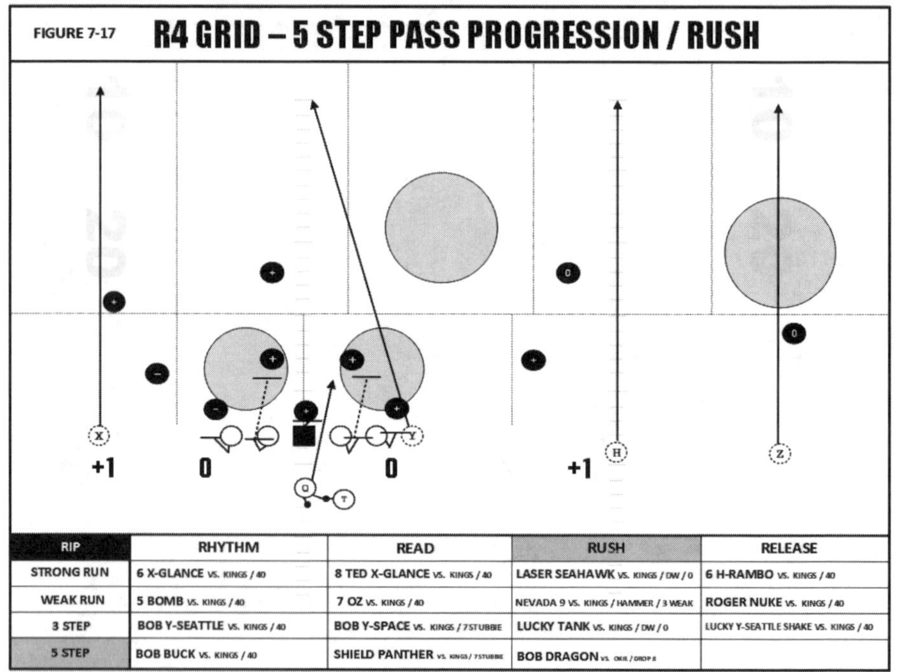

FIGURE 7-17 **R4 GRID – 5 STEP PASS PROGRESSION / RUSH**

RIP	RHYTHM	READ	RUSH	RELEASE
STRONG RUN	6 X-GLANCE vs. KINGS / 40	8 TED X-GLANCE vs. KINGS / 40	LASER SEAHAWK vs. KINGS / DW / 0	6 H-RAMBO vs. KINGS / 40
WEAK RUN	5 BOMB vs. KINGS / 40	7 OZ vs. KINGS / 40	NEVADA 9 vs. KINGS / HAMMER / 3 WEAK	ROGER NUKE vs. KINGS / 40
3 STEP	BOB Y-SEATTLE vs. KINGS / 40	BOB Y-SPACE vs. KINGS / 7 STUBBIE	LUCKY TANK vs. KINGS / DW / 0	LUCKY Y-SEATTLE SHAKE vs. KINGS / 40
5 STEP	BOB BUCK vs. KINGS / 40	SHIELD PANTHER vs. KINGS / 7 STUBBIE	BOB DRAGON vs. OKIE / DROP 8	

5 STEP PASS / RELEASE

The final play to game-plan in the 5-step category is the Release play. The Release play is the trick-or-tag play that is set up off the Rhythm play. (FIG. 7-18)

The Rhythm Boundary Smash concept contained a Glance route by the H receiver. This receiver has a neutral safety who is positioned over and inside his alignment. A Sluggo tag is added to this concept to form an explosive Release play option if the safety becomes aggressive at capping the post-snap route.

This is an example of how to fill a 5-step Pass Progression storyboard. (FIG. 7-19)

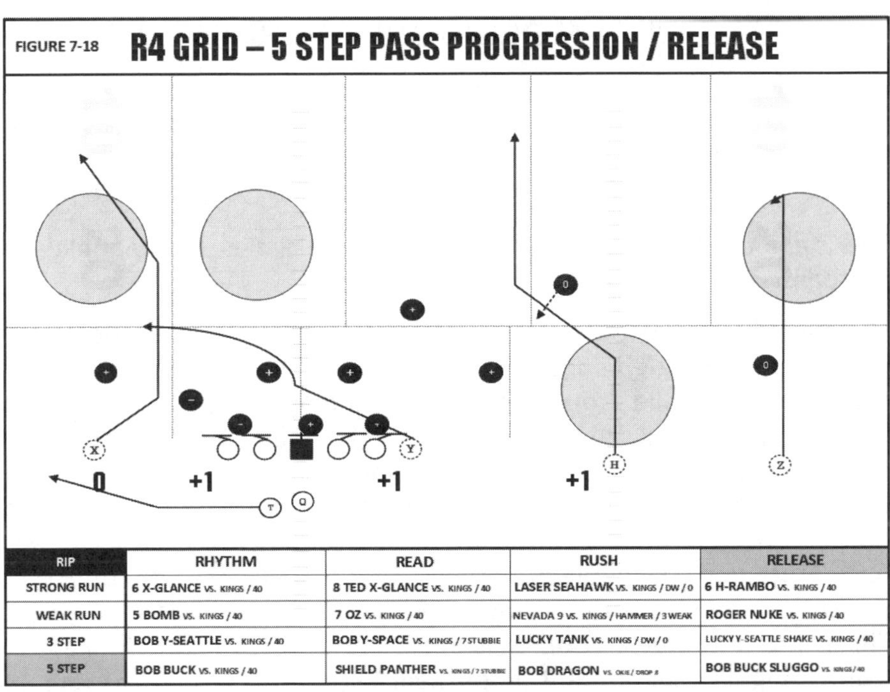

RIP	RHYTHM	READ	RUSH	RELEASE
STRONG RUN	6 X-GLANCE VS. KINGS / 40	8 TED X-GLANCE VS. KINGS / 40	LASER SEAHAWK VS. KINGS / DW / 0	6 H-RAMBO VS. KINGS / 40
WEAK RUN	5 BOMB VS. KINGS / 40	7 OZ VS. KINGS / 40	NEVADA 9 VS. KINGS / HAMMER / 3 WEAK	ROGER NUKE VS. KINGS / 40
3 STEP	BOB Y-SEATTLE VS. KINGS / 40	BOB Y-SPACE VS. KINGS / 7 STUBBIE	LUCKY TANK VS. KINGS / DW / 0	LUCKY Y-SEATTLE SHAKE VS. KINGS / 40
5 STEP	BOB BUCK VS. KINGS / 40	SHIELD PANTHER VS. KINGS / 7 STUBBIE	BOB DRAGON VS. OKIE / DROP 8	BOB BUCK SLUGGO VS. KINGS / 40

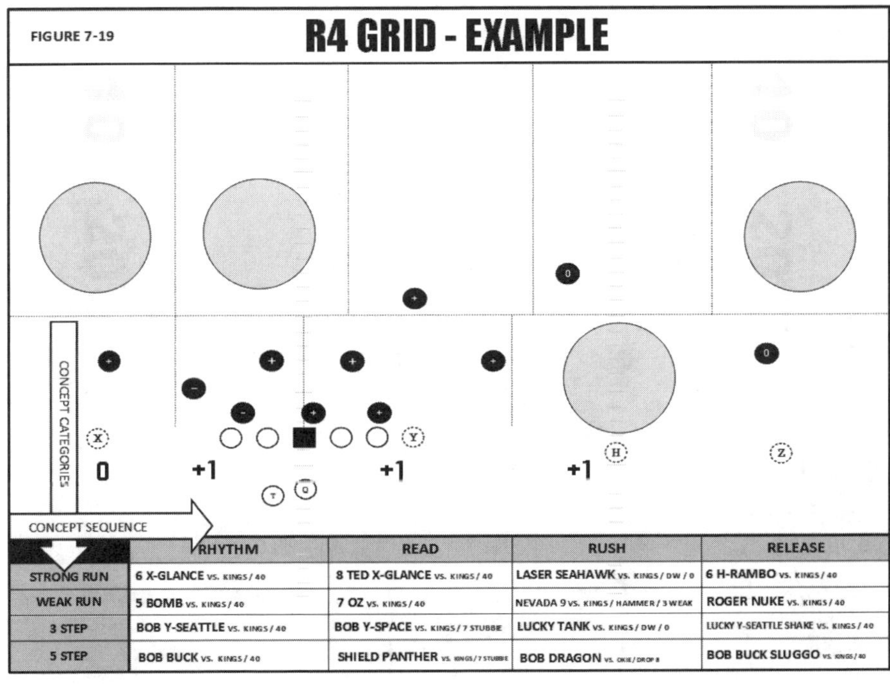

	RHYTHM	READ	RUSH	RELEASE
STRONG RUN	6 X-GLANCE VS. KINGS / 40	8 TED X-GLANCE VS. KINGS / 40	LASER SEAHAWK VS. KINGS / DW / 0	6 H-RAMBO VS. KINGS / 40
WEAK RUN	5 BOMB VS. KINGS / 40	7 OZ VS. KINGS / 40	NEVADA 9 VS. KINGS / HAMMER / 3 WEAK	ROGER NUKE VS. KINGS / 40
3 STEP	BOB Y-SEATTLE VS. KINGS / 40	BOB Y-SPACE VS. KINGS / 7 STUBBIE	LUCKY TANK VS. KINGS / DW / 0	LUCKY Y-SEATTLE SHAKE VS. KINGS / 40
5 STEP	BOB BUCK VS. KINGS / 40	SHIELD PANTHER VS. KINGS / 7 STUBBIE	BOB DRAGON VS. OKIE / DROP 8	BOB BUCK SLUGGO VS. KINGS / 40

NETWORKING THE R4 GRID

> *Your network is your net worth.*

This is a famous quote often heard in business circles. It also applies in football.

The best offenses in football are built around a base play. The base play is supported through constraint plays that protect it. This is nothing revolutionary. While sequencing constraint plays around a base play is effective and sound, it does not provide the coach with the ability to navigate the best play-call within the variability that occurs within a game. A coach's highest need is a formational network of base plays that are interconnected into a whole with the constraints included. Furthermore, a coach needs a process that reveals the symbiotic relationships between various concept categories and their sequences. This is the only way an offense can survive in the uncontrollable and ever-changing environment of football.

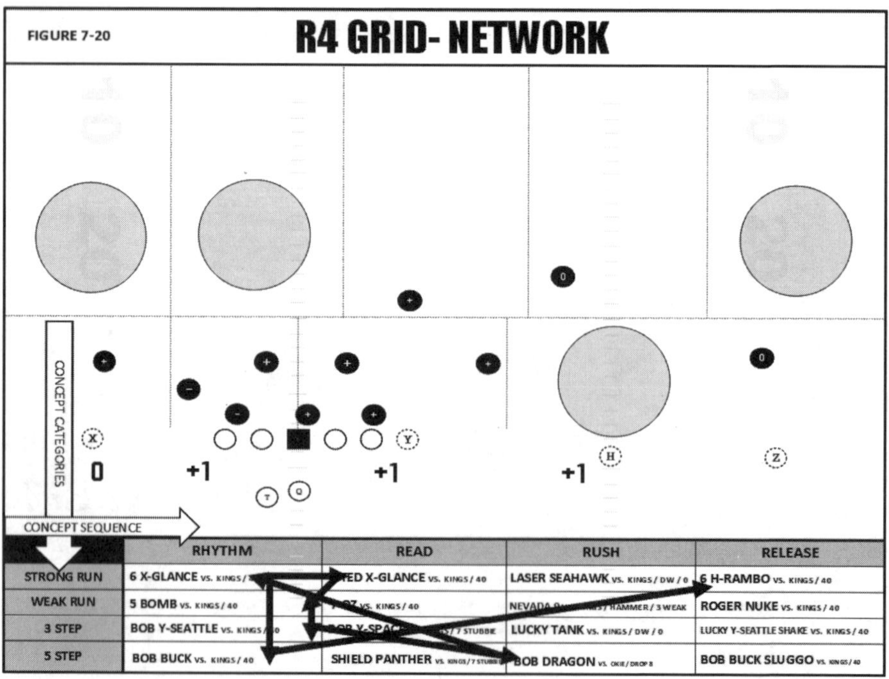

The R4 formational grid provides this solution. It provides the coach with the ability to operate within the reality of the game. (FIG. 7-20)

The R4 grid builds the framework that allows coaches and players to become the main character in their *Choose Your Own Adventure* story. A coach is now empowered with the versatility to make better decisions when the defense adapts. The grid provides more freedom to move in and out of categories and sequences without getting lost. Furthermore, a coach can explain and understand the "why" behind each move to the next "best" play-call.

The categories of Strong Run, Weak Run, 3-step and 5-step provide the most common methods of attack within any offense. These core categories are still in place even if some offenses or formations may not have concepts to occupy them. Likewise, The R4 progression platforms Of Rhythm, Read, Rush and Release provide the IF/THEN reasoning responses to the most common CAP action by the defense. This sequencing is still in place even if some game-plans or formations do not possess a concept to occupy them.

It is important to note that most R4 formational grids may not contain a play for every sequence and category available. The 16-box framework establishes guardrails to keep a game plan operational with the frequency and time limits of a game. We will discuss this more in detail later. The goal of this chapter is to show how an entire R4 grid can be game-planned and played out if, in fact, the coach deemed it necessary.

CHAPTER 8

STRING THEORY & SECTIONS

R4 Play-Call Sheet

STRING THEORY & SECTIONS

R4 Play-Call Sheet

We previously covered how to game-plan an R4 grid within a single formation and personnel group. However, it is very rare to play an entire game in one formation. Additionally, many offensive game-plans will consist of plays that use different personnel. The next step in the game-planning process is to learn how to take multiple formational grids with different personnel to network a play-call sheet.

Science can reveal some parallels to help learn how to organize a multi-formational and personnel play-call sheet. Advancements in technology have allowed scientists to discover particles that were once unseen. They are called strong nuclear force and weak nuclear force. These interactions did not play by the rules of the old school laws of physics. The old law of physics was focused on the seen interactions of gravity and electromagnetism. The seen measurable forces were founded by Galileo and Isaac Newton.

String theory is modern idea in physics that was proposed as an attempt to model the four known fundamental interactions between seen and unseen forces. In nutshell, this theory explained how the forces of gravity, electromagnetism, strong nuclear force, and weak nuclear force operate within a network. This theory was sought to end the conflict between the classical absolute certainties of the measurable world of physics with the probabilities of the uncertain and unseen world of quantum physics.

This is precisely where we are at in the modern game of football with game-planning and play-calling. As a result, the R4 String Theory was developed. The R4 String Theory is a set of attempts to model the measurable situations of a game with the often unseen reactions during a play into one theory. This theory tries to resolve the conflict between classical down and distance game-planning and accelerator-driven game-planning.

Just as Isaac Newton and Galileo set the foundation of physics for our natural world, so did Vince Lombardi, Bill Walsh, and many more, who established the foundation of game-planning and play-calling for the coaching world. And just as Gravity and laws of motion are absolute and consistent in the natural world, so is Down, Distance, and Field Zone in the football world.

The problem is that most coaches are still game-planning and play-calling based on down, distance, and field zone measurables. There is nothing wrong with this method. However, the ability to read the reality and make the right play-calls and adjustments to what is actually happening on the field is often missed. Instead, coaches are calling a game based on static Xs and Os that are seen from paper.

R4 goes deeper into a quantum/DNA unseen level by looking through the lens of the HALO and the CAP accelerators. Even though the HALO and CAP accelerators are speculative and probable, they work in synergy with the down, distance, and field zone situations to accelerate better play-call decision-making.

This synergistic relationship between the seen and unseen world is built, connected, and maintained through the R4 grid and play-call sheet. Before a play-call sheet can be built, the coach must understand the R4 string theory in a more specific way. The R4 string theory is defined as a set of 2 – 4 plays that interact with each other based on defensive CAP actions. It takes a minimum of 2 plays that complement each other to make a string.

Nonetheless, running a base play to set up 1 or 2 complementary plays is nothing new. It's the ability to connect multiple plays and formations together in a quick mental sequence based on anticipated defender movements that makes a great play-caller. These play sequences are called strings. The more we understand the R4 grid and play-call sheet, the more strings we can process and the more accelerated our play-network and game-plan become.

There are two R4 String types. The first one is called a Closed Loop String. A closed loop is a string of 4 plays that are linked together in a Rhythm, Read, Rush, Release sequence, or a Strong Run, Weak Run, 3-Step and 5-step sequence.

Here is one grid example of a Closed Loop String. (FIG. 8-1)

There is a Rhythm, Read, Rush, and Release play filled in for the Strong Run row. This would be a closed loop "IF/THEN" string sequence of play-calling that can stand alone in a game.

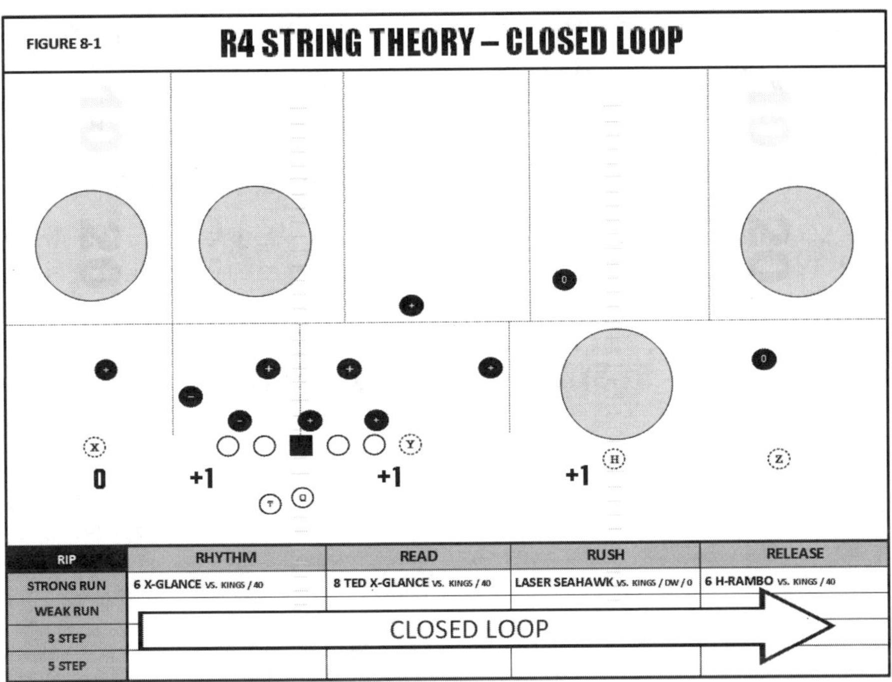
FIGURE 8-1
R4 STRING THEORY – CLOSED LOOP
X
Y
H
Z
T
Q
0
+1
+1
+1
RIP
RHYTHM
READ
RUSH
RELEASE
STRONG RUN
6 X-GLANCE VS. KINGS / 40
8 TED X-GLANCE VS. KINGS / 40
LASER SEAHAWK VS. KINGS / DW / 0
6 H-RAMBO VS. KINGS / 40
WEAK RUN
3 STEP
5 STEP
CLOSED LOOP

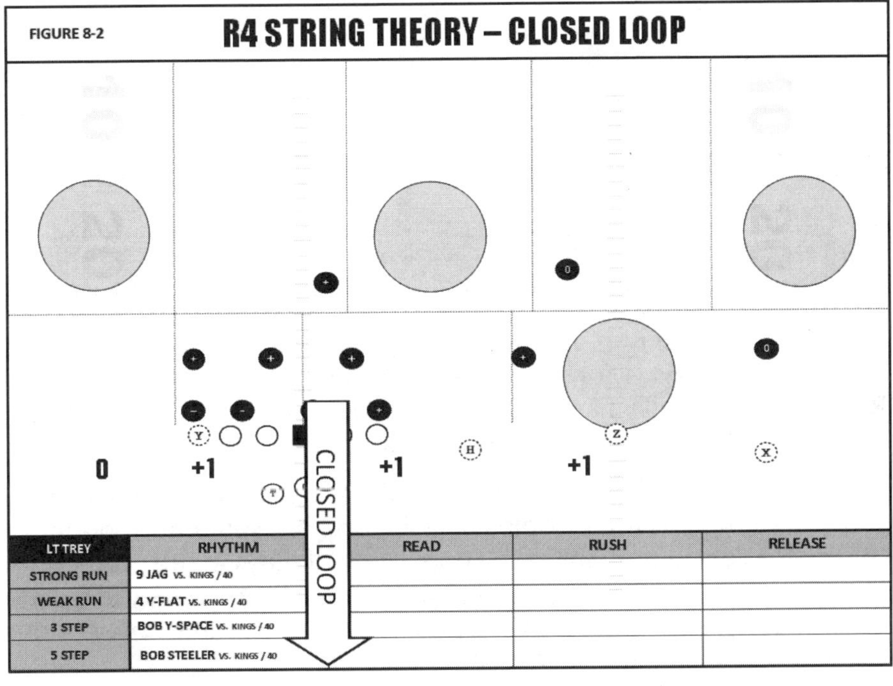
FIGURE 8-2
R4 STRING THEORY – CLOSED LOOP
Y
H
Z
X
T
0
+1
+1
+1
LT TREY
RHYTHM
READ
RUSH
RELEASE
STRONG RUN
9 JAG VS. KINGS / 40
WEAK RUN
4 Y-FLAT VS. KINGS / 40
3 STEP
BOB Y-SPACE VS. KINGS / 40
5 STEP
BOB STEELER VS. KINGS / 40
CLOSED LOOP

Here is another example of a Closed Loop String of plays out of a different formation. (FIG. 8-2)

In this formational grid, there is a Strong Run, Weak Run, 3-step and 5-step play filled in the Rhythm column. This is also considered a closed loop "IF/THEN" string sequence of play-calling that can stand alone in a game.

The second-string type is an Open Loop String. An open loop is a string of 2-3 plays that are linked together in any category or sequence. Here is one example of an Open Loop String. (FIG. 8-3)

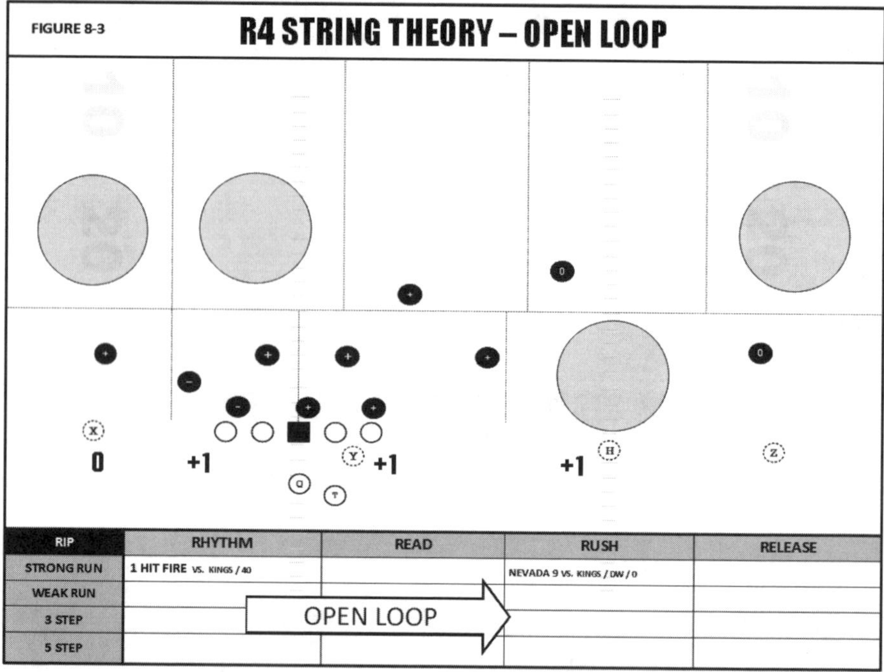

There is a Rhythm Run play and a Rush play-action play in the Strong Run category. This is considered an open loop because there is not a Read or Release play filled in to allow it to stand alone in a game. Here is another example of an Open Loop String. (FIG. 8-4)

There is a Strong and Weak Run along with a 3-step pass in the Rhythm sequence. There is no 5-step pass in the Rhythm sequence, therefore this is also considered an Open Loop String of plays in the grid. The goal of game-planning is not to attempt to fill in every grid for the sake of doing so. It's to fill in the grid to the best of the ability of our personnel and concepts allow against an opponent.

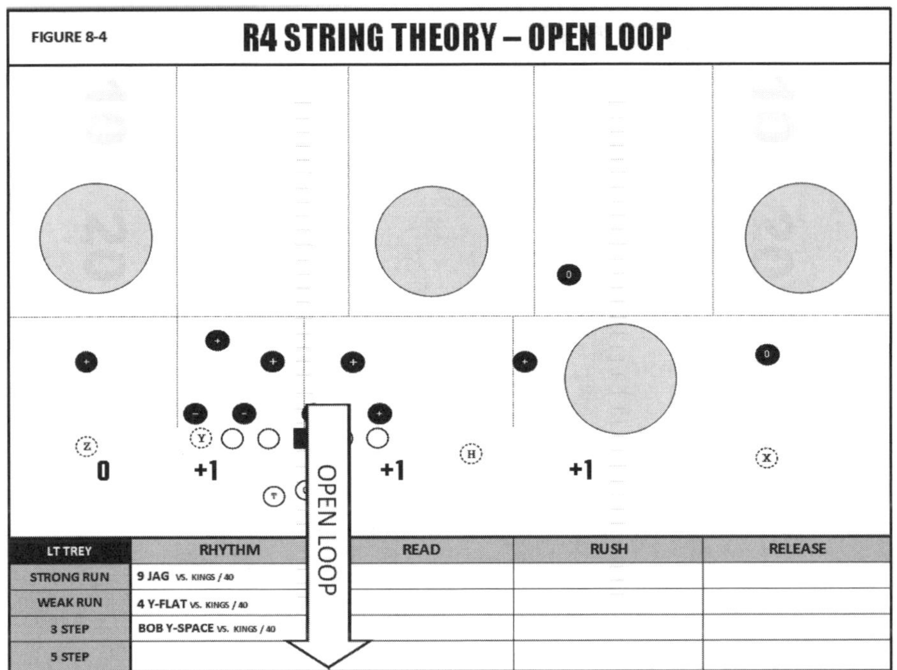

FIGURE 8-4 **R4 STRING THEORY – OPEN LOOP**

LT TREY	RHYTHM	READ	RUSH	RELEASE
STRONG RUN	9 JAG vs. KINGS / 40			
WEAK RUN	4 Y-FLAT vs. KINGS / 40			
3 STEP	BOB Y-SPACE vs. KINGS / 40			
5 STEP				

BUILDING THE R4 PLAY-CALL SHEET

The first step in constructing the R4 play-call sheet is determining which personnel and formational grids are best suited to attack a defensive opponent. Some formational grids will have more plays filled in than others. Other formational grids may only have a few plays out of different personnel. A coach needs infrastructure and workflow to help determine the placement and validity of each grid.

The R4 play-call sheet is segmented to help facilitate this process. (FIG. 8-5)

The play-call sheet is set up in 3 columns. This is to orient the play-caller into a position as if viewing the playing field. The columns are structured left to right. The first column to the left represents a field position placement on the left hash. The middle column represents a field position placement on the middle of the field. The right column represents a field position placement on the right hash. The horizontal field position placement is critical in determining what formations and plays work best from these relative locations. Most plays are hash dominant in high school and college. Therefore, those grids are going

FIG. 8-5

R4 PLAY CALL SHEET – HASH COLUMNS

VICTORY CHRISITAN	WEEK 1 -	VS. OPPONENT
LEFT HASH COLUMN	MIDDLE OF FIELD COLUMN	RIGHT HASH COLUMN

FIGURE 8-6

R4 PLAY CALL SHEET – GRID SECTIONS

VICTORY CHRISITAN	WEEK 1 -	VS. OPPONENT
	RHYTHM GRIDS	
	READ GRIDS	
	RUSH GRIDS	
	RELEASE GRIDS	

to be more complete. The middle of the field grids will usually have minimal plays filled in.

The play-call sheet is next divided into four rows. (FIG. 8-6)

These rows organize grids based on specific properties. The location of grids is critical to the setup and understanding of the R4 play sheet. Formational grids placed in the 1st segment row are called Rhythm Grid Sections. Formational Grids in the 2nd segment row are called Read Grids Sections. Formational Grids in the 3rd row are called Rush Grids Sections. Formational Grids in the 4th row are called Release Grids Sections.

RHYTHM GRID SECTION

Let's take a closer look at the properties that position a formational grid in a Rhythm Grid Section. Rhythm Grid Sections contain the following:

1. They have a minimum of 10 out of 16 concept boxes filled in
2. They have a minimum of 2 Closed Loop strings in the grid
3. They use the best offensive personnel

This is an example of the grid that was game-planned in the previous chapters. (FIG. 8-7)

This grid is classified as a Rhythm grid because it contains 2 Closed Loop Strings of plays. It also has a minimum of 10 play boxes filled in and uses our best personnel for the season. This grid would not be placed in the Rhythm grid section if one or more of these criteria is missing.

The primary goal of game-planning is to determine the best personnel and formations to attack an opponent. The Rhythm grid section places the best formational grids at the top of the play-call sheet to highlight this priority. Most play-calls in a game will come from the Rhythm grid sections if a coaching staff has game-planned effectively.

Each section of the play-call sheet can hold up to four game-planned formational grids. (FIG. 8-8)

Over game-planning occurs when a staff has created more than four grids that contain Rhythm properties. There are not enough plays in a game to set up and sequence the plays when this overage occurs. The staff should rank the top four Rhythm formations and place them in the Rhythm grid section on the play-call sheet.

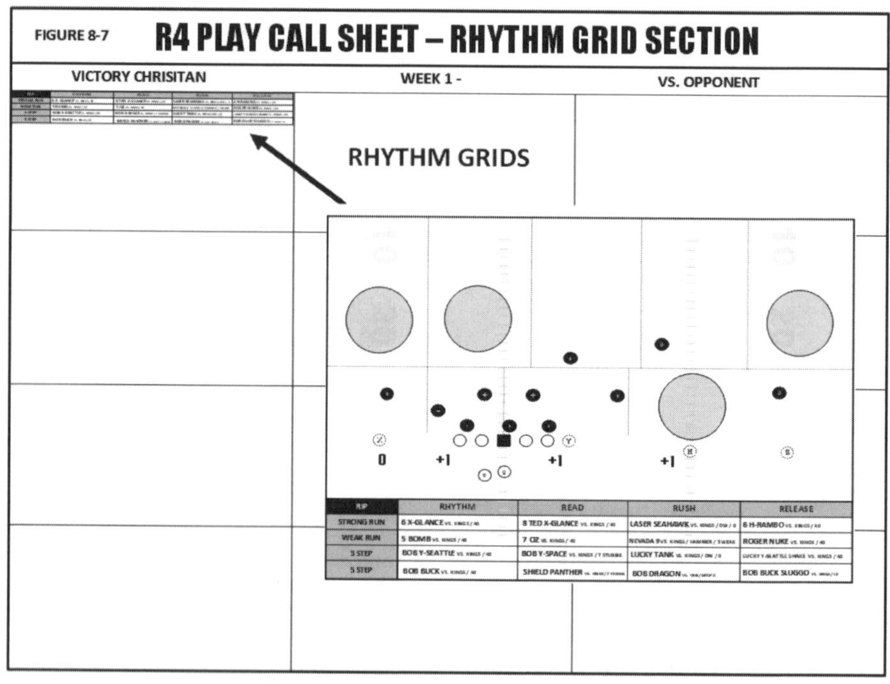
FIGURE 8-7
R4 PLAY CALL SHEET – RHYTHM GRID SECTION
VICTORY CHRISITAN
WEEK 1 -
VS. OPPONENT
RHYTHM GRIDS
0
+1
+1
+1
RIP
RHYTHM
READ
RUSH
RELEASE
STRONG RUN
WEAK RUN
5 STEP
5 STEP
6 X-GLANCE
8 TED X-GLANCE
LASER SEAHAWK
6 H-RAMBO
5 BOMB
7 OZ
NEVADA 9
ROGER NUKE
BOB Y-SEATTLE
BOB Y-SPACE
LUCKY TANK
BOB BUCK
SHIELD PANTHER
BOB DRAGON
BOB BUCK SLUGGO

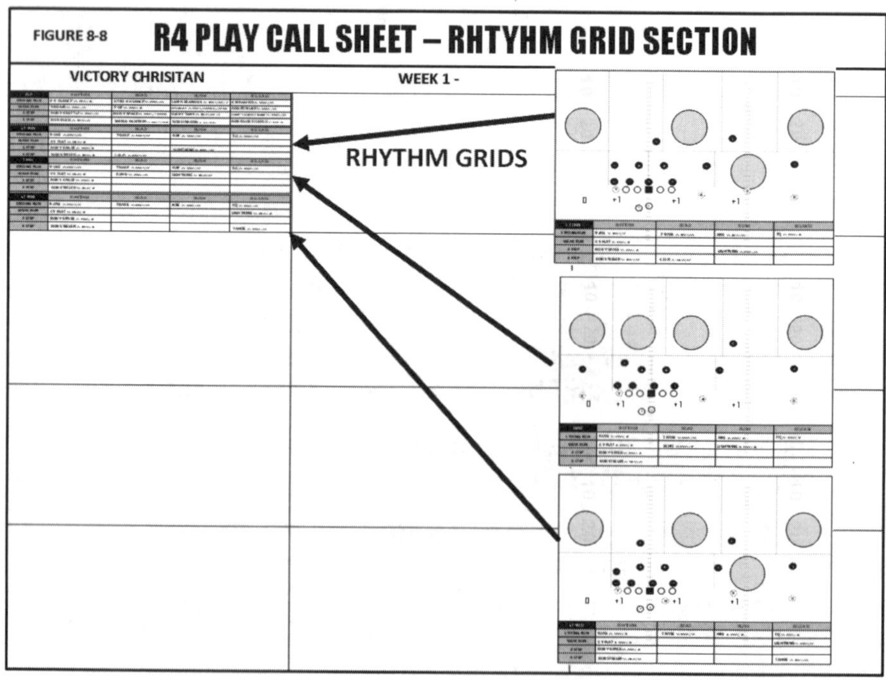
FIGURE 8-8
R4 PLAY CALL SHEET – RHTYHM GRID SECTION
VICTORY CHRISITAN
WEEK 1 -
RHYTHM GRIDS

READ GRID SECTION

Next, let's look at what places a formational grid in a Read grid section.

Read grids contain the following:

1. They have a range of 2 to 8 boxes filled in
2. They have a minimum of 1 Open Loop Strings in the grid
3. They use secondary personnel

This is an example of a Read grid. (FIG. 8-9)

This grid falls within the range of 2-8 plays. There are 4 plays filled in here. It contains 2 Open Loop Strings and uses a secondary 12 Personnel grouping for offensive formation. This grid would not be placed in the Read grid section if one or more of these criteria is missing.

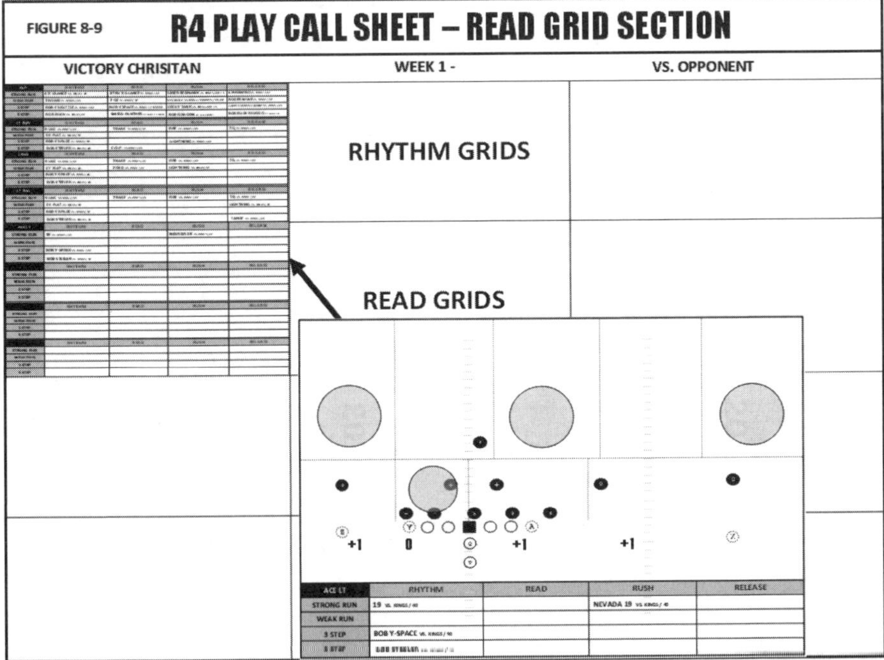

The Read grid section provides a position on the play-call sheet for personnel, formations, or concepts that may not be a part of the base offense. They can also provide a grid location for teams that use a multi-personnel offense. Some teams that only use one personnel and a few formations may not have any Read grids. No grids would be filled in here if this is the case. The Read grid section is available if a team needs space on the play sheet for them.

RUSH GRID SECTION

Next, let's look at what places a formational grid in the Rush grid section. Rush grids contain the following:

1. They have a range of 2 to 8 boxes filled in
2. They have a minimum of 1 Closed Loop String
3. They contain concepts that are used primarily for specific game situations. Some examples would be Blitz downs, 3rd downs, Red Zone and Goal line or short yardage situations.

This is an example of a Rush grid. (FIG. 8-10)

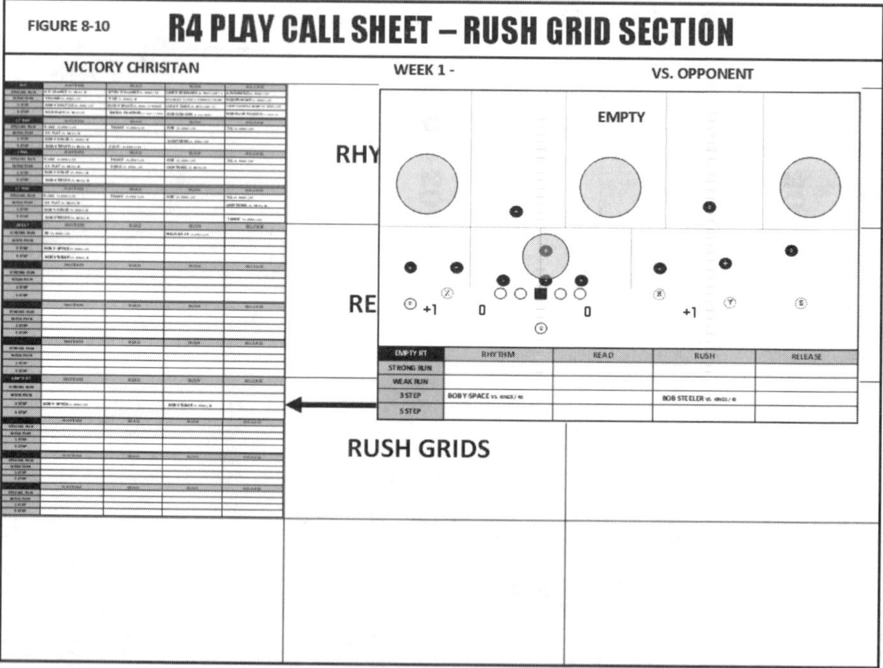

This grid is in the range of 2-8 plays with 2 total plays filled in on the grid. It also contains 1 Closed Loop String that is found in the 3-step Pass Play row. These plays are also contained and called out of a formation that is used primarily for Blitz and Red Zone downs. This grid would not be placed in the Rush grid section if one or more of these criteria is missing.

The Rush grid section provides a placement for grids that contain personnel, formations, and plays that are used specifically for pressure situations. Many offenses will adjust away from their base offense in these situations. (FIG. 8-11)

For example, in a goal line situation, an offensive staff may want to run a 22 Personnel double tight end formation. This personnel and formation may differ from a team's base offense. Therefore, only a few plays are required to address this situation.

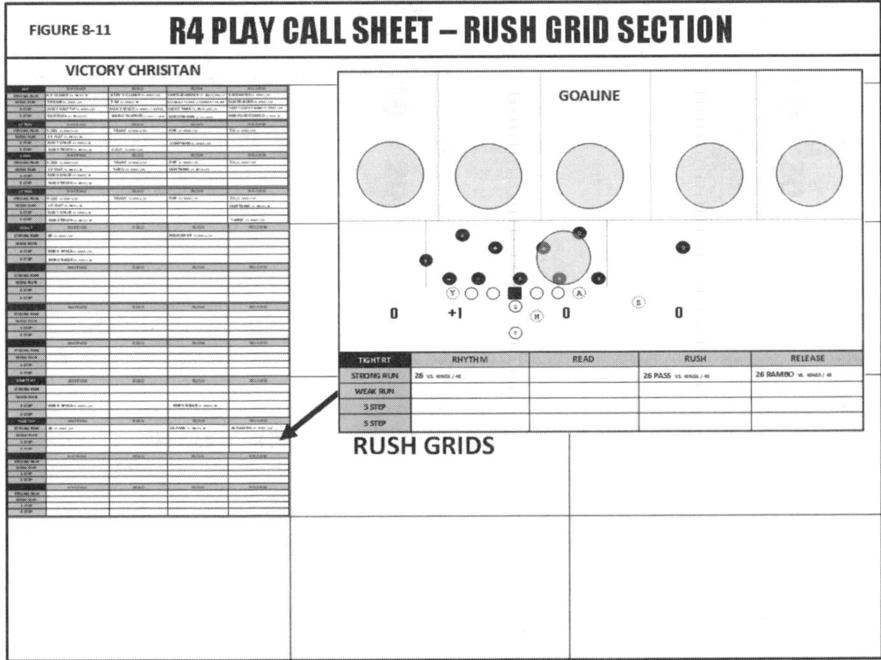

RELEASE GRID SECTION

Finally, let's look at what places a play in the Release Grid. (FIG. 8-12)

Release grids are situational grids that contain the following:

1. They have formations and plays for specific in-game situations
2. They are not bound by strings
3. They can be plays that are pulled from other grids so you can locate them for a specific situation in-game faster.
4. They use formations and plays that may not be in your base offense. These could be game-planned concepts, tweaks, and adjustments for a specific opponent.

FIGURE 8-12

R4 PLAY CALL SHEET – RELEAS GRID SECTION

VICTORY CHRISITAN	WEEK 1 -	VS. OPPONENT
	RHYTHM GRIDS	
	READ GRIDS	
	RUSH GRIDS	
	RELEASE GRIDS	

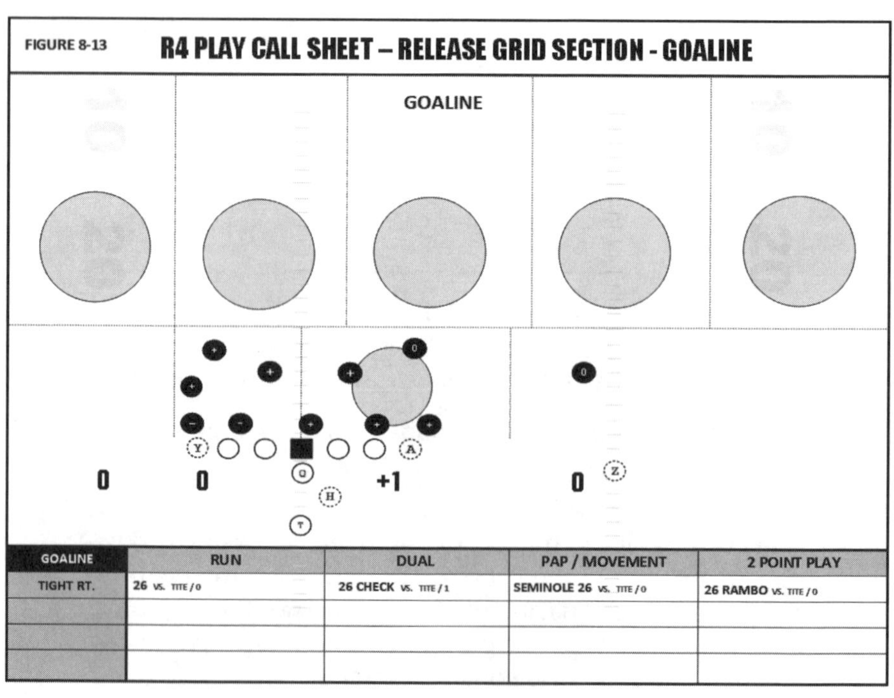

FIGURE 8-13

R4 PLAY CALL SHEET – RELEASE GRID SECTION - GOALINE

GOALINE	RUN	DUAL	PAP / MOVEMENT	2 POINT PLAY
TIGHT RT.	26 VS. TITE / 0	26 CHECK VS. TITE / 1	SEMINOLE 26 VS. TITE / 0	26 RAMBO VS. TITE / 0

It is important to note that one purpose of the Release grids is to help a coach isolate situations where game pressure will be the greatest. Release grids will more than likely contain many plays that have already been game-planned in the Rhythm, Read, and Rush grids. However, having those situations located in a specific section helps accelerate a coach's ability to locate the play under pressure. In addition, many of the situational game-pressure plays require calls that may be outside the base offense. Therefore, a coach may be less likely to remember the call when that situation arises.

If a Rhythm, Read, or Rush grid sections do not contain the best play for a situation, then a coach will scheme a play and locate it in the Release grid.

The Release grid section is set up a bit differently than the Rhythm, Read, and Rush grid sections. We break down the 4 release grids by the 4 most common situations in football. Goal line, Red Zone, 2-minute/last plays of the game, and 3rd downs.

RELEASE GRID SECTION – GOAL LINE

Goal line is the first grid in the Release grid section. (FIG. 8-13)

The Goal line grid is separated into 4 play sequence. The first play in the sequence is Run. This box contains the best runs that have been schemed based on the anticipated goal line CAP of the defensive opponent. This formation and plays were already game-planned in the Rush grid section of the play-call sheet. Therefore, we copy those plays in again here. (FIG. 8-14)

The next sequence is the best dual-call. A check-with-me play is scripted here. The next sequence is a play action or movement play-call. There is a power pass play in the Rush grid section that was copied here. The final sequence is the best two-point plays. A reverse play is scripted here.

RELEASE GRID SECTION – RED ZONE

Red Zone is the next grid in the Release grid section. In this game-plan, a 20 Personnel Pro formation was used for the Red Zone. This formation was game-planned only for this situation. (FIG. 8-15)

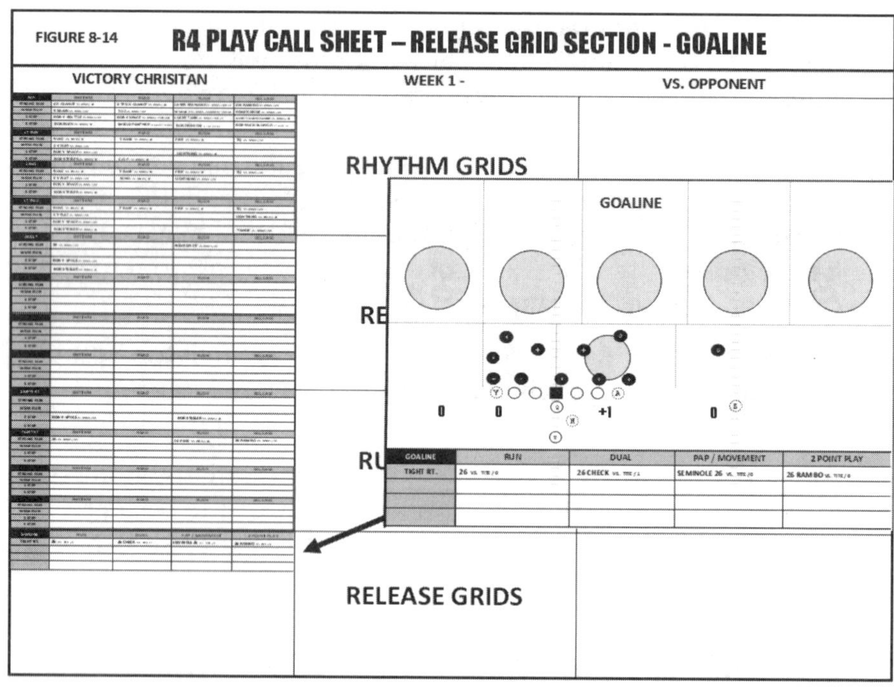
FIGURE 8-14
R4 PLAY CALL SHEET – RELEASE GRID SECTION - GOALINE
VICTORY CHRISITAN
WEEK 1 -
VS. OPPONENT
RHYTHM GRIDS
GOALINE
RELEASE GRIDS
GOALINE
RUN
DUAL
PAP / MOVEMENT
2 POINT PLAY
TIGHT RT.
26
26 CHECK
SEMINOLE 26
26 RAMBO

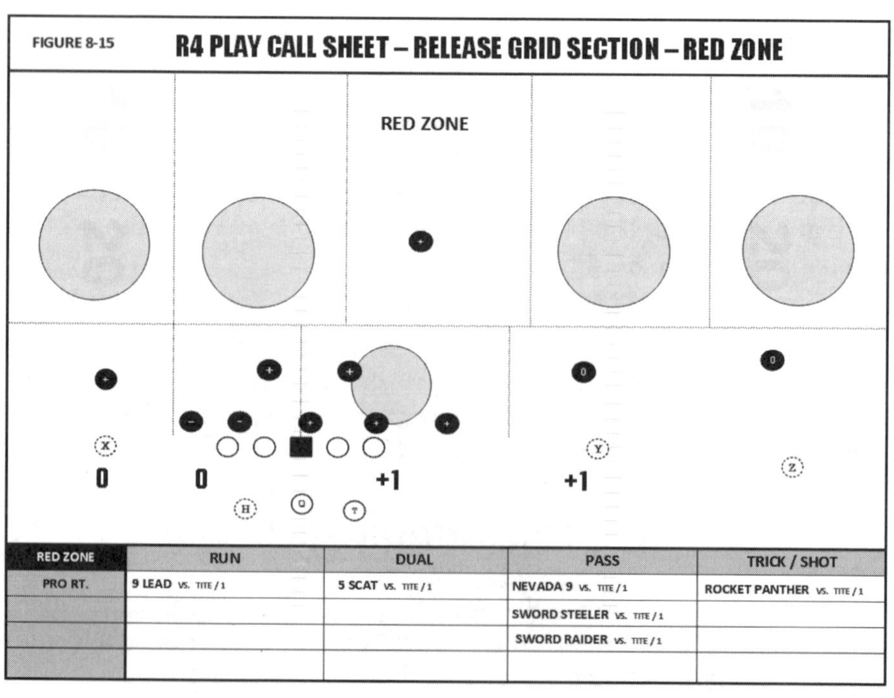
FIGURE 8-15
R4 PLAY CALL SHEET – RELEASE GRID SECTION – RED ZONE
RED ZONE
0
0
+1
+1
RED ZONE
RUN
DUAL
PASS
TRICK / SHOT
PRO RT.
9 LEAD vs. TITE / 1
5 SCAT vs. TITE / 1
NEVADA 9 vs. TITE / 1
ROCKET PANTHER vs. TITE / 1
SWORD STEELER vs. TITE / 1
SWORD RAIDER vs. TITE / 1

The Red Zone grid is separated into a 4-play sequence. The first play in the sequence is Run. This box contains the best runs that have been schemed based on the anticipated Red Zone CAP of the defensive opponent. An outside zone lead play was scripted here. The next sequence is the best dual-call. An R.P.O. concept was scripted here. The next sequence the best Red Zone pass play-call. There were three pass concepts scripted here. The last sequence is the best trick or shot play-call. A post-wheel concept was scripted here. (FIG. 8-16)

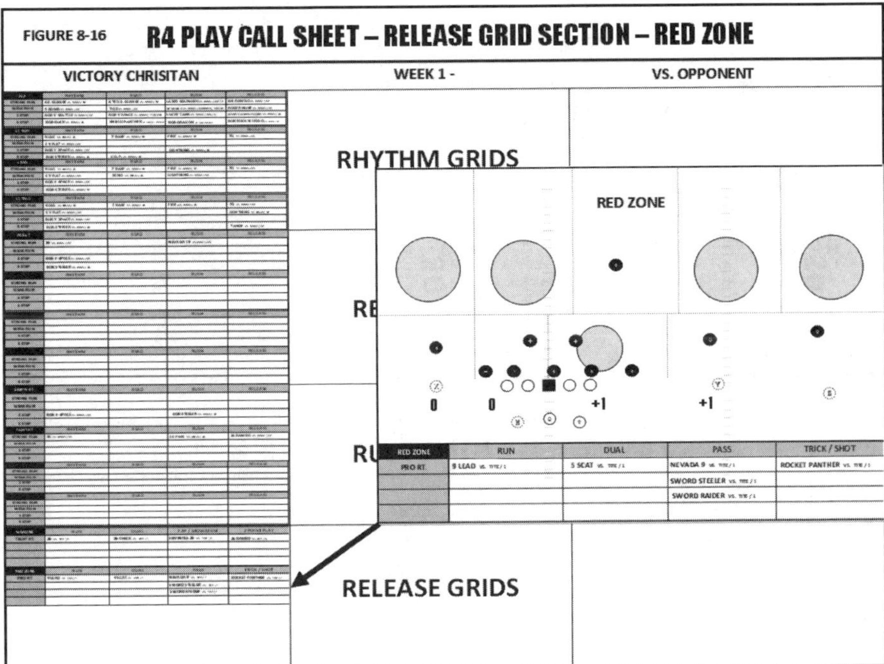

RELEASE GRID SECTION – 2 MINUTE OFFENSE

A 2-minute situation is the next grid in the Release section. The 2-minute section is separated into the same sequence as the Red Zone grid. This sequence will consist of the best runs, dual-calls, passes, and shot plays that answer the time deficient environment of 2-minute situations. (FIG. 8-17)

It is critical to reiterate that the plays a coach may script in the Release situational grid sections may be a formation, motion, or personnel tweak that doesn't fit in anywhere else on your play sheet. Some of-

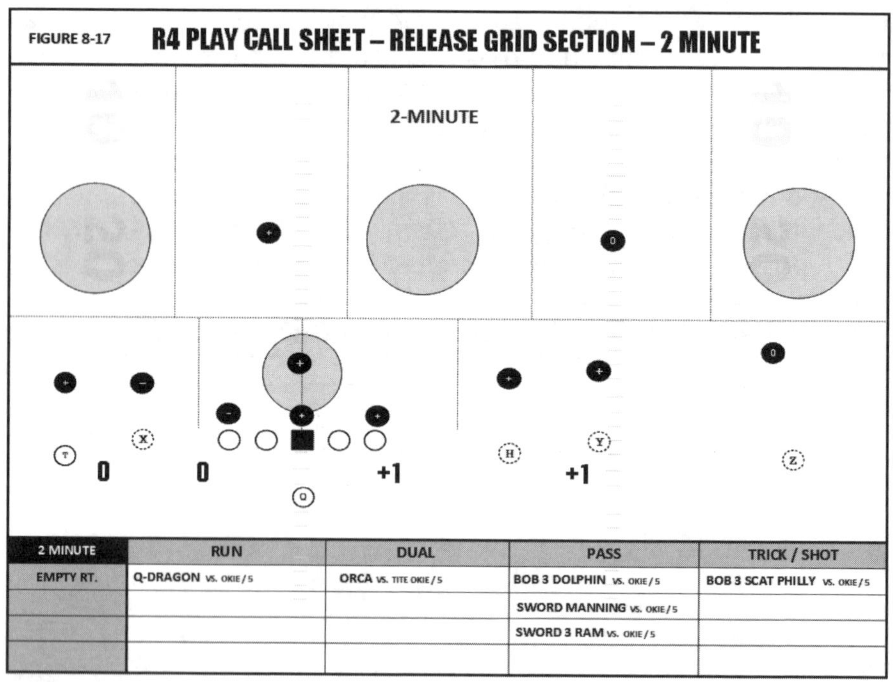

2 MINUTE	RUN	DUAL	PASS	TRICK / SHOT
EMPTY RT.	Q-DRAGON vs. OKIE / 5	ORCA vs. TITE OKIE / 5	BOB 3 DOLPHIN vs. OKIE / 5	BOB 3 SCAT PHILLY vs. OKIE / 5
			SWORD MANNING vs. OKIE / 5	
			SWORD 3 RAM vs. OKIE / 5	

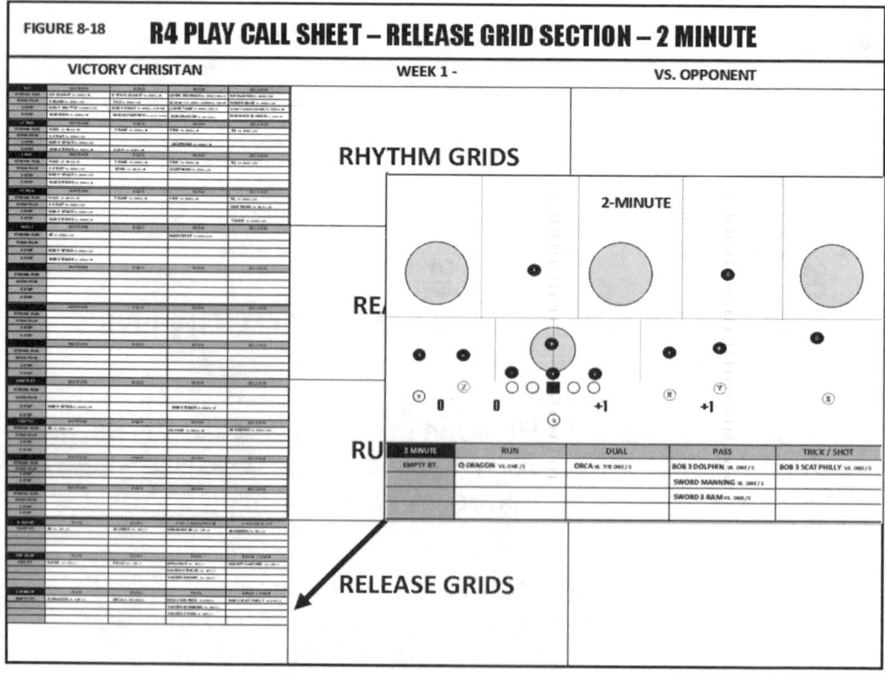

fenses operate strictly at 2-minute tempo and therefore may not need a 2-minute situational grid filled in. However, it is necessary to include concepts here that attack 2-minute defensive actions like prevent-defense or man-under-halves coverage. Another thing to script here is concepts to be used at the end of a half or game and you only have time for 2 or 3 plays. (FIG 8-18)

RELEASE GRID SECTION - 3RD DOWNS

The final situational grid is for 3rd downs. Converting 3rd downs is critical and therefore requires special attention to defensive CAP situations. Defenses will usually change CAP actions on 3rd down. Therefore, 3RD down situational plays are scripted by down and distance here. 3rd down plays may also be repeated plays pulled down from the above grids. This allows a coach to locate the plays faster under pressure.

3rd down is one of the highest priority downs to convert for an offense. Consequently, this grid is set up differently from the other Release grids. (FIG. 8-19)

FIGURE 8-19 **R4 PLAY CALL SHEET – RELEASE GRID SECTION – 3RD DOWNS**

3RD DOWNS

3RD DOWN	3RD & 1-3	3RD & 4-7	3RD & 8-10	3RD & 11+
	TIGHT RT. 26 VS. TITE/0	LEAD OLE VS. OKIE/40	TRIPS BOB GIANT VS. OKIE/5	EMPTY BOB MONEY VS. OKIE/5
	TIGHT RT. SEMINOLE 26 VS. TITE/0	LEAD BOB SPACE VS. OKIE/40	TRIPS SWORD BUCK VS. OKIE/5	
		SHARK BOB RAM VS. OKIE/40	TRIPS SHIELD EAGLE VS. OKIE/5	

There are only 4 columns to sequence for 3rd down plays. They are 3rd and 1-3, 3rd and 4-7, 3rd and 8-10, and 3rd and 11+. A coach will script the best formations and plays that address each down and distance situation accordingly. (FIG. 8-20)

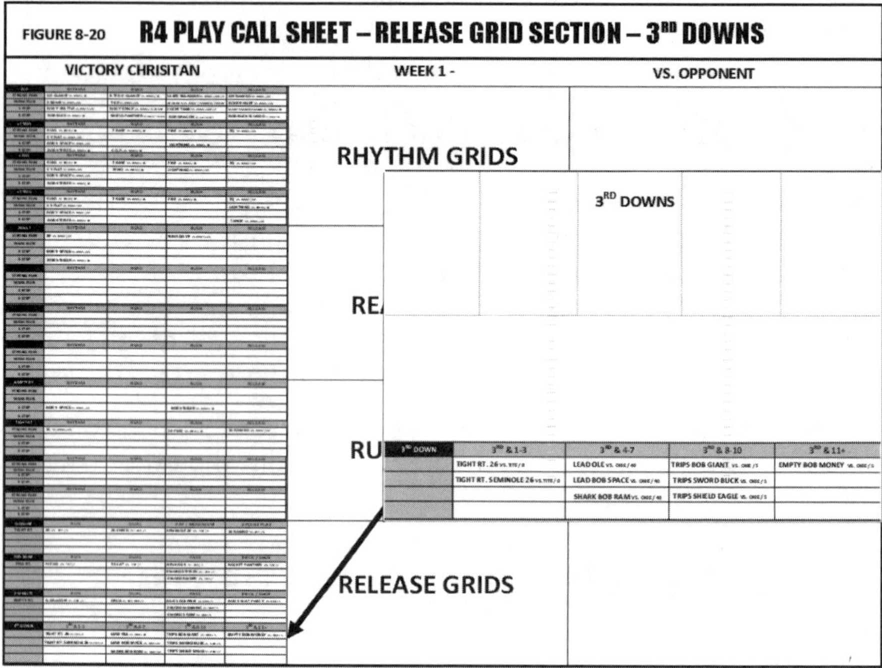

FINALIZING THE R4 PLAY-CALL SHEET

The left hash R4 grid sections are now complete. The right hash columns will mirror the R4 grids from the left hash. (FIG. 8-21)

However, there may be formations or concepts that are better served being run on a specific hash. For example, the ball is on the left hash and a weak-side counter scheme is run into the boundary. The same play may not be as effective when the formation is flipped to the right hash and run into the boundary. Most offenses that flip formations when on a different hash do not move the linemen. If this is true, then the personnel of the linemen pulling on a counter scheme may not have the same advantages on both sides.

These situations would call for different plays to be schemed within formational grids to address the personnel deficiency on that side of

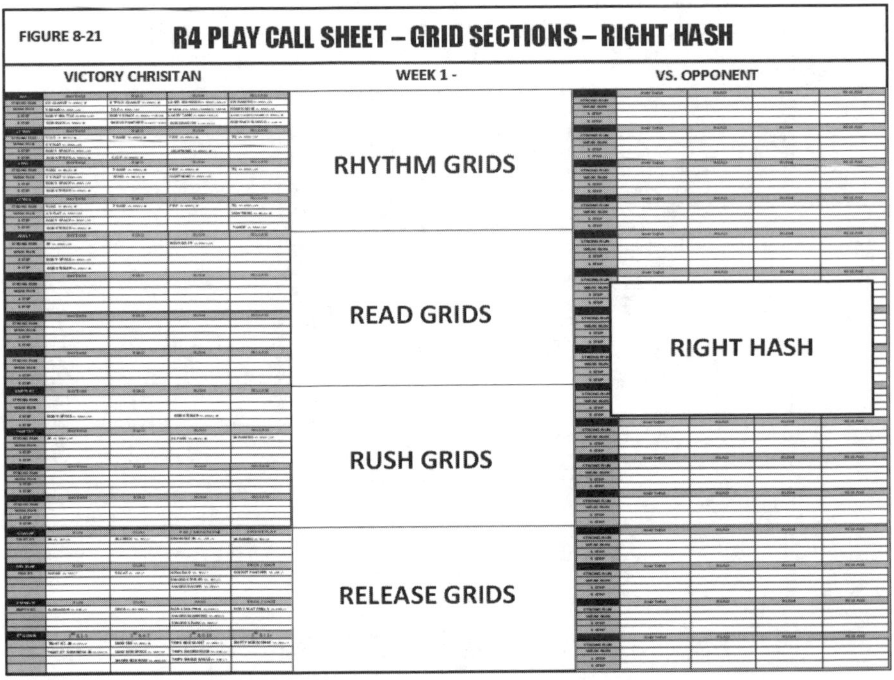

FIGURE 8-21 **R4 PLAY CALL SHEET – GRID SECTIONS – RIGHT HASH**

VICTORY CHRISITAN | WEEK 1 - | VS. OPPONENT

RHYTHM GRIDS

READ GRIDS

RUSH GRIDS

RELEASE GRIDS

RIGHT HASH

space. In some cases, these deficiencies may require an entire formational grid to be dismissed from a hash on the play-call sheet.
The last part of the play-call sheet to be filled out is the Middle-of-the-Field column. (FIG. 8-22)

The middle of the field requires the least amount of game-planning time. The average number of plays that occur in the middle of the field in a high school or college game are 8-12 plays. Most of the game occurs on a hash mark. Therefore, coaches do not need to spend as much time game-planning plays for the middle of the field.

Conversely, the middle-of-the-field position places equal space to each side of a formation. This can work in favor of some formations and concepts. Schemes that take advantage of this equal formational field space have limited opportunities to be called. This is where the middle-of-the-field grids come into play. The formations and concepts that are scripted in the middle-of-the-field grids should be specific. They should only be plays that take advantage of the equal space availability to each side of a formation.

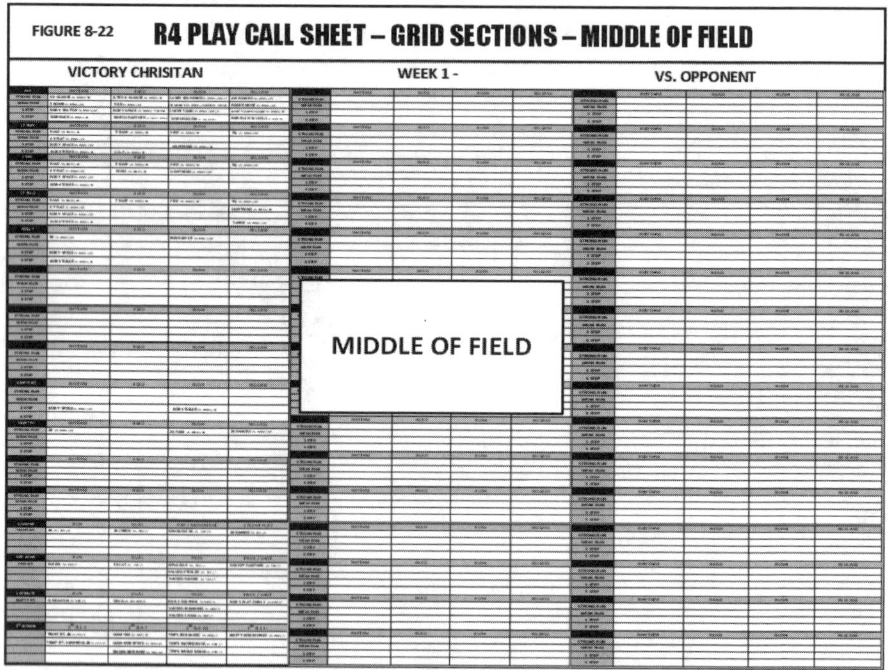

FIGURE 8-22 **R4 PLAY CALL SHEET – GRID SECTIONS – MIDDLE OF FIELD**

This finalizes the layout of the R4 Play-call Sheet. It may look overwhelming. However, If the R4 game-planning process is used correctly, more than 75% of the play-calls will be made from the Rhythm Grid Section.

The R4 system allows formations and plays to be networked and accelerated faster than before. The result is adaptability and versatility through simplicity.

Once the R4 play-call sheet is complete, a coaching staff and players now have the roadmap to navigate play-calls throughout a game. (FIG. 8-23)

ACCELERATOR DRIVEN VS. DOWN AND DISTANCE DRIVEN

Change is hard. Humans are creatures of habit. It may be difficult for coaches who have been using a specific play-call sheet to suddenly change. Acceptance of change usually occurs when the pain of staying the same outweighs the pain of changing. I experienced this in a major way in my first year as an offensive coordinator.

In my first year, we had a veteran group of offensive players returning. We went undefeated through the regular season and set the all-time

FIGURE 8-23

R4 PLAY CALL SHEET - FINALIZATION

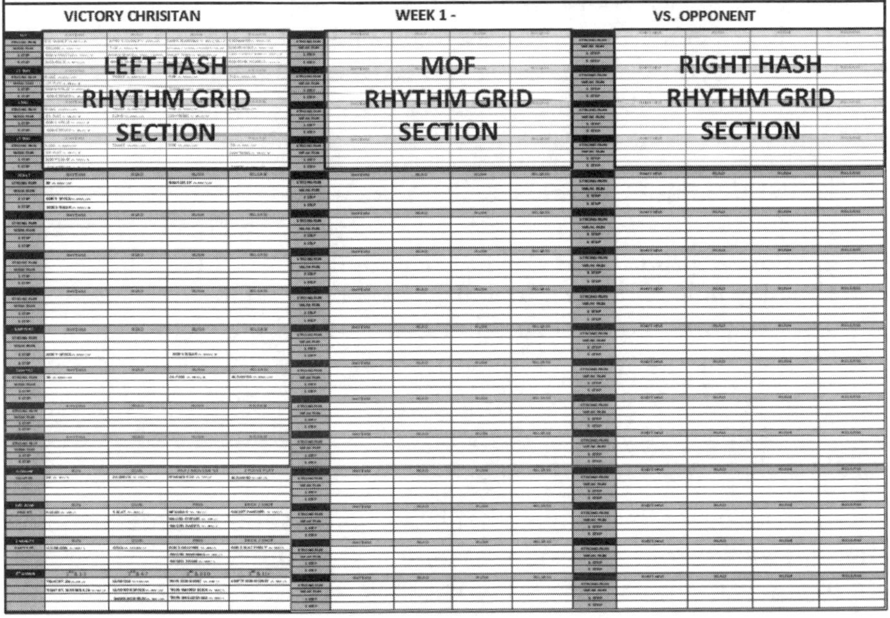

VICTORY CHRISITAN	WEEK 1 -	VS. OPPONENT
LEFT HASH RHYTHM GRID SECTION	MOF RHYTHM GRID SECTION	RIGHT HASH RHYTHM GRID SECTION

state scoring record at 53.4 points per game. I remember thinking that this coordinator job is not as difficult as I thought it was going to be. In the state championship game, we faced our rival who we had previously beaten earlier in the year. We went up quickly and went into half-time with a 21-7 lead. However, in the second half, things changed. After a turnover, some defensive adjustments, and a late 4th quarter trick play by the opponent, we quickly found ourselves behind. There was a minute and 30 seconds on the clock. We were down by 3 points.

That is when everything changed for me. The lights became brighter, the stadium was bigger, and the 25,000 fans were louder. In that moment, the pressure of an undefeated season, state championship, and relationships with an exceptional group of seniors flooded my decision-making ability. I will never forget looking into the eyes of the 11 starters as we huddled on the sideline to go out for one final drive to win it all. All of a sudden, every eye was on me for the answers. I quickly looked down at my play-call sheet and I couldn't find the answers. There were plays on the sheet. There were even ones that were scripted for this 2-minute situation.

The problem was that the play-call sheet wasn't constructed in a way that mirrored the reality of the immediate environment. The play-calls were down and distance-driven instead of accelerator-driven. Furthermore, the play-call sheet didn't provide a language and process that allowed the offensive coaching staff to understand what was going on in my head throughout the game. I desperately needed help in that situation.

I looked at the offensive line coach and asked him what he likes here. I asked our booth coaches what they liked here. The response was silence. I had one good play-call left. The offense went out on the field and the play failed. The remaining six play-calls where in desperation. We lost the game 50-47. I couldn't even get us into field goal range. That game was the most painful loss that I have ever experienced. I didn't sleep all night after that game. I am still not over it. I never wanted to be in that situation again. The R4 game-planning and play-calling system was born from the pain of that loss.

Prior to that event, everything that I had learned about game-planning and play-calling was driven by data, down, and distance. Many programs still use this as their method today. The rise of using data analytics in sports has surged in the last 20 years of sports. The use of big

FIGURE 8-24 **TRADITIONAL GAME PLAN & PLAY CALL SHEET**

Openers	1st and 2nd Down		Base Runs	Base Pass	Coverage Beaters
			Draws	Quicks	
Short Yardage	3rd Medium	3rd and Long	Nickel Runs	Play Action	Blitz
			Screens		
Red Zone	End Zone	+10	2 Minute "O"	Action Pass	Best Player
	3rd Down	Goaline	4 Minute "O"	Backed Up	
	Pressure	2 Point Plays	Last 3 Plays		

data to drive decision-making has been credited to the turnaround of many professional sports organizations. Legendary coach Bill Walsh is credited as one of the innovators in using data to drive game-planning and play-call decision-making. Many game-plans and play-call sheets follow his model of organization. (FIG. 8-24)

This is an example of a West Coast offensive play-call sheet. It is segmented into many different categories:

- **Openers**
- **1st and 2nd down plays (some sheets have 2nd and medium / 2nd and long sections**
- **Short Yardage**
- **Red Zone**
- **3rd Down & Short, 3rd Down & Medium, 3rd Down & Long**
- **Pressure plays**
- **+10 and in plays**
- **Goal line plays**
- **2 Point Plays**
- **Base Runs**
- **Base Passes**
- **Draws**
- **Nickel Runs**
- **Screens**
- **2-Minute Offense**
- **4-Minute Offense**
- **Last 3 Plays**
- **Quick Game**
- **Play Action Passes**
- **Action Passes**
- **Backed Up play**
- **Specific Coverage Beaters**
- **Blitz plays**
- **Best Player plays**

Most game-planning and play-call sheets are situationally driven by down and distance decision-making. Down and distance data can reveal key tendencies of a defense. This can better inform the offensive coordinator's best play-call. However, basing an offensive game-plan and play-call solely on situational data ignores the 3 key elements that erode data-driven decision-making.

1. Risk
2. Uncertainty
3. Multiple Variables

This three-headed monster caused the financial crises in 2008 and why the biggest banks in the world failed. The banks couldn't calculate the risk because they were operating from an excel sheet of data that ignored the real-world of uncertainty. There is no way to calculate all the alternatives or effects of a decision. The risks are very hard to estimate because the real-world environment is full of dynamic domino effects that cannot always be predicted. Similarly, the myriad of variables that occur in the game of football makes it difficult to rely solely on analytics for decision-making.

Calculating risk in the game is a challenge because of the uncertainty to predict what the 11 defenders (variable) will do. The uncertainty to predict what 11 defenders (variables) will do make calculating risk a challenge. Furthermore, even if a defensive coordinator makes a call, there is no certainty that all 11 players will execute the call in the manner it is supposed to be done. Other variables outside of players that must be considered are weather, time, score, etc. It is easy to game-plan the best 2nd and 1-yard play on a play-call sheet. However, is that play the best play if you are losing by 14 points with 5 minutes left in the 4th quarter? The solution is that data-driven decisions must be balanced with expert intuition. Intuition occurs by reading the reality of the environment instead of what the data says the environment should be.

The R4 expert system makes this possible through the interface tools of the HALO and CAP. The R4 grids create an inference engine that provides a common language reasoning progression. This allows the user to accelerate their ability to find the best solution based on accelerators. Accelerators are the non-negotiable variables (defender) movements that reveal the reality of what is occurring live within a game. Accelerator processing allows the coach to read the reality of what is occurring in real-time. The verbal and visual frames of reference of the R4 expert system make accelerator-driven decision-making possible. More importantly, it connects the coaches and players together to create a collective intelligence. The game-plan and play-calls are now seen through the same mind's eye.

This is drastically different than the traditional game-plan and play-call sheets that are solved only through situations. This process is full of fragments that create walls through a lack of language and a process that promotes division. The R4 expert system builds a bridge that sequences formations and plays. Concepts are connected through a common language and network that allows a group of individuals to work together as a team. Finally, there is a way to accelerate everyone's ability to quickly know "What is Open."

CHAPTER 9

SPEED SCRIPTING
R4 Practice Plan

SPEED SCRIPTING

R4 Practice Plan

The final challenge in the game-planning and play-calling process is the weekend workload. The enemy is time. There simply is not enough time to get everything accomplished. At least, that is how it felt before the discovery of the R4 process. In my first years as an offensive coordinator, I struggled with delegation and defining the game-plan. This lack of communication can create a toxic environment that pollutes many staffs. This also bled over into scripting practice for the week. Most of the hours of the weekend work were spent on breaking down scout film, game-planning, and building the play-call sheet.

It was usually late Sunday evening by the time this was complete. I consistently found myself out of time on the weekend to determine how to practice all the plays within the game-plan. Scripting and ensuring that the game-plan plays get practiced is one of the most important parts of the process. The R4 play-call sheet provides the solution for efficiently organizing the scripting of practice.

RHYTHM & RELEASE DAY - MONDAY

Monday practice is the most important practice day of the week during the season. This is the day that the game-planned is revealed to the players. The R4 play-call sheet provides the practice script for this priority. Monday is Rhythm Day for practice. (FIG. 9-1)

The plays that are in the Rhythm grids provide the script. The goal is to ensure that any play that is found in the Rhythm grid can be practiced on that day. Over game-planning occurs when there are not enough practice reps to cover the Rhythm plays. This can help a staff determine when there are too many plays in the game-plan.

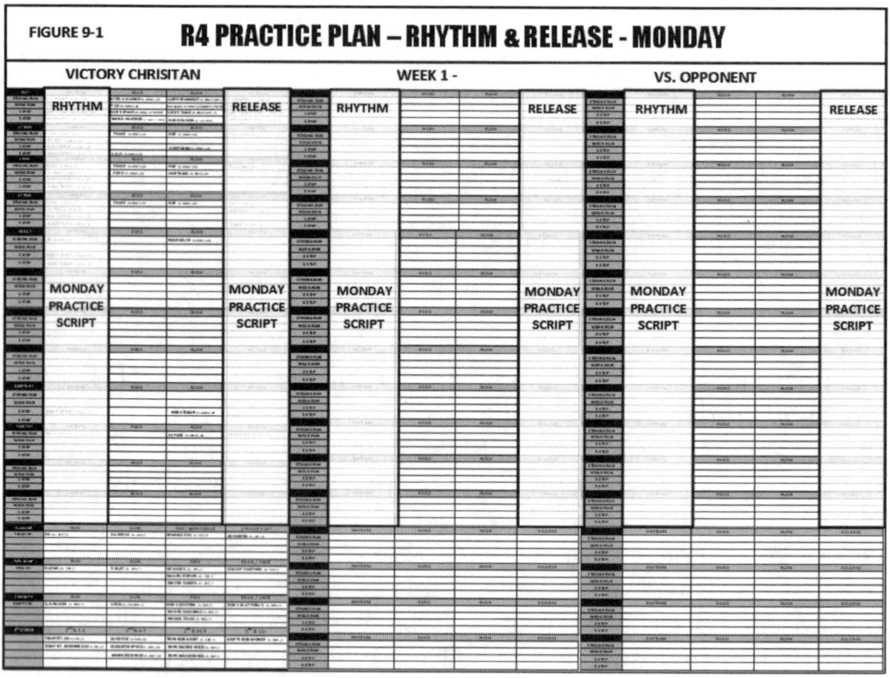

FIGURE 9-1 **R4 PRACTICE PLAN – RHYTHM & RELEASE - MONDAY**

VICTORY CHRISITAN	WEEK 1 -	VS. OPPONENT

RHYTHM	RELEASE	RHYTHM	RELEASE	RHYTHM	RELEASE
MONDAY PRACTICE SCRIPT	MONDAY PRACTICE SCRIPT	MONDAY PRACTICE SCRIPT	MONDAY PRACTICE SCRIPT	MONDAY PRACTICE SCRIPT	MONDAY PRACTICE SCRIPT

Release plays are also covered and practiced on Monday. Release plays are directly connected to a Rhythm play. Release plays are tagged-or-trick plays. They are usually new and specific for an upcoming opponent. This requires them to be practiced early in the week to provide time for players to learn the play. It also allows the staff time to determine if they want to keep that special play in the game-plan.

The focus of only covering and practicing Rhythm and Release plays on Monday removes the pressure of game-planning on the weekend. Before the creation of R4, it was originally implied that the entire game-plan must be completed and scripted by Monday morning. This forced a staff to complete everything in a compressed amount of time on the weekend. This is no longer an issue. The only part of the game-plan that needs to be complete and scripted by the end of the weekend are the Rhythm and Release plays.

READ DAY - TUESDAY

Tuesday practice is reserved for Read plays. (FIG. 9-2)

This allows the staff an extra day to watch film and determine the best plays to attack the most anticipated adjustment to the Rhythm plays. It also provides a sequence of installation with the players in a pattern of the play-call events that will more than likely occur in the game.

Furthermore, some schools that two-platoon their players may have to split practice time between offensive and defensive installation game-plans. Read Day on Tuesday can consist of a shorter script of plays. This makes it easier to have reduced offensive practice periods on Tuesday, which gives the defensive side more time to install their game-plan.

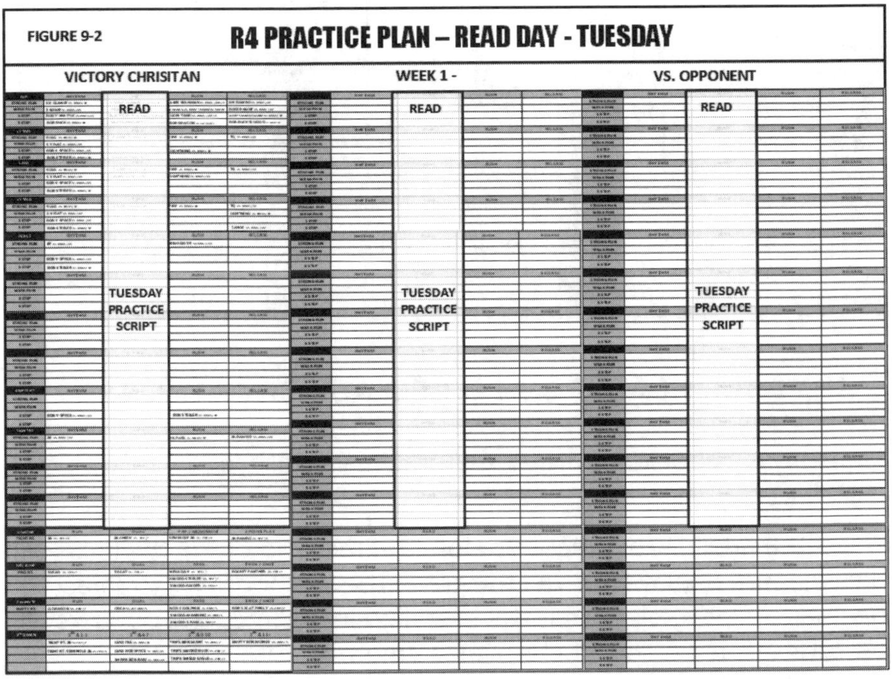

FIGURE 9-2

R4 PRACTICE PLAN – READ DAY - TUESDAY

VICTORY CHRISITAN — WEEK 1 - — VS. OPPONENT

READ	READ	READ
TUESDAY PRACTICE SCRIPT	TUESDAY PRACTICE SCRIPT	TUESDAY PRACTICE SCRIPT

RUSH DAY - WEDNESDAY

Wednesday is reserved for Rush plays. (FIG. 9-3)

This again provides another extra day to watch film and determine the pressures and blitzes defenses will use to overload space. Rush Day also includes field situations in which more pressure is applied. This practice includes plays for 3rd downs, Red Zone, and goal line pressure situations.

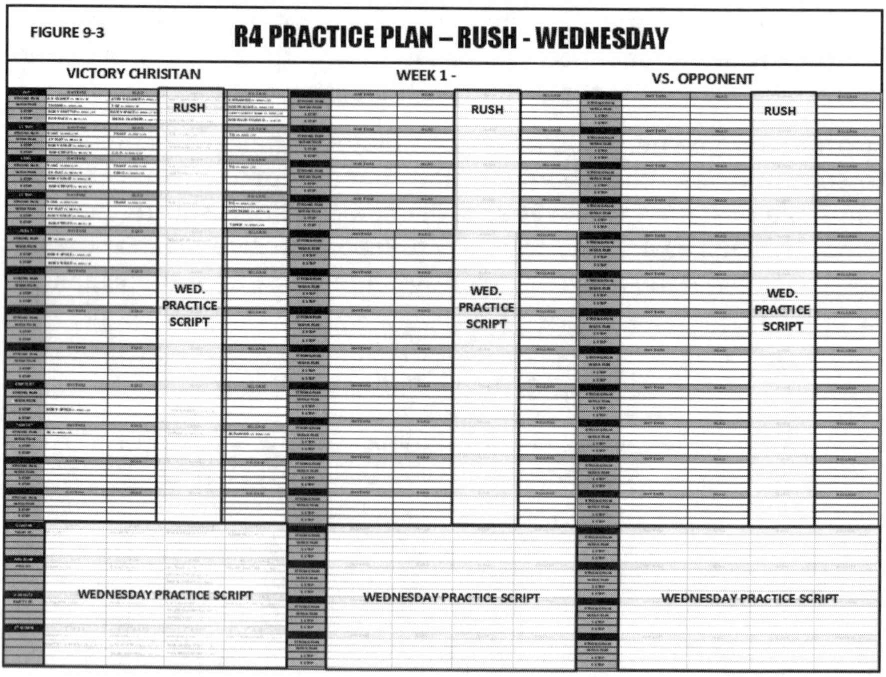

FIGURE 9-3

R4 PRACTICE PLAN – RUSH - WEDNESDAY

VICTORY CHRISITAN | WEEK 1 - | VS. OPPONENT

RUSH

WED. PRACTICE SCRIPT

RUSH

WED. PRACTICE SCRIPT

RUSH

WED. PRACTICE SCRIPT

WEDNESDAY PRACTICE SCRIPT

WEDNESDAY PRACTICE SCRIPT

WEDNESDAY PRACTICE SCRIPT

RHYTHM, READ, RUSH & RELEASE DAY - THURSDAY

Thursday is a conglomerate of Rhythm, Read, Rush, and Release plays. (FIG. 9-4)

This is the final day of practice before a game. Therefore, the focus will be a mixture of plays from all the grids. The top priority is to select the opening script of plays that will be called in a game. The openers will be scripted from the Rhythm play columns. The validity of game-planned Rhythm plays must be established early in the game. This is to determine if the game-planned CAP predictions (coverage, alignment, and personnel) hold true. The remaining plays to practice on Thursday will be high priority Read and Rush plays along with a review of the Release plays that need additional reps.

The prioritization that the R4 play-call sheet provides for practice planning accelerates a coaching staff workload for the weekend. There is no longer a need to complete the entire plan and practice script in two days. Furthermore, coaches are empowered to contribute and collaborate more efficiently during meetings. Football seasons require an extraordinary amount of time commitment to the game. This often requires a sacrifice of time away from more important roles of husband, father, teacher, and friend to important people in the coaching circles. R4 helps buy back time and moments that have often been missed during the season.

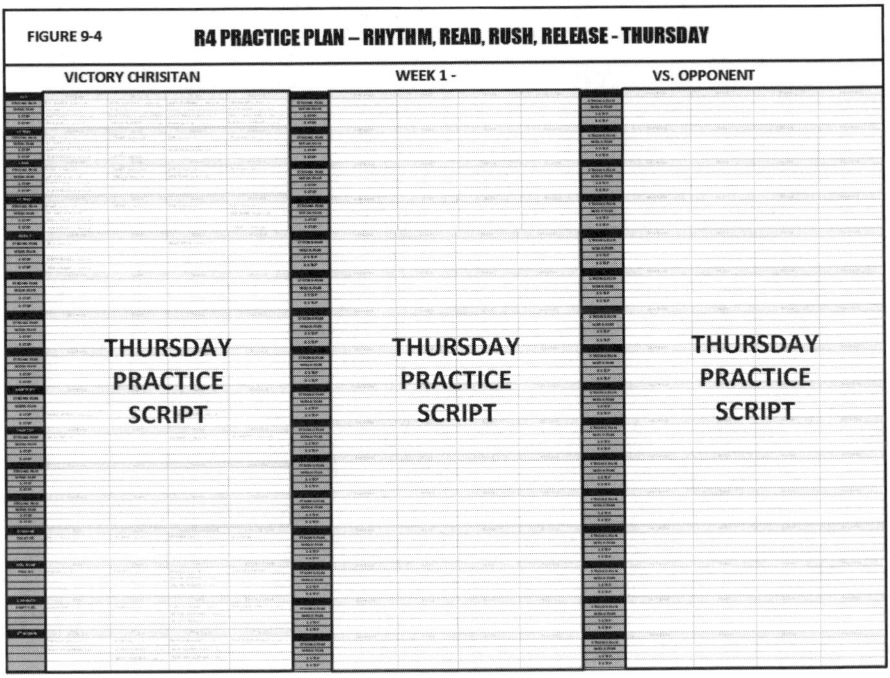

FIGURE 9-4 **R4 PRACTICE PLAN – RHYTHM, READ, RUSH, RELEASE - THURSDAY**

VICTORY CHRISITAN	WEEK 1 -	VS. OPPONENT
THURSDAY PRACTICE SCRIPT	THURSDAY PRACTICE SCRIPT	THURSDAY PRACTICE SCRIPT

CHAPTER 10

BREAKING BEHAVIOR BARRIERS

R4 Culture

BREAKING BEHAVIOR BARRIERS

R4 Culture

Culture is a hot topic in modern day football. It is one of the most commonly discussed topics in the game today. Many coaches work hard to create a championship culture within their players. What is often ignored is the culture of the coaching staff. I believe a focus on the staff culture should be considered a higher priority before the players.

An example of this is seen in families. Families that stay together and possess a great culture are rooted in the quality of the relationship between the husband and wife. Parents can preach all they want on the characteristics that they wish their children to develop. However, if they don't practice what they preach, the transfer will be diminished.

Equally, there is nothing that can derail a team faster than inner staff turmoil. Football coaches have a propensity to quickly create toxic environments due to the ego and competitive nature that naturally occurs with many dominant male coaches in the game. Most coaches, like their players, want to be the lead dog. The title of coach is not enough. This need to feel validated inhibits the ability for coaches to work together. Time is spent gossiping, backstabbing, and positioning for higher ranks and roles that a coworker my already obtain. This destroys a staff's ability to work together to better the players on the team.

In fact, many of the traits and qualities that I ask for my players to exude are the same characteristics that I struggle with myself. Over the years I have been in many war rooms where coaches spend most of their time together. I have witnessed both great ones and toxic ones. The toxic environments consist of personality conflicts that prevent the staff from working together. Humorously, there are five different personality types that you will find in coaching staff offices.

1. Hoarder – This is the coach who wants to be the smartest in the room. He has a high level of knowledge but does not want to teach or share his knowledge with others out of fear that he may create competition for himself in doing so. He desires to receive all the credit for team success and must have his ego stroked regularly. In game-planning meetings, he usually keeps to himself in a corner and ignores the rest of the staff.

2. One Trick Pony – This is the coach who is knowledgeable in one specific area. He is more open to teach and share this information with others. However, this coach feels that his area of expertise is the only way of doing things. He is not open to change, and he shuts down when challenged on his area of specialty.

3. Postman – This is the coach who is disgruntled and feels he is not valued and getting the attention that he deserves. He has often been passed over for a title or promotion to a higher role within the staff. In game-planning meetings, he will usually sit with his arms crossed and have a scowl on his face. This coach will usually instigate rumors or attempt to look for opportunities to throw fellow staff members, coordinators, or head coaches under the bus.

4. YouTuber – This is the coach who lives in an online world instead of reality. He is usually a people-person and may often suffer from A.D.D. Most of his time is spent in the office on his phone, watching funny videos or checking social media. A five-minute task will usually take fifty minutes because he cannot stay off his phone.

5. Ghost – This is the coach who is listed in the football program but rarely seen by the staff. He can remain unnoticed even while he is present in the office. He offers no value in staff meetings and is usually the first coach to leave, often mysteriously.

Throughout my coaching career, I have encountered these five different personality types of coaches. The irony is that I can easily identify them because I have been them all myself at some point. I never realized how these profiles can negatively impact a staff until I became a coordinator. A coordinator or head coach must create an environment that allows everyone to work as a team. I quickly discovered that I needed a way to remove the waste that these walls contain and create a working environment that promoted growth.

The two key elements that will remove the waste and promote growth are:

1. **Empathy** – The ability to feel what others feel.
2. **Empowerment** – Giving the freedom, knowledge, and responsibility to do a job.

Empathy and empowerment are the two most common traits in teams that win consistently in any domain. Empathy is the glue that holds the individuals together through adversity. Empowerment is the energy that drives individuals to perform a job to serve others. R4 is the operating system that provides transfer for empathy and empowerment through a staff.

HOW THE R4 SYSTEM TRANSFORMS TOXIC ENVIRONMENTS

Leading others through the transition from self-centered to others-centered requires patience and a process. Empathy is needed to help lead a coach out of his self-centered mindset. Empowerment is needed to help a coach develop his gift of greatness. As a coordinator and head coach, I can better empathize with others and empower them. R4 allows me to better understand a coach's frustration. At the same time, it provides a process to empower their ability to get better. This keeps every individual on staff connected and valued on the team. Here's how:

HOARDER

A hoarder is more open to sharing information and responsibilities when he can trust his coworkers. The R4 system empowers a hoarder with an ability to easily share information with others. I was a hoarder early on in my coordinating career because I didn't have a language and process to communicate and share the information in my head. R4 has allowed me to overcome this issue. I am now better equipped to trust the coaches I work with. We can finally see football and the game-plan through the same lens.

ONE TRICK PONY

A one trick pony becomes open to more ideas when he can see the relationship and patterns within the game. The R4 system empowers a one trick pony to step out of his comfort zone. I was a one trick pony early in my coordinating career because I didn't understand how everything in football fit together. I was extremely knowledgeable in the pass game. However, the run game was a foreign language. I didn't possess a common language and process that could cross-connect the running game knowledge to the same level in the passing game. R4 has allowed me to overcome this issue. I can now see the space and scheme relationship patterns between both and can teach it easily to others.

POSTMAN

A postman is no longer a disgruntled coworker when he realizes that he might not be as good as he thought. The R4 system empowers a postman to see the game in a whole new way. He becomes excited at a process that gives him the ownership and inclusion that he desires. Furthermore, he now has the tools that can help him finally achieve leadership goals that keep passing him by. There were times early in my coaching career where I was a postman. The feelings of not being valued pushed me to complain about decisions from leaders who I was working under. R4 would have helped me in those situations. I would have been less likely to complain about and discredit decisions. Instead, I would have been spent time improving my craft by using the R4 process to develop as a coach.

YOUTUBER

A YouTuber is no longer distracted when he understands his roles and responsibility. The R4 system empowers a Youtuber to clearly stay on track with definitive tasks when game-planning. He is less distracted from the excitement of being able to contribute to the workflow process. I was a YouTuber before I became a coordinator. I would lose focus in game-plan meetings because there was no real workflow or direction. Coaches were given assignments but connecting the process into a whole was missing. R4 would have fixed this issue. I would have been more engaged in meetings and focused on my responsibilities by seeing how they fit into the big picture.

GHOST

A ghost is no longer invisible when he is given the ability to accelerate his knowledge of the game at a level that is equal to the veteran coaches in the office. The R4 system empowers a ghost to remove his insecurities and become seen and heard. His inexperience is countered with a knowledge base to understand what the experts in the room are talking about. I was a ghost early in my coaching career. I was mentally lost in game-plan meetings. I would constantly look at the clock to see how much time was left until I was free to disappear and leave. R4 would have eliminated this. I would have been able to follow the work-flow and offer legitimate ideas that could have helped the game-plan.

"WHY CHANGE?"

The five personality profiles of coaches on a staff must change to create a team culture. The reasons for refusing to change are often ego, lack of knowledge, ignorance, lack of trust, and lack of communication. The R4 system removes all these roadblocks except ego. Ego is the ultimate enemy and blinds the belief system of a coach. An egocentric coach is usually not open to change until he is humbled through pain.

Pain can quickly change perspectives. Changing perspectives can change beliefs. Changing beliefs can change behavior. Changing behavior creates a culture. This is a non-negotiable process in creating a championship staff culture. The change starts with a question to understand the perspective of a coach. "Why are you here?" The answer to that question reveals his belief system. That belief system drives his behavior. A coach who is on a staff for himself will align with some of the selfish behaviors just covered. You cannot get a coach to change a behavior until you change his belief.

The belief that greatness comes from being "better than others" by rank, records, and rewards is a lie. This will only lead to an empty grave of regret at the end of a career. Milestones that are measured by numbers will never be satisfied because there will always be another number or level to attain. There is no finish line for greatest that is gaged in this way.

True greatness comes from being "better for others." A coach who is driven to get better, so they can serve others, becomes transformational. A coach's true purpose is to be great so he can help others get what they need. This realization propels a belief and behavior to change. Motivation is no longer about numbers. It is about the names of the people who can be served.

This is a leader's constant battle. Everyone has a self-centered default button. We don't have to remind ourselves to think about what we want. However, if we can remember the pivotal question in those moments, "Why are we here?" and answer with, "To serve others," then we can refocus our efforts to fulfill the purpose of the coaching position. The result is a real finish line full of people who will be waiting to pay their respect for the gift you gave them.

R4 accelerates the explicit knowledge transfer into an implicit approach that every person on a staff and team can understand. The result is unity. We still have disagreements but those can be worked through much faster because everyone is seeing the same space and speaking the same language. This helps to create an egoless environment that permeates to the players. They simply see the coaches happy and having fun as a team. Finally, we can truly practice what we preach and agree on the answers to "What is Open?"

CONCLUSION

The one constant in life is change. I hope this book inspires you to change or at least question the need for change. I hope it helps you the way it helped me. R4 was formed from my failures as a coach. The goal is to help serve others through those failures. I wasted many years of my career trying to make sense of the game. The different perspectives and languages that experts used to explain the game led me to get lost on the journey. Thankfully, the R4 system helped me to find "What is Open?" and my journey has accelerated forward ever since. I wish the same for you.

Reading this book is the first step to a new journey. The good news is that there is so much more. We have created an online professional development center at **www.r4footballsystem.com** This website is an online, modular, sequential teaching platform that fills in the knowledge gaps in each staff, affirms the best practices already in place, and gives a simple R4 process that provides a:

- Common language that defines defensive space, intent, and technique during film breakdown,
- Template that guides and influences playbook design, practice-scripting, and play-calling,
- Platform that maintains scheme simplicity, flexibility, and adaptability that isn't personnel dependent,
- Source code for tagging and enhancing existing schemes without having to replace them, and
- Sequential set of procedures that increases staff/player productivity and efficiency

The website contains video courses and downloadable documents that drive the concepts in this book even deeper. Coaching staffs now have a streamlined learning engine for sustainable improvement in all phases of the offense...Pass Game, Run Game, Film Review, Game-Planning, and Play-Calling.

This isn't just a library of content, plays, drills, and schemes... it's a language of connection with your players and staff like never before. If you are interested in diving into a better way to accelerate everything you do in the game of football, go to **www.r4footballsystem.com** and become an online member today.